A Feminist Ethnomusicology

NEW PERSPECTIVES ON GENDER IN MUSIC

Editorial Advisors
Susan C. Cook
Beverley Diamond

A list of books in the series appears at the end of this book.

A Feminist Ethnomusicology

Writings on Music and Gender

ELLEN KOSKOFF

Foreword by Suzanne Cusick

University of Illinois Press
URBANA, CHICAGO, AND SPRINGFIELD

Library of Congress Cataloging-in-Publication Data
Koskoff, Ellen, author.
A feminist ethnomusicology : writings on music and
gender / Ellen Koskoff ; foreword by Suzanne Cusick.
pages cm. — (New perspectives on gender in music)
Includes bibliographical references and index.
ISBN 978-0-252-03849-5 (hardcover : alk. paper) —
ISBN 978-0-252-08007-4 (pbk. : alk. paper) —
ISBN 978-0-252-09640-2 (e-book)
1. Ethnomusicology. 2. Feminism and music. 3. Sex role
in music. I. Title.
ML3798.K67   2014
780.82—dc23   2013040306

To Rebecca, Lydia, and David, with the hope
that you and your children will make a better world
where we can be all we want to be

Contents

Foreword

SUZANNE CUSICK

With *A Feminist Ethnomusicology,* Ellen Koskoff has given us an intellectually eclectic, rigorously self-aware, lucidly written, and sometimes hilarious guide to how the paradoxical interdiscipline of feminist ethnomusicology has developed over the past forty years. Koskoff herself describes the book as a kind of intellectual memoir that shows the process of change in a thoroughly intersectional professional life, but I would argue that it is more like an autoethnography, for it is firmly based in her own participant observation amid the creation of a feminist ethnomusicology from multiple disciplines, conversations, and concerns over a lifetime of "face-to-face talking, laughing, listening, eating, musicking." To Koskoff, such shared interactions between embodied, constantly changing human beings constitute the essence of fieldwork, which she posits as an ideal method both for ethnomusicology and for feminism—as well as the method for acquiring and developing knowledge that is the "most fun."

There is ample fun in this autoethnography, and not only because Koskoff has peppered some of the essays with sidesplitting anecdotes that present moments of shared, nonverbal recognition of sameness-difference as explosions of laughter. Koskoff's chronological account of her own path to a feminist ethnomusicology tacks deftly between such anecdotes and brilliantly distilled, utterly reader-friendly exegeses of the political, theoretical, and disciplinary concerns that shaped her own thought and practice, as well as that of her sisters in feminist music scholarship. The result is that complicated, emotionally, and politically fraught encounters between music and anthropology, ethnomusicology and gender studies, historical musicology and ethnomusicology, any and all of those and cultural studies, literary theory, or the several "post-" disciplines are made easy to grasp. They seem like the personal and intellectual adventure of one engaged (and highly engaging) person. Once a little girl whose curiosity was piqued by the joy-filled faces of singing men whom she passed on her way to school, and who would later be troubled by a teacher's instruction to make her *whole* native state one color on a map, that person would spend her adulthood pondering, in the real and virtual company of others, music, gender, sameness-and-difference, and what it meant to feel both inside and outside a picture that ought rightly to be rich with differences.

As a text, *A Feminist Ethnomusicology* is rich with differences, whether interrogated intellectually, mediated by laughter or music, angrily refused, or respectfully acknowledged. By far the most significant of these is the stark contradiction between feminism's inherent commitment to political action on behalf of gender equality and ethnomusicology's equally inherent commitment to the dispassionate understanding of music's importance in human lives. Although this contradiction seems to have bedeviled Koskoff through many years of fieldwork, it haunts her book very productively: her essays show how she negotiated it by bravely confronting other differences that, in their overlapping, both constituted the contradiction and implied its possible resolutions. Among the most important conflicts fruitfully explored are the conflicting yet overlapping histories, premises, and aims of Western-oriented feminist theory versus mainstream anthropological theory; historical musicology's emphasis on textwork and elite Western musics versus ethnomusicology's emphasis on fieldwork and nonelite, non-Western musics; "second-wave" versus "third-wave" feminisms; performance theory versus performativity theory; "genderist" versus "feminist" analysis; knowledge developed from fieldwork versus the desire to create broad, cross-cultural theories of gender's interaction with musicking; insider versus outsider perspectives; academic versus activist feminisms; Lubavitcher versus non-Lubavitcher understandings of the sound of a woman's voice; cultural studies theory versus anthropological theories of culture; and recent ethnomusicology's fascination with global systems of commodified human and cultural circulation versus fieldwork's emphasis on "everyday, sometimes tedious, sometimes miraculous human interactions," with their "gendered lessons of compassion, respect for the individual and for the process of life."

Koskoff works through these differences from a position of being "in between" discourses—a condition she learned to theorize as characterizing both women and music by a combination of textwork with anthropologist Sherry Ortner's writing and fieldwork among Lubavitcher Jews, for whom music is "the language of the heart," mediating between the corrupt and the pure, the earthly and the divine, the inside and the outside. In the end, she affirms feminism and ethnomusicology as always having shared certain qualities that she valued—a commitment to social justice, to understanding others, and to the struggle for equilibrium in relationships based on difference. In the end, she succeeds in presenting the sometimes vexed and contentious, sometimes harmonious or playful, always productive relationship of feminism with ethnomusicology as a parable of just such equilibrium.

But this book is richer than all that. It is a magnificent (and, dare I say, wonderfully historicized) survey of the field; a stunning textual performance of clear-headed, down-to-earth, rigorously self-aware thought in the act of engaging intensely with real human life; and a passionate argument for the continuing importance of encounters between human persons, in all our complexity. It adumbrates theoretical moves that have yet to be developed. To read *A Feminist Ethnomusicology* is to witness a person of great intellect, empathy, and honesty think, with love and humor, about music, gender, social justice, and power: it is, therefore, to encounter the sensibility that makes a feminist music scholar. Most of all, to read it is like "face-to-face talking, laughing, listening" with Koskoff herself, a privilege I have intermittently enjoyed over many years. Koskoff challenges readers to think new thoughts, rethink old ones, remember long-buried feelings, and open ourselves more to the astonishing variety of the world—and she makes it fun.

But don't trust me: read her for yourself.

Preface

While it is certainly an honor to have one's articles published in a collection such as this, the preparation of this manuscript has also resulted in a curious moment for me. In assembling these articles for publication, I have had to go back over the past forty years of my life, to revel again in excitement and hope, to sigh over missed opportunities, to reconnect with the work of old friends and colleagues—some of whom have passed on—to lament upon awkward arguments or turns of phrase, and to reflect upon shared progress and continuing challenges. Though written for others, this book has also allowed me to reconnect with my earlier self—always a worthwhile experience.

Although I am hopeful that scholars in other fields will read and use this work, its primary focus, orientation, and perspective is that of ethnomusicology—that music discipline I love and that I define here as a close, yet sometimes contentious, marriage between music and anthropology. Central to this endeavor is fieldwork. Although far from perfect, fieldwork—the face-to-face talking, laughing, listening, crying, eating, musicking, and all the rest—is still, for me, the best and most direct way to learn about others and their musics, and I privilege it here over other methods of learning and documenting.

More than anything else, though, this collection presents my understandings and interpretations of disciplinary and social intersections that have characterized music and gender studies over the past four decades. Of course, ethnomusicology has changed considerably since I entered the field in the 1970s: other disciplines, such as cultural studies, literary criticism, women's studies, and poststructural and postcolonial studies, among many others, have entered the picture and have reframed our discussions, causing us to rethink basic concepts such as music, man, woman, gender, and fieldwork. Many of these changes are reflected in the essays in this volume, which represents my knowledge and my understandings of these intersections and of their impact on ethnomusicology. Thus, this book is neither complete nor exhaustive in its scope—but it is true to my own experience, and, I hope, some of it will be true to yours.

Acknowledgments

We all know that it takes a community of colleagues, friends, and family to produce a book, especially one that covers four decades of thinking and writing. Literally, hundreds of people have contributed to this collection, from those feminist scholars I have come to know through their wonderful work to many colleagues and close friends whose support and love I greatly value. I would, however, like to acknowledge a few people here who have been especially important to me over the years.

First, I would like to thank Laurie Matheson, editor in chief of the University of Illinois Press, for asking me to undertake this project. I am honored by this request and grateful to her and to longtime friend and colleague Beverley Diamond, general editor of the Women and Music Series, for their support and for their faith in me and in this work. I am also grateful for the earlier help and support received from my "ethno-mother," Carolina Robertson, who walked part of this path with me.

I am especially grateful to the "FemEth Group" (you know who you are!) for your continued support, great conversations, and a lot of laughter—from the early days, when we squirreled ourselves away in hotel rooms, talking in low voices, to the present day, when we celebrate with loud, boisterous dinners. I could not have done all of this without you. Special thanks and love go to Suzanne Cusick, Pirkko Moisala, Zoe Sherinian, Elizabeth Tolbert, and Deborah Wong, who often talked with me into the night about all sorts of things, and, to Charlotte Frisbie, my "ethno-sister," for all of those wonderful talks, walks, and tears.

Thank you also to two of my graduate students, Jennifer MacKenzie and Nawa Lanzilotti, for their eagle eyes and for their willingness to do some very tedious, yet necessary, tasks. You have all helped immeasurably in the preparation of this manuscript.

Finally, I give my love and heartfelt thanks to my best friend, Bonnie, who was always there when I needed her—and even when I didn't.

Introduction

This book resembles what some might call an intellectual memoir, in that it traces my personal journey from the early 1970s to 2012 through a maze of social history and scholarship examining music and gender. Using the word *feminist* in the title immediately positions me as an inheritor of the political and ideological views of those in the 1960s and '70s—the so-called second-wavers—who accomplished much but also left much undone; the word *ethnomusicology* orients me and this research within the methodological frames of fieldwork and musical ethnography.

As an intellectual memoir of sorts, this collection mirrors my understandings of certain political and social events that shaped my thinking as I grew up in the 1940s and '50s within a left-wing, upper-middle-class, white, Jewish family living in the Squirrel Hill neighborhood of Pittsburgh, Pennsylvania. People like me (sometimes referred to as "red diaper babies")[1] were children of parents either active in or sympathetic to the ideals of the American Communist Party. My father, a doctor, would often tell the story (with some pride) of how he was refused a job at the local veterans' hospital because my mother's name had been found on a list of people who had given money to the communists. Himself a child of immigrants, my father had a deep appreciation for America and its many opportunities, sometimes recognizing the relative ease with which he had slid into these opportunities, being white and male, and thus, although Jewish, privileged nonetheless.

I first became conscious of feminism and the so-called women's liberation movement in the early 1970s through participation in discussions and arguments with friends and colleagues. In fact, I trace the beginning of my first feminist consciousness to one such moment.

January 1973: First Consciousness

I am in my second year of graduate school at the University of Pittsburgh, studying historical musicology. I have been spending a good deal of time lately talking with my friends about all the fuss in the news and on radio talk shows about our so-called sexist language, like the use of "he" meaning "he and she," or "man" signifying also "woman," or of "history" being cleverly parsed as "his story," and so on. I think this is pretty silly—these are, after all, just words!

And I do not really like musicology. I mean, some classes, like fourteenth- and fifteenth-century notation are fun—the music is wonderful, and the notation exercises satisfy my desire for puzzles. But the genre classes (Opera in the Nineteenth Century and so on) are not really my cup of tea, with all of that oppressive Great Masterwork language in the literature and in the mouths and minds of my professors. I am beginning to get a bit squirmy about devoting my life to this path.

I have a friend who is not a musician. Actually, she is the mother of one of my piano students. A young African American woman, she is working on a Ph.D. in psychology and is a single parent. When I first began teaching her daughter a few months ago, she would strike up conversations with me about the new "women's liberation movement," "consciousness-raising" groups, and why men and women did X or Y. I had no patience for this and would dismiss these attempts as amusing rants. What, exactly, did "liberated" mean, anyway? Liberated from what?

Today, as I enter her home for her daughter's lesson, she calls me into the kitchen. She is hunched over a little and hands me a book, using a strange secretive gesture as if it were a package of drugs, or some other illegal substance. She says in a low but insistent voice, "Read this, and then we'll talk." It is Phyllis Chesler's *Women and Madness* (1972), an examination of the historical and contemporary practices of psychiatry and psychology as they had developed in the United States and Europe.

As I read, I find the book is based on interviews with incarcerated and institutionalized women, with lesbians, and with sexually, economically, and politically active women, who have become hopelessly marginalized and stigmatized by their male, and sometime female, therapists. Categorizing and labeling them

as chaotic and out of control, these doctors have created an entire class of women deemed "mad," chronicling stories from the
seventeenth-century witches in Salem, Massachusetts, to the
"sexually insatiable" women of the late nineteenth and early
twentieth centuries, who were incarcerated in asylums (or at-
tics), or psychiatric practices ranging from psychiatrists having
sex with their patients as a form of therapy to Freud's notion of
the Electra Complex—an analogue to his Oedipal Complex for
boys—developed in the face of many female patients' memories
of childhood sexual abuse. This book jolts me into a sudden consciousness, a powerful moment of clarity, which, like a shaken
kaleidoscope, takes the bits and pieces of one stable world and
clicks them into another, never to go back.

*   *   *

What This Book Is and What It Is Not

When I was first approached by the University of Illinois Press to put this
collection together, I realized that part of what I wanted to do was to convey
some of the excitement, anger, and joy that I experienced through the decades
of my rising political consciousness. I sometimes lament today that my students are, for the most part, unaware of (or uninterested in) the history and
revolutionary fervor of feminism in the United States, or in the gains that
were made toward gender equality, especially in the last half of the twentieth
century—gains that are largely taken for granted by today's generation.

So, I began to conceptualize this book as a chronological presentation of
my work on gender and music, framed by general discussions of contemporaneous social and political events occurring in the United States, as well
as emerging strands of American and some European feminist scholarship
that were important to me at the time. These chapters—chapters 1, 4, and
10—are designed to show how certain issues "out there" became crystallized,
filtered into the academy primarily through the disciplines of anthropology
and ethnomusicology, and, ultimately, were inspiring to me.

Framing the chapters, these sections do not present a complete history
of the women's movement, the various feminisms that developed over the
decades, or an exhaustive literature review of all the important historical and
contemporary intersections between music and gender; nor do they even
present a complete review of all of the relevant works in anthropology and
ethnomusicology. Rather, together they create a personal map of the different

paths I have taken over the decades and how and why they inspired, informed, and gave clarity to my work. Along the way, I have inserted little anecdotes, like the story above, that highlight moments when I suddenly became aware of some of my underlying assumptions, leading me to a sudden conscious awareness or clarity.

I realized early on that the amount of literature dealing in some way with historical and contemporary feminism, gender, and music had become so vast, complex, and interconnected that dealing with it exhaustively here would soon become overwhelming and chaotic. Thus, I made three important choices that ultimately led to the paths seen here:

- As a result of my disciplinary inclinations, I deal mainly with feminist literature based on fieldwork, generated primarily within the disciplines of anthropology and ethnomusicology. In privileging the ethnographic method, I necessarily exclude most discussions of gender and music based primarily on document or literary analysis, such as those from the disciplines of historical women's and gender studies, most ethnic studies, popular music studies, and those of historical and critical musicologists.
- I have chosen to offer literature reviews only when they assist me in clarifying specific themes that were important to my work at the time, such as the use and abuse of power, the symbolic weight of language, ritual studies, and interdisciplinary politics.
- Stemming from the above decisions, the scope of my discussions is limited largely to intersections of gender and music, rather than other important intersections, such as those between music, race, class, ethnicity, or age.

By limiting myself to these three research and methodological areas, I am not suggesting that I find other scholarship irrelevant or uninteresting; I fully recognize that all scholarship on genders and musics is ultimately interconnected and often speaks to one another, creating different communities, different paths, and differently framed pictures. Along the way, I will try to point the reader in some directions not dealt with directly in the text. In privileging fieldwork and the ethnographic method, however, I am suggesting that, for me, the face-to-face, direct interactions with living people result in more satisfying pictures than those of more critical and interpretive studies where one is often distanced by time and space.

My understanding of, and preference for, fieldwork grew alongside my feminist consciousness, and perhaps that is why they are so connected in my scholarship. While working on my dissertation in the early 1970s, for example, my fieldwork among Hasidic Jews in Brooklyn often revealed to me a completely different picture from that presented in the historical and contemporary literature describing Jewish culture and music.[2] Most of what

I had read about Hasidic musical culture had focused exclusively on men and had been written by non-Hasidim. These accounts presented Hasidim either as overly pious men whose music was uninteresting aesthetically or as caricatures whose musical practices were childlike, and sometimes dangerously out of control.

Further, I was completely surprised to learn that women had any kind of musical life within Hasidic practice. Nothing had been written on the very visible musical activities of the women I was observing. It was, in fact, this wonderful discovery that led to my interest in gender and music. If the women I worked with could be so easily written out of the literature, what did this mean? Soon I began to rely less and less on historical and contemporary outsider accounts and more and more on my own observations and on what I was learning from the Lubavitchers themselves, especially women.

I delved into the contemporary Jewish feminist literature for some answers, which pointed toward a millennia-old history of male dominance and the erasure of most women from this history.[3] But, again, during the fieldwork process, I began to encounter inconsistencies with these written sources: the women with whom I worked did not appear to be oppressed, nor did they want anything changed, in spite of my repeated attempts to save them with my constant questioning and comparisons from secular culture. They were generally happy and fulfilled in what I perceived as their rather constrained lives, often laughing at me, saying, "Ellen, you are completely missing the point here." What point? What was I missing? Perhaps they were not yet conscious of their own oppression? How would I deal with this?

I soon realized that I did not want to necessarily change Jewish gender relations, or save my Lubavitcher sisters from their obvious (to me) subordination; I just wanted to understand how the Lubavitcher belief system worked. How could this system, so different from my own, exist so happily and productively? Although it took some time to fully process, I ultimately came to see that fieldwork was essential to my understanding of gender and music precisely because it allowed for the possibility of real-time negotiation (sometimes argument) between informant and fieldworker—and thus for a direct and intense interaction with difference itself. Many of the ideas and questions I was asking then may seem naive today, but they give a sense of the ongoing issues I have dealt with throughout my life that have led me to make the methodological and disciplinary choices I offer here.

Who, then, is the audience for this book? I see my main audience as younger scholars within the field of ethnomusicology, as well as a more general audience seeking to gain a historical understanding of the connections between feminism, gender studies, and music. More seasoned scholars, including those who have not previously connected to feminist approaches in ethnomusicology, may also enjoy reviewing parts of this history, or seeing it unfolding within the context of my work. Certainly, a wide audience outside music studies will also benefit from this collection, which is perhaps the first book to offer a historical perspective on the integration of feminism, ethnomusicology, and gender.

As these reflections suggest, I do not necessarily see other feminist ethnomusicologists—those women and men who walked with me on my paths and who often inspired me through their own work and personal conversations—as my primary audience, except insofar as they may wish to reflect with me upon a shared scholarly trajectory. Much of what I have written here is already known to such specialists, and I hope my work has already contributed something to their own understandings of gender and music, just as theirs has to mine.

The Organization of This Book

The articles in this collection are arranged chronologically in three parts. These divisions should not be taken too literally, however; obviously, there is some overlap between the sections, as certain ideas took longer to mature than others, and occasionally older research proved valuable in highlighting a newer contemporary theme in my work. Each of the three parts begins with a chapter (chapters 1, 4, and 10) that examines certain themes of interest to me in the feminism, anthropology, and ethnomusicology of that time. Finally, in chapter 13, "Imaginary Conversations," I reflect upon the preceding chapters, focusing on interconnected themes. Of the thirteen chapters presented here, seven have been published elsewhere (see notes for each chapter at the end of the book). All references cited throughout the book are listed in the references section.

Some Basic Terms and Definitions Used Here

Throughout this collection, I use terms that have become commonly associated with music and gender discourses over the decades. Many of them, such as *gender, biological sex, feminism,* even *music,* have been hotly contested and deconstructed over this period of disciplinary activity, so I would like to make my own position clear concerning how I am defining and using these terms here.

I regard gender primarily as a socially constructed and performed category of human differentiation. I say primarily because I am somewhat convinced by biological and brain studies showing that men and women are different in some ways—but these ways seem to me to be largely irrelevant to individuals as everyday social actors. Further, I applaud the efforts of gender-studies scholars who have attempted to deconstruct and destabilize centuries-long notions of gender as a binary system solely based on biological sex; I see gender as they do, as more or less an ever-changing continuum of intertwined socially constructed and negotiated categories, as well as biological categories of many varieties and performances.

However, I am of an age (and generation) where I still regard one's biological sex as pretty much a given, although I am sensitive to people born with merged or ambiguous sexual traits and also to ideas, such as those of Judith Butler and others, who posit that the biological category of one's birth takes on a specific meaning and significance only through repeated performances defined and delimited by one's culture. Thus, I believe that although what we are born with largely determines our early socialization, how aware we become of these constraints or privileges or both, and how we are driven to validate or protest them, can alter our prescribed gendered path.

The word *feminism* has taken on many new meanings as it has passed through the decades. Many in today's generation avoid using it, seeing it for some time now as the new *F* word. Feminism implies groups of angry, screaming, man-hating women of their mothers' or grandmothers' generation. I define feminism here as essentially a political philosophy, where *political* is taken in its broadest sense to describe both social and individual belief and action directed toward unequal power relations based on gender. Feminism, as a politically active movement today, has changed and modified itself into a multistranded, inclusive, and diverse set of movements common to the postmodern condition. The history of feminism over the past decades has been complicated, with successes and failures of different kinds in evidence; thus, I use the word here not only to position myself politically, but also to reclaim and reevaluate its usefulness in today's gendered discourses.[4]

I consider myself a feminist, but I am more interested in the relationships between women (of all varieties) and men (of all varieties) than in espousing a particular case for either women or men. I am far more interested in why women and men have not achieved gender equality than in decrying the fact that they have not. Thus, the word *feminism,* for me, does not imply "for women only," but, rather, points to and exposes the obvious reality that it is women, after all, who are most often the unequal partners in these power relations. To me, all people who resist inequality based on gender are feminists. Thus, the study of gender is the *lens through which I most clearly see inequality,* but feminism is *how I enact the knowledge* I have gained in this work to resist and dismantle it.

The Wave Metaphor

Today, it is common to refer to the history of feminism in the United States as unfolding in three generational waves, or sometimes in various thematic concentric circles (Scholz 2010). Based on the generational model first proposed by Kate Millet in her 1970 *Sexual Politics* to distinguish between activities of the second wave and those of the early-twentieth-century first wave, it was later borrowed by Julia Kristeva (1979) and others, eventually becoming an accepted parsing of feminism's history. Although heavily critiqued (see below), the wave metaphor seems apt here, as, among its many definitions, a wave can be seen as a periodic disturbance that flows through space and time, characterized by a transfer of energy (a common definition in physics). Over the past two hundred years, this perpetual flow, with its awkward and uncomfortable disturbances, has led to massive legal, social, economic, and other changes in the United States and elsewhere for both women and men, changes still not fully understood or realized today.

What exactly are the three waves of feminism alluded to above? Briefly, first-wave feminism is said to have begun in the United States in 1848, with the first Seneca Falls Convention in western New York, and to have ended in 1920, with the passage of the Nineteenth Amendment to the U.S. Constitution, granting women suffrage, or the right to vote. But the roots of this first wave had begun at least fifty years earlier with Mary Wollstonecraft's *Vindication of the Rights of Women,* published in England in 1792, and with Margaret Fuller's *Woman in the Nineteenth Century,* published in the United States in 1845. These texts became the catalyst for America's suffragettes, such as Susan B. Anthony, Elizabeth Cady Stanton, and many others at the beginning of the twentieth century, who used them not only to help secure women's right to vote, but also to gain control over their own bodies and reproductive rights, to allow shared ownership of children through the Married Women's Property Act, to legally recognize marital rape, and to grant rights of inheritance to women, among other gains.

Second-wave feminism is generally thought to have begun in the late 1940s, with the publication of Simone de Beauvoir's *Second Sex* (1949), one of the first texts to posit the notion of woman as a constructed other. (See more in chapter 1.) But its major legal and cultural gains were made largely in the 1960s and '70s, when sweeping legislation made marital rape and sexual harassment in the workplace illegal and legalized abortion and no-fault divorce.

In addition, a new consciousness of women as a separate, underprivileged class resulted in the passage of Title VII of the Civil Rights Act of 1964, preventing discrimination on the basis of sex, race, and other identity markers, and Title IX of the Education Amendments Act of 1972, prohibiting discrimination in education, especially in sports. Further, the founding of the National Organization for Women (NOW) in 1966, the creation of domestic-abuse shelters, and the formation of countless other support systems all provided new safe zones for women. The publication of Betty Friedan's *Feminine Mystique* (1963) and Kate Millet's *Sexual Politics* (1970), among many other texts, spread significant underlying ideas, such as outlining historical and contemporary relationships between patriarchy, sexuality, reproductive rights, and work roles, to the broader culture.

The beginnings of third-wave feminism are under contention, partly because there is debate over whether events and ideas following the second wave actually constitute a distinct wave or are merely a continuation of the second. Those who believe that a separate third wave now exists see it beginning with the publication of Rebecca Walker's article "Becoming the Third Wave" (1992) and Jennifer Baumgardner and Amy Richards's *Manifesta: Young Women, Feminism, and the Future* (2000). The main issues presented by the third-wavers deal with what they see as the second wave's insistence on essentializing women for political gain; reifying binary contrasts, such as men/women; and avoiding intersections between gender, race, social class, and sexuality. They also challenge the white American-centric efforts of the second wave, which almost exclusively focused on middle-class white women. Today, they concentrate on creating networks with women of color in the United States and elsewhere and on appealing to the politics of younger women and girls.

The wave metaphor, however, has been unpopular for some time. Although it has been useful in its articulation of continuing feminist ebbs and flows, and in aligning younger feminists with various postcolonial communities worldwide, it has also made the discussion of parallel, or intersecting, waves more difficult (Gillis et al. 2007, xxiii). The third-wave label was chosen, for example, precisely because it made an explicit statement against what younger feminists saw as the limits of the second wave: "Having learnt the lessons of history, [third-wavers] prefer contradiction, multiplicity, and difference" (ibid., xxiv).

Critics of the third wave, such as Henrietta Moore (1999) and others, however, point to the overall effectiveness of second-wave constructions of woman as a monolithic category, by asserting that the third wave, in all of its fragmentation, has lost its political core. Finally, the use of this metaphor by third-wavers to distinguish themselves from their mothers' generation has created somewhat of an adversarial, reactionary stance, and "the question of who 'owns' third wave feminism remains a contentious one" (Gillis et al. 2007, xxiii). Thus, how these questions will be resolved remains in the realm of conjecture.

*   *   *

Ultimately, my hope is that this collection of essays and its historical and conceptual framing will accomplish three things: that it will help its readers answer questions about the historical intersections of feminism, gender, and music; that it will inspire readers to question and critique various assumptions about these intersections; and that it will help those who question to feel more comfortable about leaving many issues unresolved. To those who follow and forge new paths, I wish you luck as you continue to make uncomfortable and awkward disturbances that, together, help us all to reach a freer, more equal world.

PART I

1976–1990

1. From Women to Gender

I begin my academic journey in 1975, the year I wrote the last chapter of my dissertation on Lubavitcher music. Entitled "The Musical Experience of the Female Lubavitcher," it was, to my knowledge, the first scholarship based on fieldwork that documented the presence of Hasidic women's music and musical activity. That is not to say that all of my thinking or research on gender and music miraculously began there, but, rather, that this date and this writing mark my entry into the feminist literature of the day and its applications to music. After my initial "consciousness raising" in 1972 (see the introduction), one that seemed to expose the universal subordination (or at least undervaluation) of women, I spent the next few years working on my dissertation and gradually becoming more and more angry, seeking answers to the questions of if so, then why? And even more important, just who was responsible?

I began to see female oppression everywhere—from inside my own family to my educational institutions, from my own socialization as a heterosexual white American female to worldwide marriage and courtship negotiations, from Lubavitcher women's constrained musical activities to gendered musical contexts more globally. In short, I became simultaneously politicized and overwhelmed by the enormity of the problem.

I began to seek the company of other women, especially those involved in musical scholarship. In the early 1980s, for example, Marilyn Mason, professor of organ at the University of Michigan, began organizing conferences on women and music.[1] I attended these, along with the Berkshire Conferences on Women's History. Although I found them useful, I was also beginning to become aware of the white upper-middle class and Western-centric focus of these conferences, along with a growing consciousness of my own hetero-sexuality as a blinder to other forms of female sexual identity.

Here is a story that, like the first one a decade earlier, illustrates a sudden aha moment of new feminist consciousness.

March 13, 1982: "Ann Arbor, Michigan: The Women and Music Conference"

I am here at the first University of Michigan Conference on Women and Music, sponsored by the School of Music. There is a small population attending the conference, but composer Edith Borroff (1982), who is chronicling this, estimates that participants have come from at least fifteen states of the United States, as well as parts of Canada. I am sitting through many sessions of "compensatory history," getting to know many (Western classi-cal) women composers and performers who have been "erased by history." I am beginning to wonder if issues of why this has happened (not only that it has happened) will ever surface. And what about all of the rest of the women in the world and all of the rest of their musics?

I have recently met Suzanne Cusick, who is also at the confer-ence. She now lives near Rochester (where I live), in Seneca Falls, New York, at the National Historical Park for Women's Rights. It is Saturday evening and time for the conference banquet. We are all sitting at our assigned places and listening to the kudos and thank-yous for conference organizers. Suzanne and I are but one table apart and eye each other periodically, nodding and smiling.

Marilyn announces that the University of Michigan's Women's Glee Club will now present a small concert of music by and for women. I remember only the finale. The glee club is performing "Thank Heaven for Little Girls," by Alan J. Lerner and Frederic Lowe, composed for the musical *Gigi* (1958)—for me, the absolute epitome of sexist lyrics! When the lyrics round the chorus with "Thank heaven for little girls . . ., for, without them, what would little boys do?" Suzanne and I make eye contact. Both of us are convulsing with laughter. Neither of us knows how to respond to this, but both of us are sharing an awkward yet satisfyingly bonding moment—is this some form of extreme irony on the part of the conference's organizers or just plain ignorance? Or . . .

might we also be laughing because one of us (me) cannot believe that such sexist lyrics exist or, even worse, would be performed at an academic conference on women and music (!), and the other (Suzanne) because she is delighting in little girls growing into desirable women (but not for little boys)? I am laughing so hard that my stomach hurts and tears slip down my cheeks. I leave the banquet, energized both by anger and by a new consciousness of different female sexualities and their many performances.

*   *   *

Feminism's Second Wave

By the early 1970s, the second wave of feminism was rising in the United States. Many of the rights women had won by the end of the first wave (ca. 1920), such as the right to vote, to have joint control over their children, to inherit property, and to be protected from (some) sexual harassment in the workplace, had become largely accepted, but the attitudes and cultural norms of gender imbalance still prevailed. The post–World War II period of economic growth (ca. 1945–60), along with powerful cultural myths of stability and domesticity, created a cozy picture of a contented white American middle class and a largely patriarchal prosperity. But many were dissatisfied. Both men and women, encased in the tightly fitting prescribed roles—breadwinner/homemaker—were finding it increasingly difficult to live under such constraints. Alcoholism, drug use, and suicide, especially among white suburban middle-class women, rose substantially as efforts to revive old prewar patriarchal values increased in their intensity.

Many scholars cite the publication of Betty Friedan's *Feminine Mystique* (1963) as the beginning of a wider second-wave consciousness—referred to in the late 1960s as the "women's liberation movement." But other works, such as Simone de Beauvoir's *Second Sex* (1949) and Kate Millet's *Sexual Politics* (1970), cited earlier, had already begun to expose the patriarchal system as the norm, where women were always an other to a normative male self. Friedan's contribution, though, brought many of these ideas home to a larger public. Primarily attacking various media, such as advertising and television, Friedan exploded the notion of an idealized female domesticity, seeing women's entrapment in the sheltered home environment of the predominantly white middle-class suburb as a tremendous waste of talent and potential.

In the same year as the publication of Friedan's book, President John F. Kennedy released his first Presidential Commission on the Status of Women Report on Gender Inequality.[2] Created at the prompting of Eleanor Roosevelt, this report became the basis of many local, and eventually national, discussions, in the form of consciousness-raising groups, coffee klatches, and more formal groups, such as the National Organization for Women (founded in 1966). Finding discrimination against women in all aspects of American society, this report did much to bring these issues to light and to educate both women and men on the political and social ramifications of gender imbalance in the United States.

During the 1960s and '70s, important legislation, such as Title VII of the Civil Rights Act of 1964 and Title IX of the Educational Amendments Act of 1972, prohibiting discrimination on the basis of sex in employment and in educational opportunities, respectively, opened the gates for women and girls to enter the workforce in large numbers and to participate in sports and other educational activities previously denied them. Further legislation dealing with marital rape, domestic abuse, the right to abortion, the use of contraceptives, no-fault divorce, and much else led to substantial and deep legal changes, as well as changes in attitudes toward women and toward gender relations more generally.

One interesting stumbling block during this period (and to the present day) was the drafting and failed passage of the Equal Rights Amendment (ERA). The modern version of this bill was first introduced in 1972.[3] Its simple language states: "Equality of rights under the law shall not be denied or abridged by the United States or by any State on account of sex" (117 *Congressional Record* 35815). Yet, for various reasons, this bill has repeatedly failed to be ratified in all fifty states.

Early criticism of the bill foreshadowed later divisions within the movement. One of the most powerful of these concerned the relative status of women and men as separate groups. If the ERA were to be passed, critics held, women would not only become no different from men as a group (i.e., they would be drafted and so on), but also *lose* important rights and privileges they had gained previously as a special group (i.e., maternity leave and so on). In other words, women would lose their status as a protected class. This larger question of women's sameness or difference in relation to men came to define the end period of the second wave.

Early Feminisms of Color

Although the connections between race, ethnicity, and gender were not a primary focus of the second wave, many African American, Latino, and Native

American scholars in the United States began to address these issues early on. In the early 1970s, for example, black, predominantly lesbian, feminists had begun to meet in Boston to protest what they saw as a double oppression: that of gender and race (and later class). Much of their dissatisfaction grew not only from their treatment by the white middle-class women's movement, but also from earlier civil rights and Black Nationalist movements where women of color had largely been excluded.

The Combahee River Collective Statement of April 1977 used, perhaps for the first time, the term *identity politics* in connection with this double situated identity, defining it as "a politics that grew out of our objective material experiences as Black women . . . [that] led to the need to develop a politics that was antiracist, unlike those of white women, and antisexist, unlike those of black and white men." Although the collective ended in 1980, it formed the foundation for a black feminism that understood the intersections of various subject positions and sought liberation for all oppressed peoples. Thus, a black feminist agenda grew that began to address three new challenges: to prove to other black women that feminism was not only for white women, to demand that white women share power with them and affirm diversity, and to fight the misogynist tendencies, especially of Black Nationalism (Burns 2006; see also Hull, Bell Scott, and Smith 1982; and Davis 1981).

The late 1960s and early 1970s also saw the growth of a new interdisciplinary focus on ethnicity, and this growing awareness of racialized and nationalized identities led to the development of ethnic studies departments in the United States, but did not include the racialized category of whiteness, which was to come later. The National Association for Interdisciplinary Studies, later to become the National Association for Ethnic Studies, brought historians, anthropologists, social justice advocates, feminists, and many others together to discuss intersections between all forms of identity, including, but not limited to, gender.

Early feminists of color also sought a central place in a larger Marxist revolution, one that would liberate all oppressed groups worldwide (Weathers 1969). One of the results of this more widespread agenda was a connection that many African American women felt toward other women of color: Latinas, Native Americans, and Asian women in the United States, as well as with women worldwide. This later led to a fruitful partnership with feminist groups outside the United States and with a growing consciousness of unequal, gender-based practices in other parts of the world, especially those that had been colonized by various Western powers. Together, these partnerships furthered the argument that gender was not a single-faceted issue, but, rather, intersected with race, social class, ethnicity, sexuality, and many other identities, creating a matrix of overlapping, intersecting selves that understood gender differently in different cultural contexts and at different times. Thus, the term *gender*, like *woman*, began to be deconstructed and individualized.

The Ebbing of the Second Wave

By the 1980s, the term *postfeminism* had entered discourses surrounding the second wave. Early postfeminists believed that the major issues of outright discrimination against women had largely been solved. Legislation prohibiting marital rape and sexual harassment in the workplace, as well as that permitting legalized abortion, coeducation, and a host of other successes garnered in the second wave, was now seen as the new normal, and much of the energy that fueled the second wave began to ebb.

Three issues, however, rose to the surface near the end of the second wave that caused a rift within the larger feminist community, signaling its end. The first focused on the sameness-difference debate that had been ongoing since the 1970s. The second dealt with female sexuality, sexual pleasure, and differences between hetero- and homosexual women. And the third developed within the growing African American and other feminist communities of color, focusing on intersections between race and gender. Thus, in the 1980s, certain issues dealing with identity politics and difference began to emerge. These would lead, in the late 1980s and beyond, to feminism's third wave.

The Sameness-Difference Debate

The sameness-difference debate initially focused on the passage of the Equal Rights Amendment, but quickly grew to address basic underlying philosophical issues. Many felt—given the successes of the second wave's women's liberation movement—that equal protection was already in place and that the special status accorded to women as child bearers and primary nurturers was now adequately recognized in the law. Thus, proponents of the difference side claimed that women were both equal under the law *and also* different and separate as women, a class of humans defined primarily by biology, as well as by a believed-to-be-shared history of oppression. With protections now in place, they reasoned, we had reached a postfeminist state and there was no longer the need for an Equal Rights Amendment.

Perhaps the most widely known proponent of the difference side of the debate, psychologist and ethicist Carol Gilligan, suggested in her widely acclaimed study of women and girls, *In a Different Voice* (1982), that women tended to think and respond differently from men to intimate relations and moral choices and that this difference should be taken into account in any feminist discourse. This work gradually developed into a new subfield of feminism that came to be known as the ethics of care (Scholz 2010, 92–94), where the very differences between women and men were studied and honored.

Sameness proponents, on the other hand, felt that it was essential to see both men and women as the same under the law and that neither women nor men should be held as a special class and treated differently. Sameness supporters further claimed that continuing to define women by their biology and their supposed universal oppression, that is, those aspects that had largely been responsible for centuries of discrimination, only continued to highlight and perpetuate those differences. Passage of the ERA would ensure that both women and men would have the same rights and privileges in both legal and everyday life. Stopped in its tracks just three states short of passing into law, the ERA still languishes in the American Congress.

The sameness-difference debate, though, began to touch upon an issue that would become prominent in later critiques of the second wave and would lead to exploring the notion of the "universal woman." If women were to be treated in the same way as men, did that mean that all women were the same? Did all women experience and deal with oppression, patriarchy, and other so-called universals in the same way? Were all men actual participants in this inequality, and were men really privileged everywhere? The disciplines of anthropology, ethnic, women's, and cultural studies began to deal with these issues, ultimately moving toward a stance that celebrated difference— not necessarily difference under the law, but individual identity and group difference. Of course, most of this discussion during the 1980s and into the '90s emanated from Western academic discourses. Women and men from other parts of the postcolonial world had different stories yet to be heard.

The Feminist Sex Wars

Another issue that caused an awkward disturbance in the flow of the second wave came to be known as the sex wars, a sometimes heated battle between radical and mainstream feminists over issues of female sexuality, sexual pleasure, pornography, prostitution, and sadomasochism. These issues came to light largely from the lesbian and transsexual communities and focused on the right to legally, socially, and morally determine sexual practices. Prominent feminists on the antipornography side, such as Andrea Dworkin (1981; Dworkin and MacKinnon 1988), Catherine MacKinnon (1987, 1989), and Susan Brownmiller (1975, 1984), among many others, argued that pornography and prostitution were essentially forms of oppression. They fought for and largely succeeded in passing massive legislation against pornography (especially child pornography) and in founding the now national "Take Back the Night" movement, where women and men continue to protest issues of rape, incest, and other sexual abuses.

Proponents on the sex-positive side, such as Robin Morgan (1970), Gayle Rubin (1975), and, later, Nadine Strossen (1994), argued a number of basic issues. If, for example, women were to be totally free of patriarchy, they should be able to define their own sexual practices, which for so long had been positioned within heterosexual norms that privileged male needs (see Adrienne Rich, for example, on compulsory heterosexuality [1980]). Further, they argued, one person's pornography was another person's erotica. Why should one's private sexual practices be subject to legislation? Finally, prohibiting pornography and other printed sexual representations violated basic freedoms of speech and ultimately amounted to censorship.

Black Feminist Critiques

Two women of color were especially important to me and to many others in signaling the growth of a black feminism in the 1980s: author and social activist bell hooks, whose books *Ain't I a Woman? Black Women and Feminism* (1981), *Feminist Theory: From Margin to Center* (1984), and *Talking Back: Thinking Feminist, Thinking Black* (1989), among other writings, became foundational texts. These examined various issues, such as the portrayal of black women (and men) in the media, the failure of the American education system, and the lack of theorizing that privileged intersecting identities.

Writer Alice Walker's work over many decades also helped to bring awareness of the oppression of women of color in the United States and elsewhere. Her early collection of essays *In Search of Our Mothers' Gardens: Womanist Prose* coined the term *womanist,* which she defined as "a black feminist or feminist of color. From the black folk expression of a mother to female children and also a woman who loves other women, sexually and/or nonsexually. Appreciates and prefers women's culture. Committed to survival and wholeness of entire people, male and female" (1983, ix). This term and its association with second-wave feminism would later become a locus of disagreement between Alice Walker and her daughter, Rebecca, one of the young leaders of the third wave.

The end of feminism's second wave left many issues unsettled, and new discussions began dealing with issues of the body—often seen through the lens of women's bodies in relation to eating disorders, sexual violence, and prescribed standards of beauty, as defined and controlled by various media.

Other older issues, such as difference in terms of race, class, ethnicity, religion, and other forms of identity, and those surrounding sex and gender as analytic categories, continued, and evolved, in new ways. But perhaps the most important issue growing in the late 1980s and into the '90s was the deconstruction of the essentialist, ahistorical, universal woman. Unraveling and celebrating differences between and among women (and men) would become a hallmark of the third wave.

Early Feminist Anthropology

Today, there are many fine books discussing the histories and ideas of feminist anthropology,[4] but in the late 1970s there were few. Major questions that interested me as I began my journey: Where were all the women in the anthropological and ethnomusicological literature I was reading? Why were most informants male? Was the male experience also that of the female in the cultural contexts we studied? And were male privilege and power a universal?

The anthropological literature has always included both women and men as social actors in the cultures it has documented, although women, until recently, were seen largely as an afterthought or as an extension of men. Issues of kinship, weddings, childbirth and child rearing, and other activities also contributed to anthropological theory, but were generally integrated into studies focusing on bride exchange, ownership of children, and sexual and ritual practices.[5] Ethnographies and theories specifically focusing on women as a separate group, however, were difficult to find before the 1970s.

What was becoming clear by the late 1970s was that anthropology itself was largely dominated by a male perspective, and questions began to arise concerning how women were being represented in the ethnographic literature. One of the most important first understandings of male bias in anthropology exposed the resonance between gender structures witnessed in the field and those of American society, the institutional home of anthropological inquiry. As most world cultures of the early and mid–twentieth century (including that of the Western academy) were seen and experienced as patriarchal, both male and female fieldworkers tended (mostly unintentionally) to privilege male informants, seeing them as more accessible, more public, and better representatives of their specific cultural norms. In short, male bias in anthropology had been largely invisible to its practitioners.

This resonance further biased the interpretation of data, pushing it seamlessly into Western-friendly analytical categories, such as woman, man, gender, and personhood, categories that sometimes did not fit comfortably with indigenous, especially non-Western, systems. Finally, male bias in anthropology itself tended to privilege male theoretical approaches, so that female anthropologists were largely invisible or unimportant in the early ethnographic and theoretical literature (with some notable exceptions, such as Margaret Mead).[6] Thus, prompted primarily by a new consciousness of gender bias, anthropology began to look inward, in what became a long self-reflective and critical analysis of itself as a discipline.

One of the first steps taken to remedy this problem was to begin constructing women and men as separate analytic categories and to position women's culture in the center of a new subfield, soon to become known as feminist anthropology. Scholars such as Sherry Ortner (1974), Michelle Rosaldo and Louise Lamphere (1974), Eleanor Burke Leacock (1981), and many others began to question basic underlying assumptions in the literature. Four significant and interrelated questions emerged at that time: Are women universally subordinated in all world cultures? If so, what is the origin of this subordination? If not, what other kinds of gender structures existed historically or in contemporary times? And finally, if universal patriarchy exists today, has there ever been matriarchy? These and other questions soon resulted in an explosion of literature, creating many different analytical streams that continue to examine gender imbalances and their histories, cross-culturally, today.[7]

Some Shifting Paradigms

In her book *Feminism and Anthropology*, Henrietta Moore summarized mainstream anthropology's reaction to feminist challenges in the 1980s and earlier by first presenting a three-part chain-reaction model of male bias within the field, as seen in earlier ethnographies dealing with gender cross-culturally. The first link in the chain concerned the anthropologist her- or himself, who, having been raised and educated most often in Europe or the United States, or in countries colonized by European or U.S. interests (or both), brought into the field, perhaps unintentionally, unconscious assumptions about men and women as separate and unequal social groups. This led to a second link: a certain blindness in recognizing different arrangements, or misinterpreting them, where concepts of specific gender categories, or gender hierarchies in their field sites, might be fuzzy or irrelevant.

This, in turn, led anthropologists (both male and female) to see these unequal relationships in the field as analogous to those of Western society. Thus, it was important, wrote Moore, to move from an "anthropology of women," which was "more remedial than radical," to a feminist anthropology, one that studied gender and gender relations (1988, 6). This was important because it could expose the previously hidden assumptions of both the fieldwork method and anthropology itself. This resulted in a new literature in the 1980s concerned with rethinking categories, such as woman, man, and gender cross-culturally, and in reevaluating social relations in terms of difference in many layers: difference between women and men; difference between and among women and men; difference in class, race, in families, and so on; and, perhaps most important, difference in understanding notions of "personhood," including access to resources, degrees of autonomy, and styles of power found within social groups.[8]

Certain scholars began to generate important questions: Were categories such as women and men important signifiers in all cultures?[9] Were women really universally subordinated? What were the crucial differences in humans that needed to be addressed in a feminist anthropology? What theoretical approaches were best suited to address sameness and difference? And how could one be both an anthropologist (observing, participating) and a feminist (challenging, protesting)?[10]

The Anthropology of Power

Another area of inquiry, the anthropology of power, also began to take on new life and became especially important for me at this time. Of long-standing interest to anthropology, discussions of power had begun to diverge in the late 1970s and '80s from a primarily (monolithic and hierarchic) Marxist model, branching out to address inequalities embedded within race and gender, as well as class constructs (Leacock 1981). One of the first books I read that helped me more deeply understand power dynamics as they related to gender was Raymond Fogelson and Richard Adams's *The Anthropology of Power* (1977), a collection of essays analyzing power relations among Melanesians and Native Americans, where power was negotiated, not only between and among humans, but also between and among humans and spirits.

Perhaps the most important thing I took away from that book when I first read it in the early 1980s was the notion that power was not something one *had* over another, but, rather, something inherent in social interactions of all kinds—a force that was embedded in all human constructs, such as religion, ritual, language, and music, a force that resulted, through persuasion, coercion, or violence, in the dominance of one entity over another. The resulting power-powerlessness binary also seemed to resonate with other binaries (female-male, nature-culture, private-public, and so on) that I had come to see as structuring my 1980s worldview.

Ideas questioning these binaries, such as those of Michel Foucault and Pierre Bourdieu, among many others, also began to surface more broadly in the anthropological writings of the 1980s. Foucault, for example, saw power and powerlessness not as a binary, but, rather, as a constant process of interaction,

circulation, and mediation that strategically positioned individuals and institutions in complex situations where certain people or groups came to be per-
suaded of their own powerlessness and others of their own power (Foucault
1977, 1995, in Kingsolver 2002). Once established, maintenance of this system
could be ensured through language, ritual, and everyday interactions, among
many other forces. Bourdieu (1977) concentrated primarily on what he called
symbolic capital (prestige, honor, and so on) as a primary source of power and
focused on how language and other human interactions legitimized power
structures, seeing subordinate groups and individuals as somewhat complicit
in their own powerlessness.

   Although there is no doubt that philosophers, such as Foucault and Bourdieu, began to have a tremendous influence on anthropology, some feminist
theorists quickly began to critique their ideas, especially Foucault's (1975)
reduction of the powerless to "docile bodies," a concept developed early on
in his study of prisons.[11] Anthropologists, such as Nancy Fraser (1989) and
others, soon pointed out that in not providing enough structure to the "big
stories" of power relations, there was no place in Foucault's philosophy for
resistance and the ultimate overthrow of male dominance. If power was
everywhere, coming from multiple directions and sources at once, requiring
constant diligence, they reasoned, where did autonomy exist and how could
constantly created docile bodies ever become empowered?

Power Relations in Fieldwork

Yet another new area of intellectual inquiry came into being during the 1980s
that had a profound effect on my thinking. Many questions being posed by
those interested in gender and in systems of power began to filter into the
fieldwork process itself and into the underlying assumptions and narrative
structures of ethnography. Ultimately, this led to a moment of extreme self-
reflection in anthropology, now called the "crisis of representation," where the
role of the fieldworker was deconstructed. Led by George Marcus and Dick
Cushman (1982), Marcus and Michael Fischer (1986), and Clifford Geertz
(1988), this debate centered primarily on issues of representation: How could
anyone represent an other or a group of others adequately? How did just
being there change the societies with which we worked, causing people to
perhaps become "self" conscious under our gaze in ways they had not been
before? And, perhaps most important, were the ethnographies we wrote
simply fictive narratives of our own power?

   Some feminist anthropologists, though, would come to see this self-reflexive moment as destructive to their purpose: just when power imbalances
between women and men were beginning to be uncovered in the field, and

just when women were beginning to speak in their own voices, they were effectively silenced in the wake of a new theoretical paradigm (proposed largely, they pointed out, by male leaders in the field) that put fieldwork and ethnography into question as viable methods of data collection and presentation (Mascia-Lees, Sharpe, and Cohen 1989). What had happened to women and men as analytic categories and to fieldwork as a core method of experiencing and learning a new culture?

Thus, feminist anthropology in the 1980s was beginning to rethink and critique older understandings of woman, man, and gender; develop new theories that could address different gender structures and how they were enacted cross-culturally; and take on a sort of political activism that protested theoretical positions not explicitly dealing with real women's actual oppression. Rich ethnographies, such as *Nisa: The Life and Words of a !Kung Woman,* by Marjorie Shostak (1981), and *Crafting Selves: Power, Gender, and Discourses of Identity in a Japanese Workplace,* by Dorrine K. Kondo (1990), as well as many important collections, appeared in a veritable explosion of literature. No longer content with the older, remedial model, where women were simply recognized as a human category, and perhaps placed in the center of a study, this work opened up new paths for theorizing gender, focusing on the relational, interactive, intersubjective, and negotiated aspects of gendered human relations.

But an even more fundamental shift was also occurring in these earlier days of postmodernist and feminist thinking in anthropology—a shift in focus from a high level of abstraction, where differences were often blurred or ignored, to a more differentiated level of specificity, where difference itself became the focus. This shift from a top-down, all-encompassing, and often monolithic theoretical approach, largely producing essentialist and ahistorical thinking, to a bottom-up, more specific theoretical focus allowed real people to emerge as agents in their own lives, a notion that ultimately became the bedrock of feminism's third wave. For me, this resonated with my strong commitment to fieldwork—actually living with and connecting to individuals whose complicated identities, musical and otherwise, were constantly in flux and whose lives were lived absorbing and producing similarities and differences of all kinds, aligning them here and differentiating them there from others in their orbits.

The Beginnings of a Feminist Ethnomusicology

Much of the early literature, especially that on women and music from before the 1970s and into the early '80s, is examined more fully in the introduction to *Women and Music in Cross-Cultural Perspective* (1987), which is reproduced here as chapter 2, so I will only summarize general trends. Works began to appear in the 1970s that questioned the lack of women's representation in the literature as performers, creators, and experiencers of music cross-culturally.

These paralleled other discoveries of women's expressive cultures, especially in art history. In 1971 art historian Linda Nochlin published an important article titled "Why Have There Been No Great Women Artists?" in which she questioned underlying assumptions about men, women, and their artistic expressions, seeing the invisibility of women as a direct consequence of hierarchic values surrounding men's and women's artistic efforts, especially within the European art tradition. This article was extremely helpful to me in the late 1970s and early '80s, for it was easy to make the leap to music. So many of the issues were similar, especially in reference to Western art music, similarly burdened by the (largely invisible) gendered notions of male genius, masterwork, and canon formation. But, she cautioned, to do this questioning, we needed more documentation and better evidence of women's artistic work.

Thus, many studies began to appear in both ethnomusicology and historical musicology that fell into the category referred to today (somewhat pejoratively) as "woman worthy" or "compensatory history" (Nochlin 1971). This work attempted to fill in the gaps, documenting women's musical roles in various rituals and female-associated activities.[12] These scholars, including myself, were motivated by a growing awareness that ethnographies and monographs ignoring women were not representing the whole of musical cultures worldwide.

Four articles were especially important to me at the time, in that they assumed a basic link between women, music, and othering that led the way to deeper understandings of the importance of cultural constructions, not necessarily biological givens, for the study of music and its gender imbalances—and they were all based on fieldwork. Articles by Kenneth A. Gourlay on the sexual symbolism of musical instruments in Papua New Guinea (1970), Lorraine Sakata (1976) on the links between gender and musical practice in Afghanistan, Norma McLeod and Marcia Herndon (1975) on women's folk music on Malta, and Byong Won Lee (1979) on the Korean courtesan tradition all dealt in some way with the relationship between cultural musical norms—understood implicitly as male—and other musics, somehow defined in relation to this norm. Each suggests, first, that societies regulate cultural activities according to norms that are gender coded and, second, that women who are outside both male and female norms (i.e., shamans, prostitutes, midwives, lesbians, witches, and so on) are often awarded certain musical freedoms not given to women who adhere to their prescribed roles.

Thus, these scholars began to understand that "woman" was not one mono-lithic category, but differentiated according to ethnicity, race, class, or social position (or a combination). Their understandings were derived from their recognition that the women they were discussing were in some way "social deviants." But now the term *deviant* was beginning to lose its more negative associations and to become aligned with newer notions of difference. This understanding of difference in relation to culturally constructed and gender-coded norms ultimately became the basis of newer postmodern literature of the 1980s, '90s, and beyond.

A Theoretical Shift: From Women to Gender

As in anthropology, a theoretical shift in feminist ethnomusicology occurred during the 1970s and '80s, when scholars began to move away from an earlier form of compensatory scholarship toward a radically different conceptu-alization of gender as a socially constructed system regulating all forms of human behavior. A new form of music scholarship emerged that was heavily influenced by anthropology and social and cultural history, one that sought to understand music not simply as a product of human behavior, but also as an interpretive site for enacting and performing gender relations. A prolif-eration of studies on Western concert music, especially opera, as well as on Western or Western-influenced popular music traditions emerged at this time, as scholars began to expose powerful ideologies and systems of power that controlled gendered musical behavior and its discourses worldwide.[13] Again, as much of the literature of this period is discussed in chapter 2, I focus here on a few key works that were important to me at the time. Each of these helped me frame significant questions and begin to construct a theory that would address the ifs, wheres, and whys of gender and music imbalances cross-culturally. I treat them chronologically here.

As though through divine intervention, three works—all published in 1980—suddenly appeared on the scene: Elizabeth Wood's pathbreaking ar-ticle "Women in Music," in *Signs;* Joanne Riley's "Women and World Music: Straining Our Ears to the Silence," in *Heresies;* and Nancy Falk and Rita Gross's wonderful collection, *Unspoken Worlds: Women's Religious Lives in Non-Western Cultures.* Each work, in its own way, pointed to the lack of docu-mentation concerning women's musical practices and the need to rethink connections with other feminist scholarship in women's and gender studies.

Although Wood's article invoked the spirit of ethnomusicology, suggesting a closer look at American folk musics, it focused primarily on Western art music, presenting a solid review of previous literature on composers such as Barbara Strozzi (1619–67) and Ruth Crawford Seeger (1901–53), as well as commenting on two contemporary publications: *Unsung: A History of Women in American Music*, by Christine Ammer (1980), and *Women Making Music: Studies in the Social History of Women Musicians and Composers*, edited by Jane Bowers and Judith Tick (1986)—now a staple of historical and critical musicology. Wood called for a more contextualized research that incorporated social and cultural constraints or privileges that had traditionally affected women composers. Further, she proposed new areas of research on music and political activism, patronage systems, and institutionalized sexism (such as the face-to-face audition process common for orchestral musicians in the 1980s). In addition, Wood advised her historical musicology colleagues to adapt analytical and interpretive theories from ethnic studies, black history, and, most important, the new burgeoning field of gender studies.[14]

Joanne Riley's article in *Heresies* performed a similar service for ethnomusicologists. *Heresies: A Feminist Publication on Art and Politics* was a journal published from 1977 to 1992 by the Heresies Collective in New York City. Although primarily interested in the visual arts, issue number 10, published in 1980, was devoted to music. In addition to Riley's article, it included others on American composers and on the compositional method, a few articles on female African American composers and performers, and a number of ethnomusicology-friendly articles on music and healing, women and American Indian musics, and, to my knowledge, the first article ever published on women-identified music.

Using Ortner's finding of universal discrimination against women as the foundation of her argument, Riley surveyed the existing ethnomusicological literature and proposed that women's culture (as separate from that of men) be researched "to reveal the influence of a universal androcentric culture [in order to] give women's lives and activities the respectful attention which they deserve" (79). This article is the first I read—perhaps the first written—that clearly made a connection between ethnomusicology and gender studies.

In this same miraculous year, Nancy A. Falk and Rita M. Gross published a collection of essays that examined various case studies of women's ritual practices outside the West. To structure the essays, they linked them by women's shared strategies in these contexts, prefacing related essays with startling headings, such as "Women Explode: Ritualized Rebellion for Women" and "Up against the Wall: Women in Male-Dominated Systems." They also presented situations of relative gender equality in sections entitled "Success Stories: Women and Men in Balance or Equality" and "Womb Envy: Male Domination and Women's Power." This collection was especially helpful to me, as I was dealing with women, music, and ritual within the Lubavitcher Hasidic culture and was finding it difficult to understand what I saw then as a highly skewed musical and social system. And it also energized me—after all, these scholars seemed angry, and I shared this anger without yet truly understanding the whole story.

By the late 1980s, scholars in ethnomusicology had taken up the challenge of feminism and many other "isms" that questioned the pervasive power structures of the status quo. Four works appeared in the late 1980s that helped me better understand the breadth, complexity, and variety of gender relations cross-culturally. All of them were based on careful fieldwork and presented strategies (as in the Falk and Gross collection) that women and men used either to perform their traditional gendered musical activities or to protest them.[15] Judith Vander's book *Songprints: The Musical Experience of Five Shoshone Women* (1988) and Veronica Doubleday's *Three Women of Heart* (1990) together provide beautiful and complex pictures of specific women's musical lives, showing their resilience and integrity in situations often fraught with social and political upheaval. These works reminded me that real women had lived these lives, had names, real families and communities, real stories, and their own perspectives. Theorizing, I cautioned myself, tended to erase their realness, to make invisible their real-life musical selves.

Finally, two articles, both appearing at the end of the decade in 1989—Jane C. Sugarman's "The Nightingale and the Partridge: Singing and Gender among Prespa Albanians" and Beverley Cavanagh's "Music and Gender in the Sub-Arctic Algonkian Area"—presented some creative new models to better integrate and theorize cultural performances of music and gender, thus linking musical sounds with social structures more convincingly. Jane Sugarman states near the beginning of her article that among the Presparë, a Muslim Albanian people living in (the former) Yugoslavia,

> Singing, rather than merely reflecting notions of gender, also shapes those notions in return. . . . Through singing they are temporarily able to mold their individual selves into the form of a cultural ideal. In the process they may choose to affirm that ideal, by following closely the norms of musical practice, or they may use their singing to suggest its revision. Gender concepts and musical practice can thus be seen to exist in a dialectical relationship to each other, each functioning as a "mutually determining aspect" of the Prespa "system." (193)

The notion that gender was *performed* (like music), and that these performances informed one another at different levels of analysis, was my first inkling of what Edward L. Schieffelin (1985, 1998) and later Judith Butler

(1990) came to call "performativity," a concept I have found to be immensely useful over the years and to which I return later in this volume.

Beverley Cavanagh states outright in her article's first sentence: "This paper explores different frameworks for talking and writing about gender in relation to several Indian communities in the northeastern Algonkian area," a project she admits undertaking with "considerable apprehension." Largely using an insider perspective, based on the Algonkian language (not easy to translate into English), Cavanagh teases out three levels of performance based on gender: performances that are clearly male or female, those that are more or less egalitarian but where "gender differentiation may occur at the level of style or interpretation," and "Algonkian explanations for, on the one hand, the distinctiveness of women's roles, and, on the other, the complementarity of gender roles, the latter concept being voiced in different ways by contemporary native speakers and authors" (1989, 55–56).

With this model, Cavanagh exposes one of the most persistent problems inherent in gender scholarship: dividing the world into a binary system (male-female) leads inevitably to a rigid value hierarchy. Algonkians, however, although recognizing *difference* between the genders, also see them as *equally valuable* (complementary). Thus, Algonkians may create a binary system based on gender difference—but it does not lead to a hierarchy of value. The uncoupling of difference from value within a binary is still an undertheorized concept, but was, at the time, a new and wonderfully liberating concept for me and continues to energize my thinking today.

*   *   *

The two chapters that follow are clearly a pair: Chapter 2, the introduction to *Women and Music in Cross-Cultural Perspective,* attempts to gather together relevant music scholarship on women and gender before and during the first half of the 1980s. It also suggests a potential theory that could be applied cross-culturally. Chapter 3, "Both In and Between," focuses more specifically on women's musical activities in three widely different ritual contexts, elaborating and expanding upon the theory presented in chapter 2.

2 Introduction to *Women and Music in Cross-Cultural Perspective*

The introduction to *Women and Music in Cross-Cultural Perspective* (1987) is probably my best-known work. Certainly, it is the one most cited and quoted by others, and for many readers in the late 1980s and early '90s it presented the first collection of articles specifically devoted to gender, music, and (mostly) ethnomusicology. It was inspired by the wonderful papers I had heard at the second University of Michigan's Women and Music Conference (1983), where the organizers had responded to suggestions that the focus should be wider than simply Western art musics. Many of the papers I heard there ended up in this volume.

However, just before its initial publication, I became increasingly uncomfortable with the word *Women* in the title, wanting to change it to *Gender,* but the book was already too far along in the process and I was still unclear about the implications of this change. I was now only beginning to see the richness of a gendered ethnomusicology opening before me. My main task in this introduction was, I thought at the time, to present and organize the ethnomusicological literature I had already discovered. I also hoped to develop a general theory that could explain musical performance in terms of gendered belief systems based on notions of power, prestige, and value, cross-culturally.

Upon completion of the introduction, only one universal statement based on the existing literature I surveyed could tentatively be made: nowhere did men and women have equal access to all musical experiences and opportunities within a given society; gender-based restrictions of some sort existed everywhere (mostly for women, but also for men) from the mildest, such as gently steering a young American boy away from playing the harp in the school orchestra, to the most violent, such as threats of gang rape against the

Mundurucú women of central Brazil who see the men's sacred flutes (Basso 1987). Of course, not all of the world's musical cultures had been equally researched, and much more information was needed on all aspects of gendered musical behavior, especially among traditional cultures of Central and South America, Africa, and Asia, a gap in the research that persists to this day.

In this introduction, I focused first on gender ideologies, those often inherited systems that come to be acted out and reinforced through ritual, language, music, and other processes. I devised a continuum of gendered musical contexts, ranging from total domination-coercion to total separation-autonomy.[1] Within those contexts, I wrote, women were able to protest, validate, and negotiate gender relations. Of course, in moving to a general, highly abstract level of discourse ("Among the X, all women do Y"), I fell into the essentialist trap so common in cross-cultural surveys.

*   *   *

In this introduction, I examine the implications of gender upon music performance and address, either explicitly or implicitly, two central questions. First, to what degree does a society's gender ideology and resulting gender-related behaviors affect its musical thought and practice? And second, how does music function in society to reflect or affect intergender relations? I begin by asking whether gender-specific music cultures actually exist. Is not culture a homogeneous whole, an integrated system? Recent studies of women's folklore and culture[2] have suggested that in many societies, women and men do appear to occupy separate expressive spheres, creating not necessarily two separate and self-contained music cultures, but rather two differentiated yet complementary and overlapping halves of culture.

Until recently, though, ethnographers have tended to focus primarily on the more public, more easily accessible sphere occupied by males. Why this is so may reflect the worldview and resulting methodologies of anthropologists more than the lack of women's musical activities in the societies we study. Bruno Nettl, for example, asks in *The Study of Ethnomusicology* (1983, 334) whether the large proportion of women in ethnomusicology has had an effect on the nature of research. In answering, he hints at some of the factors that may account for an unbalanced picture of world music, heavily weighted toward male musical practices. He notes, for example, the possibility that "this may result from the dominant role of men in determining approaches and methods," that both males and females in the field have collected information primarily from male informants and assumed that the picture was complete, or that the use of male fieldworkers inhibited female informants, especially those unused to (or prohibited from) performing in the presence of men or in a public setting (ibid., 334–35).

Some of these problems have also been addressed recently by anthropologists, now concerned with the complexities of gender issues and their effect on other cultural domains. Such studies have begun to uncover some of the problems associated with Western-oriented anthropological thinking and training.[3] Rayna R. Reiter, in her introductory essay "Toward an Anthropology of Women," sees a double male bias in anthropological accounts. First, ethnographers bring to the field the bias of Western anthropology, which has "developed a theoretical perspective that separates biology from culture in the investigation of race," but has not done so for gender; this has, in effect, prevented us from seeing the second category of bias: expressions of male dominance in the societies we study (1975, 14). Sally Slocum echoes this concern when she comments that too often when the word *man* is used (as in "The Study of Man"), "supposedly meaning human species, it is actually exactly synonymous with 'males'" (1975, 38).

Until recently, few of us were aware of the impact of our own or any other society's gender structure on all sorts of behavior. In fact, until the late 1960s and 1970s, both male and female fieldworkers seemed to accept uncritically the androcentric theoretical models (see Stack et al. 1975 and Rosaldo 1980 for more insights into this problem). "If an unbalanced picture of world music has been presented, scholars of both sexes bear the responsibility" (Nettl 1983, 337). Many anthropologists now feel that developing newer investigative techniques that collect corresponding data from women will help explain the "seeming contradictions and internal workings of a system for which we have only half the pieces" (Reiter 1975, 15). These views are shared by many others, notably Judith Hoch-Smith and Anita Spring (1978), who caution fieldworkers to look toward women's groups for clues to cultural notions of power and cooperation.[4]

Review of the Ethnomusicological Literature

In spite of the picture presented thus far, references to women's music and musical practices are not uncommon in the ethnomusicological literature. When ethnographies focus on female initiation rites, birth, or child care, women's musical activities associated with such events are frequently noted. Usually descriptive in nature, many do not explicitly address issues of women's status, intergender relations, or the effects of a society's gender arrangements on women's musical behavior. Most often encountered are passing references to women, a sentence here or there that hints at musical activity or the lack of it.[5] Other studies that do attempt a fuller cultural description of women's musical activities are relatively fewer in number, and some are exceptionally rich in ethnographic detail.[6] Still others have focused on women's instrumental practices or vocal genres where data were collected primarily from female informants.[7]

Many authors have noted the links between women's sexuality, their culturally perceived sex role, and music behavior; some describe performances that include licentious sexual behavior, ranging from flirting to actual copulation during performances. Among the Yoruk, for example, Richard Keeling discusses the explicit sexual nature of Yoruk light songs (1985, 199); Carol Campbell and Carol Eastman, among the Swahili, describe all-female gatherings where the young women do hip rotations to learn the "right" sexual movements (1984, 477); Usopay Cadar describes the Maranao Kulintang tradition of the Philippines, where women performers must learn correct female body positions ("Head and torso are in a position that should pass the old test of letting a water-filled glass stand on the top of the head . . . without spilling the water" [1973, 240]). All of these examples and many others point to musical behavior associated with or heightening female sexuality, specifically citing gestures, erotic dance movements, and various constricting, yet correct, body positions for women performers.

Others have commented upon the frequent association of women's musical activities with implied or real prostitution. Norma McLeod and Marcia Herndon, for example, in their article "The Bormliza: Maltese Folksong Style and Women" (1975), show how Maltese concepts of women and music intersect, creating two basic categories: women who do not sing in public places and those who do, and by that very act are considered prostitutes. Lorraine Sakata (1976) notes the association of professional singers in Afghanistan with the courtesan tradition; Byong Won Lee, in his article tracing the changes in role and status of Korean female performers (1979), delineates a three-tiered grading system used traditionally to rank such performers, ranging from one, the highest (women of correct moral behavior who receive the most status and remuneration), to three, the lowest (prostitutes).

If performances by young (mostly unmarried) women tend to heighten sexuality, those by older women (past childbearing years) often downplay this aspect of gender identity, frequently resulting in women's loss of musical interest or in added musical responsibilities. Charlotte Frisbie among the Navaho (1967, 1980), Barbara Hampton among the Ga (1982), and Joann Kealiinohomoku (1967), describing female dance genres in Polynesia, among many others, comment upon the changing musical roles of women as they advance in age.

Acceptable environments for women's musical performances of all kinds have also been noted by researchers who, by moving away from public, male-dominated musical domains to the private domains of women, have discovered a variety of musical traditions. Authors such as David Ames among the Hausa of Zaria (1973), Mercedes Mackay among Nigerian Muslim women (1955), Indira Junghare in India (1983), Steven Feld among the Kaluli (1982), Jihad Racy discussing Druze funeral music (1971), Ellen Koskoff among Hasidic women (1976), and many others have described separate all-female performance contexts, styles, and genres.

Some attempts at cross-cultural examination of sex role and its relation to music behavior have also been made. Curt Sachs, for example, in *The History of Musical Instruments,* after describing a number of musical instruments associated with males and females in performance, uses a predominantly Freudian interpretation when he notes, "The player's sex and the form of his or her instrument, or at least its interpretation, depend on one another. As the magic task of more or less all primitive instruments is life, procreation, fertility, it is evident that the life-giving roles of either sex are seen or reproduced in their shape or playing motion. A man's instrument 'assumes the form of a man's organ, a woman's of a woman's organ. And in the latter case, the addition of a fertilizing object is not far off" (1940, 51).

Dennison Nash states that where male and female roles are less differentiated and where "specialization in the field of music is not far advanced (i.e., Toco, Trinidad or the society of the medieval Troubadors)," one may find women composers of note; however, in societies "where specialization in the creation of music is more advanced (i.e., Bali, among the Chopi, and in modem America), one rarely finds women among the ranks of eminent composers," presumably due to their time-consuming occupation of child rearing (1961, 82–83). Alan Lomax has noted that correlations exist between a given society's sexual sanctions and its vocal style, stating that in societies where premarital sexual activity is restricted, a high degree of "narrowing and nasality, both signs of tension," become prominent and constant features of a culture's singing style (1968, 195). And Alan Merriam, too, has noted that music "reflects, and in a sense symbolizes, male-female roles" (1964, 248).

It is not surprising that the majority of existing descriptions of women's musical activities and rationales for their behavior focus on their primary social roles, for these roles are central to women's gender identity in many societies. Further, it is also not surprising that so many descriptions exist, for musical activities surrounding such roles, presumably receiving social sanction, would be the most accessible to ethnographers. Valuable as these descriptions are, what is needed now is a deeper analysis of the relationship between a society's gender structure, what ideologies surround gender, the nature of intergender relations, and how all of these affect music behavior. Further, we must invert this question and ask how music behavior itself reflects and symbolizes gender behavior. In undertaking such an analysis, we may begin to answer some of the questions posed implicitly by the descriptions cited above. Gertrude Kurath, as early as 1960, in her study of Native American societies, recognized the need for such an analysis, stating, "The role of the sexes in ethnic dance is so eloquent of occupations and social relationships, from segregation to mutual aid, as to merit a prolonged study in itself" (4).

Gender Ideology and Its Effect on Women's Music Making

In order to introduce some of the current thinking on the effects of gender structure on other cultural domains, I begin by making certain preliminary remarks concerning sex and gender, gender ideologies, and intergender relations, by distinguishing between the biological categories of sex (female-male), the socially constructed categories of gender (woman-man), and the systems of belief that provide, uniquely for each society, an underlying conceptual framework for ideal behavior based on gender (gender ideologies) (see Ortner and Whitehead 1981, 6–9). The gender structure of a society reflects socially constructed and maintained arrangements, made between men and women largely based on inherited, culture-specific gender ideologies. Although gender structures theoretically range on a continuum from total male to total female dominance, in no known society do women dominate men (see Rosaldo and Lamphere 1974).

Margaret Mead, in her pioneering 1935 study, *Sex and Temperament in Three Primitive Societies,* proposed that seemingly "natural" behaviors associated with either sex were not founded in nature, per se, but were rather the result of ideologies and processes that were socially constructed, warning us that we must recognize that "the cultural plot behind human relations is the way in which the roles of the two sexes are conceived, and that the growing boy is shaped to a local and special emphasis as inexorably as the growing girl" (1963, x). Thus, although one's biological sex can be, and frequently is, brought into play as a rationale for certain socially defined and acceptable behaviors, aside from the obvious biological differences between females and males that allow women and not men to bear and nurture children, most other behaviors depend not so much on biological sex differentiation as on culturally conceived notions of gender and on prestige systems that accord value to one gender over the other.

General studies dealing with the distinctions between sex and gender have begun to appear in the anthropological literature. Kay Martin and Barbara

Voorhies, for example, present an excellent survey of anthropological theories concerning the "fundamental nature of the sexes" (1975, 144), Catherine MacKinnon (1982) offers a synthesis of feminist and Marxist thought that attempts to explain the origins of intergender arrangements in social class, and Carol MacCormack and Marilyn Strathern (1980) and Gayle Rubin (1975) present excellent summaries of issues raised by earlier theorists, mainly Lévi-Strauss, Engels, Marx, and Freud, concerning the role of gender relations in developing kinship systems, incest taboos, and exclusive heterosexuality.

Although there are generally two culturally recognized sex and gender categories,[8] gender structures and ideologies vary widely from society to society and from group to group within societies, so that gender-specific behaviors may, in cross-cultural comparison, seem quite opposite. Anthropologists such as Martin and Voorhies (1975) and Ortner and Whitehead (1981), among many others, have recently reiterated the need in data collection and analysis to make clear the distinctions between sex- and gender-related concepts and behaviors. Ortner and Whitehead, especially, stress the need for cross-cultural comparisons that discuss the degree to which different cultures have formal notions of gender and sexuality and whether such notions operate as "master organizing principles for other domains of life or social activity" (1981, 6).

Indeed, what are the implications of culture-specific gender ideologies on music performance cross-culturally? If we assume that in most societies, a woman's identity is believed to be embedded in her sexuality, one of the most common associations between women and music, as we have already seen, links women's primary sexual identity and role with music performance. Women's sexuality, both self- and other defined, affects their musical performance in three important ways: performance environments may provide a context for sexually explicit behavior, such that music performance becomes a metaphor for sexual relations; the actual or perceived loss of sexuality may change women's musical role or status or both; and cultural beliefs in women's inherent sexuality may motivate the separation of, or restriction imposed upon, women's musical activities.

The issue of female sexuality centers for our purposes on a basic distinction in many societies between women who are exclusively heterosexual and those who are not. Females not in this category—young girls, older women, shamans, homosexual, and "marginal" women (i.e., those who may be of childbearing years, but are perceived as "sexless" for other reasons)—may assume certain musical roles that deny or negate their sexuality. Older women especially may assume different musical roles from those they had in childhood and during their childbearing years, roles frequently accompanied by higher social and musical status. Ernestine Friedl, for example, in her excellent cross-cultural study of male and female ritual behavior, notes that older women may gain in power and status because their former status as child bearers and nurturers effectively barred them from much ritual activity. When women have lost their sexual potency, they have an opportunity to "reverse the balance of a lifetime" (1975, 85).

Women whom men claim for exclusive heterosexual activity, that is, menstruating and childbearing women, such as mates, lovers, concubines, courtesans, or prostitutes, often assume musical roles that either heighten their sexuality or restrict its display. Women's "musical talent" in the West, for example, is often defined in terms of cultural expectations of female sexuality. Elizabeth Wood notes that for musical success, however socially defined, "women must frequently serve the linked economic and erotic interests of a dominant culture" (1980, 295). In societies where males were or are the main patrons of musical performances or where male-dominated political, religious, and economic spheres call for young female performers, musical behaviors that heighten female sexuality are the norm.

Sexual identity also affects women's music performance in another important way. The belief in women's inherent and uncontrollable sexuality, often expressed in terms of menstruation taboos or in anxiety about women's insatiable and destructive sexual appetites, may lead to a separation between women's and men's expressive domains and in some societies to restrictions imposed upon certain women's musical activity. Most human societies recognize biological, sexual differences between females and males. In many societies, these sexual categories link up with other symbolic binaries, creating conceptual clusters (male-female, nature-culture, public-domestic, and so on) that provide a framework for gender identity. Because gender identity is not necessarily consistent with sex category, it is possible for males and females, although biologically one sex or the other, to cross over into opposite gender domains, displaying behaviors normally associated with the opposite sex. This subject has implications for music performance and is one to which we will return below.

Origins of the binaries surrounding gender categories are treated by various authors. MacCormack and Strathern (1980) discuss the structuralist theories of Lévi-Strauss concerning nature-culture dichotomies current in European thinking;[9] Ortner (1974) presents a theory of woman, the primary socializer of infant children (both male and female), as mediator between nature and culture; Rayna Reiter (1979) and Peggy Sanday (1974) address the issue of gender-related strategies for gaining control and power in both domestic (female) and public (male) domains, spheres of activity that can differ considerably from society to society.

The separation of men and women into two gender categories has profound implications for music thought and behavior. Many societies similarly divide musical activity into two spheres that are consistent with other symbolic dualisms. Authors have noted that the division of musical labors reflects the gender-related dichotomies discussed here. Jonathan Hill, in describing the male performance genre *jaqui* found in the Brazilian Amazon Basin, states that this rite symbolizes a "relation of dialectical opposition between the sexes as groups" and that performance "models the sexual division of labor and the opposition between insiders and outsiders" (1979, 418, 430). Mary Coote (1977), in discussing the traditional division of Serbo-Croatian songs into "heroic" and "women's songs," relates this primary division to binary contrasts noted in other social domains: public-private, actions-feelings, socially positive-negative acts, and so on. Timothy Rice (1980), discussing the Macedonian *sobor,* relates women's participation in this celebration to the basic division in Macedonian society between women, the religious observers, and men, the celebrants. Steven Feld among the Kaluli in Papua New Guinea (1982), Adrienne Kaeppler in Tonga (1970), Lorraine Sakata in Afghanistan (1976), Norma McLeod and Marcia Herndon in Malta (1975), and Anthony Seeger among the Suyá Indians of Brazil (1980) have all noted that the division of musical roles and responsibilities is conceptually linked to other culture-specific, gender-related domains. These range from the most common associations, male:female = public:private, to those of insult:compliment = inner world:outer world (McLeod and Herndon 1975, 88); urban:rural = variety:homogeneity (Sakata 1976, 13); weeping provoked by song:weeping provoked by loss = little text:extended text (Feld 1982, 94); and so on.

One result of the conceptual linking between gender, music, and other cultural domains is a separation between male and female performance environments, genres, and performing styles. Separation, perhaps the result of gender ideologies that stress contamination or other putative destructive female forces, can also act as a positive catalyst for female bonding. Sally Price (1983), in her studies of a so-called woman-dominated society (the Suriname Maroons), discusses the conscious desire of many female singers to present their own songs as "reflection[s] of their self-image" and as explanations of the gaps they perceive between the way they see themselves and the way they are seen by others (1983, 468). Feld has shown the complementarity of gender relations as reflected in Kaluli music performance, where men and women have "coordinated separate expressive spheres" (1982, 397) of equal value. The presence of secluded, all-female gatherings where many social restrictions regarding musical performance are lifted often serves the dual goals of providing women a socially acceptable, if limited, forum for musical expression as well as an environment for the expression of gender identity. Musical behavior, then, not only is enmeshed in social concepts of sexuality, but can also serve to reinforce and define one's gender.

Music in Intergender Relations

Music performance can also be an active agent in intergender relations, transforming, reversing, or mediating conflict between the sexes. At the heart of most gender (and other) relations are notions of power. In all societies for which we have evidence, males control access to most educational, political, religious, and economic institutions. Yet each society (and, indeed, each household) arranges its intergender relations in its own unique way. Thus, we find a wide range of social possibilities, from societies where men control through force or coercion to those where men and women are perceived not in a conceptual framework of opposition, but rather in terms of complementarity and where control is more or less shared.

Ortner and Whitehead state, "The study of gender is inherently a study of relations of asymmetrical power and opportunity" (1981, 4). Rosaldo and Lamphere critique two possible explanations for such asymmetry: biological differences between the sexes and evolutionary adaptive measures. The first argument is rejected on the basis that "biology constrains but does not determine the behavior of the sexes" and that "differences between human males and females reflect an interaction between our physical constitutions and our patterns of social life" (1974, 5). Evolutionary arguments, dividing ancient human societies into man the hunter (i.e., cooperative, far-wandering, public, "cultural") versus woman the gatherer (i.e., individualistic, domestic, private, "natural"), are similarly rejected because they do not adequately explain why such high value is placed on male activities.[10]

Music performance can also provide a context for behavior that challenges or threatens the established social and sexual order. The common use of such strategies of protest, disguise, or gender transformation in many diverse social and musical settings points to one of the most interesting social processes that occurs cross-culturally, namely, social deception. The word *deception* is used cautiously here, for I am not referring necessarily to a conscious intent to deceive, mislead, or hoax, although, in fact, that may be the case in certain circumstances. Rather, I use this word to highlight the seeming contradictions that result from what people say they are doing (socalled ideal behavior), what they appear to be doing (apparent behavior), and what they are actually doing (real behavior). Such deceptions, camouflages, or what Victor Turner calls masquerades (1969, 184) are often at the heart of the expression of gender relations and affect music and much other behavior. Taking on the role of the opposite gender in ritual or in everyday behavior (i.e., becoming the opposite sex, if only briefly), secretly couching sexually explicit or threatening language in lyrics, for example, or disguising one's self to hide the directness of assertive behavior involves, to a great degree, the connivance or collusion of all parties in the camouflage. Thus, men and women must actually cooperate to yield the deception.

A number of researchers have taken up the question of social deception and have attempted explanations for the seeming discrepancies between idealized behavior and everyday social action. Yolanda Murphy and Robert Murphy, in their classic study of the Mundurucú of central Brazil, for example, describe the women of this group as having in reality a high status within this society, owing in part to the preference for matrilocality and the resulting establishment of large and cohesive networks formed with other women in their families. Male ideology in this group, however, clearly states the inferiority of women and the need for men to "tame women with the banana" (1974, 94) if they enter the men's houses or view the sacred flutes. Murphy and Murphy believe that this ideology is maintained because it conceals from the men "the fragility of their own superiority; it perpetuates an illusion" (ibid., 226).

Ken A. Gourlay discusses this notion of social deception and connivance among males and females in Papua New Guinea and the role that certain esoteric musical instruments play in intergender relations that border on antagonism. In a discussion of various instrument-origin myths, Gourlay points to many structural similarities that stress four features of intergender relations characterized by secrecy and deception (1975, 104). Males preserve and protect the secrets of their instruments and rituals through various threats of punishment: death, rape, hoaxing, or other forms of social control.

Thus, the most common elements in deception, as noted by Gourlay and others, concern secrecy in performance and resulting punishments for transgressors. In almost all cases where males are the secret performers, the reputed punishment for female transgressors is rape or death. However, this is often expressed in such terms as "we did this in former times" (ibid., 13), and, in nearly all outside descriptions of these events, authors are quick to note that, in reality, women know the secrets, have heard the music, played the bullroarer, or seen the flutes and that female transgressors are not actually killed, but are instead either sworn to secrecy, fined, subjected to male initiation, or the transgression is simply ignored. Gourlay asks just who is being deceived, why this process is necessary, and, finally, why it is that the women "chose to do nothing about it" (103, 117). Gourlay echoes Murphy and

Murphy's assumption that such deceptions are needed primarily to protect the theory, if not the reality, of male superiority, a notion that helps maintain the established social and sexual order.

The question of why such deceptions occur and are maintained may have to do more with the appearance than the reality of the deception. Women may connive with men for the purpose of protecting other less obvious but more relevant value systems at work for them alone. Sue Roark-Calnek, in working among Native American groups in Oklahoma, discovered that during certain important ritual performances, the women, in appearing to take a secondary role by moving quietly on the sidelines, were actually subtly displaying the creative handiwork of their shawls, competing for prestige and higher social status with other women (1977, 321–22). Although it may have appeared that the women were allowing the men to assert their superiority, in reality the values of the music and dance performance were irrelevant for the women, as other value systems were at work, ones that were perhaps less articulated, but clearly significant. Whether such symbolic actions are truly perceived as deceptive must depend ultimately upon women's own perceptions of themselves in relation to men and to each other.

Conclusion

I have spent a great deal of time discussing intergender arrangements, especially those of asymmetry, and their effect on music behavior in a wide variety of cultural settings without directly addressing the issue of value. I have noted that the conceptual framework that underlies both music and intergender behaviors shares the common feature of power or control (or both) in many societies. What, however, is the relationship between gender, music, and social standing or prestige? It is here that we can begin to ask questions that will help us to understand why those gender asymmetries reflected in music exist and are maintained.

Sherry Ortner and Harriet Whitehead, in their article "Introduction: Accounting for Sexual Meanings," define the notion of a prestige structure that they see as deriving from a Weberian and Geertzian model of actor-mediated societies as the "sets of prestige positions or levels that result from a particular line of social evaluation, the mechanisms by which individuals and groups arrive at different levels or positions. [Such structures order human relations into] patterns of deference and condescension, respect and disregard . . . and command and obedience" (1981, 13–14). Further, they state, a gender system can be regarded as a prestige structure in itself. In all known societies, men's actions receive higher value and prestige than those of women, and frequently a loss of male status is equated with female-related behavior. Carol Robertson echoes this by stating that the domain of value is "perhaps the most elusive and most significant motivator of human interaction, meanings and performances" (1984, 451).

Charles Seeger (1977) and many others have also noted the effects of a society's value systems on music, but the fusion of music, gender, and value has only recently been alluded to in the literature. Claire Farrer, for example, addresses the issue of value in folklore scholarship when she states that in research of the past, "female genres either fit the male mold or [were] relegated to non-legitimacy" (1975, xiv). Similarly, in many societies, including those in the West, women's musical activities, genres, instruments, and performance efforts are frequently considered by both men and women to be amateurish or unimportant, or they are simply dismissed as not music.

Obviously, notions of power and value are intertwined; both must explain the prevalence of male dominance and the resulting subordination of the female in all known societies. The foregoing suggests that we should begin to construct a model that incorporates cultural concepts of power, gender, music, and value. If we see, for example, human societies ranging on a social continuum from total oppression to total equality, value existing on a separate continuum from high to low, and gender-related behaviors existing on a third dimension of relative maleness to femaleness, then we have created a multifaceted model for the discussion of music activity, one that is sensitive to the complexities of social contexts. Within this framework, we can begin to answer some of the questions of why correlations seem to exist, first, between gender-status asymmetry and resulting gender-related music behaviors and, second, between social deceptions surrounding music and the maintenance of order.

Aside from the obvious need in the future to collect data from female informants or to look toward symbolic action or language, such as ritual, myth, or metaphor, for relevant information about gender ideologies, we must also begin to address the valuative role that music and its performance play in defining and reflecting established social and sexual orders and in acting as an agent in maintaining or changing such orders. It is my hope, then, that the issues raised here will encourage future exploration of the complex and ever-changing processes that affect both gender and music making.

3 Both In and Between

Women's Musical Roles in Ritual Life

"Both In and Between" continues with the comparative approach seen in chapter 2, concentrating on women's musical performances in three very different ritual contexts: the ultra-Orthodox Lubavitcher culture I examined for my dissertation, shamanistic practices in Korea, and the Iroquois Longhouse tradition. I was, like many in the early 1990s, attempting to see if any universals existed across different gendered and musical cultures.

Each of these three case studies seemed to present major differences in women's and men's social contexts, gender interactions, and resulting musical activity. In Lubavitcher culture, men's musical activities were far more highly valued than those of women; indeed, they were seen as necessary for a communication with the divine. Women and men were separated from each other during musical performances, due to powerful beliefs in women's inherent sexuality and in men's aggressiveness, so men were never to hear or see women singing or to perform with them. In Korea women who exhibited certain psychological traits became shamans, able to summon up and speak in the language of protective spirits. Often called upon to help a struggling person or household, many shamans became well-known, powerful, and sometimes wealthy, musical-religious specialists, even using male members of their families (their husbands, sons, and so on) as their assistants (Kendall 1985; Harvey 1980). However, such shamans were also feared, and they and their families often suffered extreme discrimination within their own communities. The Iroquois, those who followed the Longhouse tradition, seemed to regard men's and women's musical performances as equally necessary for a ritual's efficacy. And although performances tended to be separate, there were no restrictions placed on either side concerning hearing or witnessing ritual performances (Shimony 1980).

Using Sherry Ortner's work (1974), I suggested that these three different cultural systems, like the ones Ortner discussed, saw women as existing both in and between nature and culture. I then elaborated upon this model, adding music into the mix, defining music in these contexts as meaningful sound that also acted as intermediary—between humans and spirits. Thus, I reasoned, if both women *and* music were conceptualized as intermediate—that is, in between binaries—they shared a powerful symbolic ambiguity. When women performed music, especially within ritual contexts, the combined power of their gender and musical performance in this context created the potential for chaos or social destruction; women (i.e., their material bodies and sexualities) and their music (even their speaking voices) must therefore be somehow separated from those of men or restricted in some way. Thus, this article explores the idea of the believed-to-be-destructive power in female performance and suggests a possible answer to why women (far more than men) have been, and continue to be, constrained within musical performance cross-culturally.

*   *   *

Women's position in many of the world's religions presents a paradox. On the one hand, codified versions of ritual practices often stress a female or feminine principle, one of equal value and weight, acting in harmony with a male counterpart. In many societies, especially those of Asia, female deities, often highly polarized as all good or all evil, have tremendous power equal to or perhaps exceeding that of males. If codified religious systems have the function of interpreting and validating the social and cosmic order, and of providing prescriptions for appropriate social interaction, then it would appear from this tendency to valorize the feminine that women, like men, would, even at the everyday, on-the-ground level of culture, have equal participation in social and ritual life.

Yet, despite this conceptual framework, in the vast majority of cases, women's actual involvement in ritual, especially as music specialists, is severely limited, and women's rituals are often described as relegated to the home or as peripheral to the mainstream. Understanding why this is so may lie in examining more of what occupies the space or gap between a culturally constructed, overarching theory that presents the idealized and generalized concept of male and female—often enacted ritually—and the everyday social reality of women and men, whose relationships and interdependencies are enacted on a daily, often changeable basis. Within this gap lie ideologies that provide frameworks for such interactions, ideologies that are often contradictory to more idealized concepts. This paper explores the notion that women and the music they perform can be seen as simultaneously "in" and "between" various domains and, further, that they derive their power and efficacy precisely from this intermediate position. Using a theory proposed by Sherry Ortner (1974) that posits women's role as mediator between nature and culture, I present three case studies that explore the relationship between women, music, and power within very different religious and social settings and suggest widely different possibilities for their interaction.

The Ortner Model

Ortner's view is that all societies construct conceptual categories, nature and culture, that are used to separate humans from nonhumans. Built into this primary binary distinction is a value system that places humans, their activities, and artifacts (culture) at a higher level than nonhumans (nature). "Thus culture (i.e., every culture) at some level of awareness asserts itself to be not only distinct from but superior to nature, and that sense of distinctiveness and superiority rests precisely on the ability to transform—to 'socialise' and 'culturalise'—nature" (ibid., 73). Women, as bearers, nurturers, and primary socializers of all children, yet existing also in the world of humans (i.e., properly socialized adults), are seen everywhere as occupying an intermediate position between the two domains and, thus, universally subordinated and devalued.[1]

There has been some criticism of Ortner's work, especially her assertion of the universality of female subordination. Many researchers, although acknowledging that societies universally differentiate (often polarize) male and female and the cultural domains over which they have control, also suggest that value systems placing females in a subordinate position to males are not always present. Societies do exist where males and females may lack access to each other's domains, yet both the sexes and the domains are equally valued. Further, many societies, such as those influenced by Confucianism or Native American beliefs, stress harmony between nature and culture and see humans as existing in balance, not in conflict, with nonhumans. Finally, Ortner does not address the spirit world, for many a real place inhabited by dead ancestors, great leaders, ghosts, or demons, all of whom can have an effect upon both nature and culture. In fact, the relationship of the mundane world to the spiritual can be seen as analogous to that between culture and nature, and it is here, too, that women in many cultures act as both in and between.

However, it is Ortner's elaboration on the intermediate position of women that is the most suggestive for our purposes. She describes three interpretations of women's intermediacy: where intermediate may have the significance of "middle status" (i.e., women exist on a hierarchy of being from culture to nature); where intermediate may imply "mediating," that is, synthesizing or converting; and where the intermediate position of women carries the implication of "greater symbolic ambiguity" (ibid., 84–85).

From Ortner's perspective, the first interpretation answers her primary question as to the whys of universal female subordination; the third interpretation helps to explain the polarized female symbolism in many world religions (as well as art, law, or ritual): "Feminine symbolism, far more often than masculine symbolism, manifests this propensity toward polarized ambiguity—sometimes utterly exalted, sometimes utterly debased, rarely within the normal range of human possibilities" (ibid., 86). It is the second interpretation, that of women's position as mediator, that I wish to explore here, for it is this aspect of (perhaps universal?) gender ideology that I believe has the most implications for women's musical roles in ritual life.

Ortner sees women's mediating position as essentially that of synthesizer or converter between nature and culture, yet there are other senses of the word *mediate* that seem to have more relevance to women's ritual roles, for these roles tend to position women both in and between the everyday world, inhabited by both humans and nonhumans (i.e., nature *and* culture) and the divine world of spirits (not addressed by Ortner). Here, the word *mediate* takes on the sense of intercede, intervene, or negotiate, and it is in this sense that I wish to address the issue of women as both in and between.

Music sound and performance also carry the implication of intermediacy, in the same sense as above. Often described as a channel or vehicle that transports humans from one psychological state to another, from the mundane to the spiritual, or from one social status to another, music has power that is believed to be only partially controlled by humans, and its use is often limited, especially in ritual contexts, to a few specialists. Thus, like women, music can be seen as existing both in and between, not only nature (i.e., uncontrollable sound) and culture (efficacious sound), but also in and between one social or spiritual state and another. In this negotiating capacity, music and its performance can be useful in communicating with the spirit world, in settling disputes, or in protesting various social actions, such as war or unwanted marriages (see especially T. Joseph 1980). Music performance can also act to mediate overt antagonisms between the sexes (Gourlay 1975; Basso 1987). Thus, when women perform music, the combined ambiguity of both women's and music's symbolic and real position as mediators creates potential explosive power. Each society attempts to regulate such power (often seen as threatening to the social and sexual order) in its own way, and nowhere is this control better manifested than in ritual practice.

Jewish Women and Music

Among Orthodox Jews, the performance of music is considered a spiritual necessity, yet many of the codified laws of Judaism exclude adult women from overt, public music making. Although many social and religious justifications exist for this, the most important stems from various legal interpretations of a biblical passage from Solomon's *Song of Songs*: "For your voice is sweet and your face beautiful" (A. Jones 1966, 2:14). Talmudic scholars, in interpreting this passage, fully elaborated upon its sexual implications. The great philosopher and medical doctor Moses Maimonides (1135–1204), for example, interpreted it as follows: "He who stares even at a woman's little finger with the intention of deriving pleasure from it, is considered as though he had looked at her secret parts. It is forbidden to listen even to the singing of a woman" (5:21:2).

Eventually, a large body of literature arose dealing with the issue of *kol isha* (the voice of a woman—both singing and speaking), which continues today to be regarded as a serious distraction to men. Any situation that would encourage a man to become *ervah* (sexually promiscuous) and might result in abandoning his true religious purpose is strictly prohibited. Although the proscription is placed on the man, that is, he is not permitted to hear the (by inference sexually attractive) woman, in reality adult women simply do not sing (or pray) in the presence of men.

One other factor must be mentioned here as affecting women's ritual activities in Orthodox Judaism. There are 613 commandments related by law and custom to Orthodox Jewish activities. Although both men and women are expected to adhere to these laws, women are given some freedom (especially during childbearing years) and are exempted from all commandments related to time and place. Thus, for example, many of the laws dictating synagogue prayer at specific times of the day are not followed by most adult females. As caretakers of the home and children, such women must be free to fulfill other commandments that have a higher priority.

These exemptions, combined with the prohibition against hearing *kol isha*, effectively prevent (or excuse) women from participating freely with men in many of the public ritual activities of Orthodox Judaism. For example, in Orthodox synagogues, men and women are separated from each other during services or other events, such as Sabbath meals or weddings, where the danger of hearing a woman sing or pray exists. Even among Reform Jews, who long ago abandoned many of the older Orthodox practices, women, until recently, have been prevented from becoming rabbis or cantors.

Among Lubavitcher Hasidim (ultra-Orthodox Jews), with whom I worked, one event, the *farbrengen*, highlights the extent to which women are barred from public ritual activity. The *farbrengen* is a gathering that unites the community with its spiritual leader, or rebbe. During a *farbrengen,* the rebbe delivers a spiritual message, usually focusing on a specific topical issue affecting the community as a whole. His talk, which can continue for hours, is punctuated at various intervals with the singing of special paraliturgical songs, called *nigunim. Nigunim* are believed to be vehicles for achieving the two emotional states, *simha* (joy) and *hitlahavut* (enthusiasm), that are essential for spiritual fulfillment, or *devekut* (adhesion). The performance of *nigunim,* especially in the presence of the rebbe, is considered to be one of the most effective ways of achieving *devekut* and, as such, is a spiritual necessity for all Lubavitchers.

Women who attend *farbrengen* sit in a gallery high above the males. The gallery is enclosed by sheets of tinted plastic, so it is difficult to hear the proceedings below. Sitting quietly in the gallery, reading from a book of prayers, or perhaps chatting with friends about family affairs, the women do not usually sing or seem to participate in the events in any way. Their surroundings have effectively removed them physically, visually, as well as spiritually from the men, the rebbe, and the *nigun* performance.

The women themselves (as opposed to the outside ethnographer) do not see this as evidence of a second-class position. They resent the perception of feminists that their status is measured in terms of "where they sit in the synagogue" (Lubavitch Foundation of Great Britain 1970, 217). Rather, they regard their exemption from many of the commandments and their lack of musical activity as a sign of their superiority: "For to the extent that the *mitzvahs* [commandments] constitute an exercise in self-discipline for moral advancement . . . , it would seem that the Creator has endowed woman with a greater measure of such natural self-discipline" (ibid., 220). Judaism, with its strong emphasis on the family unit as the prime locus of spirituality, regards women's position in the home as highly valuable and as a powerful counterpart to men's ritual activities in the synagogue.

One of the things that I began to see as fieldwork continued was a certain parallel between the Lubavitcher concept of music as a channel between the mundane and the divine and the role of woman as mediator between the religious and secular. Lubavitcher women, in a sense, have more freedom than their male counterparts to interact with the outside non-Lubavitcher environment. Many young, married women, for example, work outside the home in shops or as secretaries, often to support their husbands' studies. Most speak English among themselves (most of the men, even those born and raised in the United States, speak Yiddish); some will occasionally read popular magazines, listen to the radio, or attend a movie, activities that are usually prohibited for adult males and children. Women see themselves as both part of the Lubavitcher world and acting to protect their families from the more or less hostile nonreligious world. They are, more than men, cognizant of both worlds and function much of the time in a safe negotiating space in and between them.

Further, although all Lubavitchers recognize the effectiveness of *nigun* performance, it is rare to hear older married women singing, even in the privacy of their own homes with no men present. Young girls, before the age of puberty, often sing at the Sabbath table with their fathers and, if attending Sabbath services or *farbrengen,* may sit with male relatives (or, more commonly, run about, not paying too close attention to the proceedings) in the lower portion of the synagogue. When a young girl is to marry, her friends prepare a *forshpil* (foreplay), a large and raucous party filled with singing and dancing that marks her transition into her true adult status. From then on, there is usually little music making, most music performance now regarded as a more or less frivolous activity associated with youth and *nigun* performance described as "what the men do."

It is clear that in the Lubavitcher world, both music and women serve a mediating function. For men, music acts throughout their lives as the vehicle through which they achieve *devekut* (adherence to God); for women, though, music serves to mark their transition from one social status to another. Yet women themselves are mediators, acting on behalf of their families, existing both in the Lubavitcher world and between that and the potentially threatening secular one. Further, females also exist between two other poles: uncontrolled (i.e., chaotic, unmarried, natural) and controlled (i.e., reproductive, married, cultural) sexuality. Thus, within the context of Orthodox Judaism and Lubavitcher culture, ritually important music (liturgy, *nigun*) must remain within the hands of men, as performance by sexually active females might prove too disruptive.

Female Shamans in Korea

In Korea the traditional social position of women has, until recently, suffered under the neo-Confucian philosophical and religious system that entered Korea with the Yi dynasty (1392–1910). Whether extreme Confucianist beliefs that saw women's position to men as analogous to that of men to the gods ever took hold in Korea as they did in China is still in question, but there is no doubt that similar ideologies continue today to constrain women's social and religious activities.

Kept in relative seclusion, women of the upper classes are expected to serve males in the home by, most important, producing male heirs. Within this

social and economic context, however, females frequently dev
ful relationships with each other. Many of their ritual activities
toward family and household concerns: the birth of sons, the cur
forecasting the marriage of a daughter, appeasing dead souls, ɪ
spirits, and so on. Many household and village rituals, often descɪɪᴜᴄᴄ
male Koreans and by Western religious scholars as folk rituals, as opposed
to Confucianism—the official written philosophical system of males—are
controlled by women shamans (*mudang*) and are carried out primarily on
behalf of other women and families.[2]

Shamanism has been an integral part of Korean ritual life for centuries and
has always been primarily in the hands of women, who today represent about
95 percent of the total number of shamans. Male shamans (*paksu mudang*),
considered marginal males, will often dress in female ritual costume when
performing (Harvey 1980, 52n1).

Shamans are of two types: those, primarily from the North, whose role
is hereditary and those, from the South, who are chosen by spirits as ritual
specialists. The term *mudang* is used to denote the generalized role, whereas
mansin (literally, ten thousand spirits) refers specifically to the chosen, professional shaman who performs *kuts*.[3] A *kut* is a musico-dramatic ritual called
by a *mansin* who mediates between a client, having paid for her services, and
various spirits who enter and speak from her body during a trance. *Kuts* can
be held for individual men or women at household shrines or for an entire
village or city at a larger public shrine, thus uniting families under one concern,
such as the consecration of a new building or enduring a local drought.

Men appear to have no interest in *kuts* and will sit passively during a performance, even if it has been called on their behalf. During a *kut,* the *mansin*
acts in ways that are antithetical to prevailing notions of proper behavior for
women, both in the context of a *kut* (where she may speak directly, often
with considerable anger, and dance wildly to the accompanying music) as
well as in the larger social context of her town or village (where she is often
unmarried and considered to have an especially low social status). If married,
however, her status is considered to be higher than that of her husband, who
frequently acts as her assistant during a *kut,* performing on various musical
instruments. The relationship of a *mansin* to her husband thus further defies
Korean notions of gender relations.

Becoming a *mansin* involves a three-stage process: spirit appearance, spirit
sickness, and performance of an initiation *kut.* Often summoned by spirits
when quite young, a future *mansin* begins to act "strangely," becoming de-
pressed, perhaps sexually active, or exhibiting symptoms of mental illness.[4]
When the spirit-sickness phase begins, a family will take the child to the local

established *mansin* to determine if this is truly a forecast of the girl's status as a shaman or simply mental illness. When it is established that the girl is to become a *mansin,* she is apprenticed to the older shaman and learns the songs, dances, and pantheon of spirits that she will later invoke during *kuts.* At the completion of this spiritual training, an initiatory *kut* is held on her behalf, where she demonstrates her ability to contact the spirit world during a trance, and, having been successful, she moves into her new social and ritual role.

Kuts also fall into three categories that are distinguished by length and by the type of female who is in control: the *pison,* lasting an hour or so, performed by an ordinary housewife as well as a shaman; the *p'udakkori,* lasting three or four hours, conducted by a fortune teller or shaman; and the greater *kut,* which often lasts several days and is performed only by a *mansin* (Huhm 1980, 11–12). During the greater *kut,* a series of spirits are summoned on behalf of the client, including great male leaders of past Korean dynasties, various male and female ancestors of the client's family, and martial spirits used to drive away the evil demons or ghosts inhabiting a person who is ill or present in an unfortunate household. Trance is induced by performance on various musical instruments, including a double-headed hourglass drum, flute, gong, one-stringed fiddle, and a large wand upon which are fastened five to nine jingle bells (Covell 1986, 40–41). While in trance, the *mansin* may wield a knife, a tripointed spear, or a halberd—a crescent-shaped ax used to slice through the chest of an offending spirit.

The ritual power of the *mansin* is not questioned. In total control of both the trance-inducing music and the ten thousand spirits in whose voices she speaks, her actions can decide the fate of a childless couple or the auspiciousness of a new downtown auditorium. Further, although not officially recognized by the male-dominated Confucian and Buddhist ritual and political hierarchies, the power of the *mansin* and the efficacy of *kut* are nevertheless regarded as crucial to the running of the household and continue to be called today on a regular basis.

Thus, unlike the Orthodox Jewish women above, Korean *mansin* are the main conduits to the spirit world. As women with special power, their relative ritual position is higher than that of Jewish women, in that they have sole access to the spirit world that decides the affairs of family and household. They are, in a sense, analogous to *nigun,* in that they act to mediate on behalf of humans, intervening, placating, and negotiating in a direct way with the spirits who decide the outcome of everyday human actions. Yet unlike Jewish women, their social and official religious status is low, and families whose children exhibit early signs of spirit sickness often hide in fear and embarrassment, only reluctantly acknowledging their child's potential power.

Iroquois Women's Rites

Among the Iroquois (Haudenosaunee, or Keepers of the Longhouse), women have traditionally held positions of great power and prestige. American Indian social structure, often referred to erroneously as a matriarchy, implying women's control and authority over men, is, rather, matrilineal, that is, descent is reckoned through the mother. Upon meeting someone for the first time, the question "Who is your mother?" establishes the person within a matrilineal-extended family, a clan (families of the mother's siblings), a moiety (half or side), a tribe, and many other familial, ritual, and political networks (Shimony 1961; Allen 1986). Within this framework, women as well as men are seen as equally important and valuable to the balance of life, and although they each control specific ritual, social, and economic domains, no one domain is valued over the other, both seen as necessary and complementary.[5]

Today, the Iroquois are a league of six Native tribes (Mohawk, Seneca, Onondaga, Oneida, Cayuga, and, an adopted tribe, the Tuscorora), many of whom live at the Six Nations Reserve near Brantford, Ontario. About one-third of the current population follows the teachings of the Seneca prophet Handsome Lake (d. 1799), who founded the Longhouse religion in the late eighteenth century, a time of tremendous social and political upheaval. During this time, the Iroquois lost not only much of their land and hunting rights, but also much of their own autonomous political power. Further, white notions of male control over social, political, and economic institutions (patriarchy) and of basic citizenship, reckoned in European social organization through the father (patriliny), came into conflict with basic Native notions of family and society.

During this period of upheaval, many Iroquois suffered from depression and alcoholism, which contributed greatly to other social problems, such as wife and child abuse. It was within this social context that the Seneca prophet Handsome Lake arose with his messages of individual and social reform. Now representing a conservative element at the Six Nations Reserve, the followers of Handsome Lake continue to practice the older, more traditional rituals in the face of widespread acculturation among their Christian colleagues (Shimony 1961).

The *Code of Handsome Lake* (*Kaiwiyoh*), a collection of stories, myths, rules of conduct, and prescriptions for behavior, is believed to have been revealed to the prophet by four spirit messengers sent by the Creator. It combines elements of traditional (precontact) practices and beliefs with Christian (European) ideals, which initially allowed its followers to return to more traditional ways, thus restoring some of their former dignity and power, while at the same time subtly changing the relationships between the sexes that would have implications for future ritual and social life.

For example, in precontact times, men generally hunted and conducted large-scale intertribal wars, which removed them from the local communities, while women assumed control over agriculture (including growing and exchanging food) as well as tribal concerns, as the men were frequently away for great periods of time. One of the women's most important duties was the election of a peace chief, a member of a hereditary council that was responsible for tribal governance (Shimony 1980, 247). Women could also impeach a chief if his actions were too disruptive to tribal life. In 1924 the Canadian government insisted that the Iroquois choose chiefs and other ruling parties by general election (a point of contention and protest to this day), and, as a result of this intervention, the power of both the chief and the chief's "matrons" diminished.

Further, when hunting lands were taken from the Iroquois, the entire economic structure was upset. Handsome Lake specifically addressed this problem in his *Code,* suggesting that male Iroquois now adapt to three things that white men (referred to as "our younger brothers") did that were "right to follow": cultivate and harvest food, keep cattle, and build "warm and fine appearing" (i.e., European-style) housing (Parker 2008, 38, sec. 25). Effectively, the *Code* prescribed changing the entire social structure of the Iroquois from a horticultural society, where women had tremendous political and economic power, to an agrarian one, where the control of food production and distribution now fell to both men and women and where women's autonomy decreased (O'Kelly and Carney 1986, 50).

Although some contemporary Iroquois remain farmers, most travel to nearby cities such as Brantford, Toronto, Niagara Falls, or Buffalo for work, so the former agricultural cycle that regulated work and marked the year into periods associated with planting and harvesting no longer has the same social meaning. However, as today's Iroquois move further away from their traditional economic way of life, the importance of Longhouse rituals has grown, and within the Longhouse religion the role of women has recently taken on a dignity and power reminiscent of past times. Women are now prominent as "faithkeepers" or "deaconesses," and their duties include scheduling and conducting women's rituals and ceremonies as well as counseling or settling quarrels (Shimony 1980, 254–56).

Four Longhouse congregations exist today at the Six Nations Reserve. According to Annemarie Shimony, the roles of men and women are highlighted both in the special layout of the Longhouse itself and in the division of the rituals into men's and women's observances: "Members say that they enter by the men's or women's door and sit on the men's or women's side. During the rites themselves, action is reciprocal between the two domains, and much of the service consists of dialogue between the opposing units. Thus, on the whole, a balance is struck, and the efficacy of a ceremony depends upon the combined efforts of whatever divisions are at play" (ibid., 250–51).

One ritual, not part of the agricultural cycle, the Ohgi'we, or Feast of the Dead, highlights the powerful position of women in Iroquois society today. During the Ohgi'we, the spirits of dead ancestors are contacted and placated to ensure harmony and balance in the earthly realm. Ohgi'we also acts as a healing ceremony to cure ghost sickness or possession. Women are seen as the main channels through which the spirit world is contacted, and the Ohgi'we takes place on the women's side of the Longhouse. Yet although women schedule and execute these ceremonies, and are the main dancers, in traditional complementary fashion men are also involved in important ritual roles, mainly as assistant drummers and singers, and both sexes must be present for the ceremony to be effective.

When we compare the social and ritual position of Iroquois women to their Jewish and Korean counterparts described above, what is most apparent is the acknowledgment in Iroquois society—but not in traditional Orthodox Judaism or Confucianism—of the value and beneficial power inherent in both the women and their music, a power that is perhaps feared, but ultimately acknowledged and respected. The value accorded Iroquois women of today may stem from earlier times, when they had considerable economic and political control, yet even though their real power has diminished, their position in the traditional social and belief system as complementary counterparts to the male has not. In this position, they have equal access to ritual music and ceremony, performing their own songs and dances in their own side of the Longhouse, the center of ritual life. Here, combining the power of women with that of music is not threatening but rather seen as a necessary balance to male ritual activity.

*   *   *

From the above examples, it is clear that there is a wide range of social and religious contexts where women and music interact in a variety of ways. The position of women as more or less in and between so-called natural, cultural, and spiritual domains is ultimately related to a society's notions of gender, power, and value that regulate all aspects of life. Understanding women's ritual and ceremonial roles is impossible unless we see women, men, and ritual as interacting within the larger social, economic, and political world.

PART II

1990–2000

4 Shifting Realities

The six chapters in this part mark a change in my thinking and writing, from a predominantly comparative and theoretical approach to more of a focus on culture-specific gendered musical systems. As I grappled with postmodernism's multivocality and positioning, I began to experience a deep ambivalence: on the one hand, I was attracted to postmodernism's deeply compassionate focus and valorization of individual difference and multiple intersections of position; on the other, I wondered, if individual difference were to be privileged, where was room for sameness? Could one successfully and gracefully move back and forth between comparative and individual lenses and still say something meaningful? This ambivalence often emerged in unlikely places. Here is a story of an unusual event that highlights some of the difficulty I was experiencing at the time in holding two (or more) simultaneous perspectives.

June 23, 1993

I am involved in a weeklong College Music Society Summer Seminar focusing on feminism and music, organized by Ruth Solie and Jane Bowers, hosted by Catherine Pickar, and held on the campus of American University in Washington, D.C.[1] I am there to represent the feminist perspective in ethnomusicology. Thus, unlike other participants dealing with Western art musics (and, roughly, a three-hundred-year time period), I have a dual task—I must be a spokesperson not only for *all* of ethnomusicology, but also for *all* "other" women (outside the West) and for *all* historical periods. Needless to say, this is daunting, but I am glad that historical musicologists are finally recognizing that there is more to women and music than what happens in the salons and concert halls of the European or American upper middle class.

We are all done for the day, schmoozing in the basement of the dorm where we are staying. Someone has just turned on the television. We watch the news. "It's June 23," the announcer intones. "Today, a woman, Lorena Bobbitt, motivated by years of physical, emotional, and sexual abuse, cut off her husband's penis, while he lay sleeping. She got into her car with the severed penis and drove off with it, throwing it out of the window of the car into an abandoned field" (reconstructed from memory).[2]

What?! Did I hear that correctly? A woman cut off her husband's penis? And threw it out of a car window? We sit there, stunned. A wave of shock, tempered with a muted ambivalence, passes over the group. Is this a bad thing—or a good thing? We look at each other, measuring our own internal reactions against the others.' I see different faces expressing a wide range of emotions—horror, empathy, shock, amusement, vindictiveness, compassion.

Suddenly, a guttural, almost animal, sound begins. We all begin to laugh, deep belly laughs, loud guffaws, out-of-control hiccups! We can't stop! Tears fall from our eyes. I grab my stomach, wracked by laugh cramps, thinking I will surely throw up. Someone claps; another screams. We sit there, simultaneously horrified and bemused, each feeling the entwined and inchoate sensations of vengeance and empathy. "That must have hurt," someone says. More gales of laughter.

It was a moment when all of us, having experienced some measure of sexual harassment, abuse, discrimination, or privilege, unexpectedly came together, our differences melting. We laughed until we were weak, not knowing what else to do in this powerfully ambivalent moment.

*   *   *

Feminism in the 1990s: Into the Third Wave

By the late 1980s and into the '90s, many felt that major problems with un-balanced gender relations had been largely solved by the efforts of first- and second-wave feminists. Women were entering the workplace in higher num-bers, and some were being elected to public office; rape, domestic abuse, and workplace harassment were being taken more seriously in the courts and in the mainstream media; and a host of laws came into place, creating greater opportunities and a more equitable social structure for women.[3] Men, too, were beginning to understand how gender norms had also constrained or privileged them, and many became more involved with their children, with housework, with caretaking, and with other areas of life previously labeled women's work. Within the academy, some men began to deconstruct their own systems of masculinity; they came to be called "men in feminism" or, sometimes, "femmenists" (Jardine and Smith 1987).

Third-wave feminism grew out of the critiques of the second wave and began, in the 1990s, to take on a life of its own. Influenced by postmodernist ideas, especially deconstruction, third-wavers stressed a multiplicity of identities. In third-wave philosophy, one's gender was a fluid, blurred, and fuzzy set of identities, an entwinement of one's biology, race, sexuality, class, ethnicity, nationality, age, and so on. Further, and more important, each person had individual agency in defining and performing his or her own gender and other identities—and the more ways, the better. Thus, the norms of gender assignation and behavior, defined and theorized by the first and second waves of feminism, were completely rejected here in favor of a new subjectivity and of multivocality.

One important catalyst for this new generation of feminists was the accusation of sexual harassment made by Anita Hill in 1991 against Clarence Thomas, who was undergoing hearings to confirm his nomination to the Supreme Court. The Senate ultimately dismissed these accusations and confirmed Thomas, but the anger that these hearings generated, especially among young African American women, was enormous. Rebecca Walker, a young feminist activist and the daughter of writer Alice Walker, wrote an article in response to the hearings, called "Becoming the Third Wave" (1992), and is generally credited with naming this movement. In 1992 Rebecca Walker founded the feminist activist group the Third Wave Foundation, dedicated to the support of young women and transgender youth, ages fifteen to thirty (www.thirdwavefoundation.org).

The third wave coincided in the 1990s with the explosion of new technologies, and many advocates used new media, such as the Internet and fanzines, to spread their ideas. This is significant because third-wave feminists began to shift their focus from the older and working women of the second wave to younger women—girls, sometimes spelled "grrrls"—to emphasize a growling authority and aggression. One outcome of this new focus was the reclaiming of demeaning or derogatory words, such as *baby, bitch, whore,* and others that were previously used as tools of male control. This reclamation not only helped reduce their power, but also helped to empower young women to fight their own oppression. This sense of empowerment resulted in a creative musical scene that evolved out of punk rock in the 1990s—riot grrrl—an underground feminist movement involving concerts, fanzines, meetings, and various forms of do-it-yourself (or DIY) activism. Riot grrrl, along with queercore, an earlier punk-related movement, focused on issues of rape and on multiple sexualities.[4]

The Three Posts of Third-Wave Feminism

During the late 1980s and through the 1990s, third-wave feminism and feminist theory split into many strands, each dealing with a different set of issues and political stances. It is beyond the scope or purpose of this book to trace them all; here, I discuss some general ideas that influenced me and continually prodded me into rethinking basic concepts and relationships.

One of the benefits of second-wave feminism was a questioning and rejection of claims that gender inequalities were somehow natural, or normal. This resonated with other developing ideas critiquing the so-called truth claims of previous periods in history, such as the belief that one could objectively describe the world. Terms such as *subject position, identity politics,* and *embodiment* began to filter into general parlance, as we came to understand that although one need not always consciously assert an identity position, one always spoke and acted from one;[5] more important, this position could be used politically to achieve certain ends. These and other ideas eventually coalesced into what we now call postmodernism, our most recent philosophical turn, one that seems to have redefined reality as we once knew it.

Many postmodern strands of thought developed in the last decades of the twentieth century, especially within the humanities and social sciences, but the two that were the most significant to me were poststructuralism and postcolonialism. Poststructuralism (now almost synonymous with the label postmodernism) helped make me aware of power systems embedded in cognitive organizational schemes, language, institutions, and, indeed, all human interactions and creations. Postcolonialism centered on listening to and privileging the voices and perspectives of formerly colonized peoples. Each in its own way contributed to the growth of third-wave feminism and to basic feminist ideals of the 1990s.

Certain postmodern ideas appealed to me more than others as I continued to think and write. I was drawn, for example, to the urge to collapse binaries, those pesky cognitive models that always seemed to privilege one side over the other. Earlier in my ethnomusicology life, I had more or less adopted the structuralist views of Claude Lévi-Strauss (1908–2009). I understood his desire to promote cross-cultural understandings in asserting that all humans, even so-called primitives, structured their worlds into interrelated cognitive units and that these units could be understood as sets of binary contrasts. That seemed plausible at the time (as well as neat, from a modeling perspective).

Poststructuralists such as Jacques Derrida (1976), Michel Foucault (1977), and Julia Kristeva (1979), among many others, however, began to assert that the value hierarchy implicitly embedded within a binary was evidence of a larger, far greater problem: the structure and use of language itself. Language—a human invention—was, they asserted, an instrument of power and control. Learning how to be in the world could happen only through language. Thus, language structured knowledge and meaning. All knowledge, they said, was interconnected and fluid, not fixed (or True), constructed and negotiated from interactions between people speaking and acting from differently situated subject positions. All knowledge—even scientific knowledge based on the so-called scientific method—was situated in an a priori system of social relations (Anderson 2011).

One of the strands of thinking that arose from this idea was the notion of a feminist epistemology, one that took gender into account in the study of knowledge systems. Embodiment, cognitive style, worldview, and a host of other individual and social attributes situate a knower within a system of other knowers and influence how and what the knower learns. Gender is central to one's situated knowledge. As Elizabeth Anderson writes, "By bringing together the general account of situated knowledge with the account of gender as a kind of social situation, we can now generate a catalogue of ways in which what people know, or think they know, can be influenced by their own gender (roles, norms, traits, performance, identities), other people's genders, or by ideas about gender (symbolism). Each mode of gendered knowledge raises new questions for epistemology" (ibid.). Thus, not only does each of us hold different views or versions of reality, but these can change in real-time social interactions, resulting in a sort of fragmentation of the knower into a set of interactive knowers.

Feminist epistemology moved away from the logocentrism of earlier theorists by stressing embodiment, rather than language, as an important way of knowing. Embodiment is essentially performative; that is, one's ways of knowing are often performed or felt through the body in specific situations. This idea, further developed by Candace West and Don Zimmerman (1987), Janet Price and Margaret Shildrick (1999), and Judith Butler (1990, 1993), among others, posited that one's gender was performed into existence through repeated acts, eventually constituting a "natural" set of normative behaviors.

Postcolonial studies were also helpful to me, as they explored the effects of mainly European and American colonialism on many cultures outside the West. Like anthropologists, postcolonial scholars understood unequal power relations as socially constructed and therefore able to be deconstructed. This branch of cultural criticism was said to have begun with the publication in 1978 of literary theorist Edward Said's *Orientalism* (1978).[6] Said suggested that most Western descriptions of the East, especially of Arab cultures, were suspect, as they were written by scholars who held underlying assumptions about non-European peoples that were essentially racist. To arrive at a more accurate historical and cultural picture, one should concentrate more on indigenous voices—those voices of the people, especially those of color, who were subjected to colonialist, and imperialist, agendas, largely by white Europeans and Americans. This highly influential work became a central text in the humanities, especially within feminist studies, and was especially important to me, as it privileged insider and local knowledge.

Postcolonial feminism and its many cousins, including global feminism (focusing on the commonalities of all women, not only those of colonized areas) and third world feminism (focusing on the commonality of women's poverty throughout the world, including in the United States), developed initially as both outgrowths of the African American and Latina feminism of earlier decades and as a consequence of a rising feminist consciousness by women outside the West. Like black feminism, postcolonial feminism stressed intersections between gender, sexuality, and race, but also included nationality, ethnicity, and religion as well. Essentially focusing on the effects of European colonization over many centuries, postcolonial feminists sought to connect issues of oppression and erasure across cultures and nationalities, largely by listening to and working with women in specific non-Western cultural settings.[7]

But an even more important postcolonial feminist agenda was to expose and interrogate the assumptions of first- and second-wave feminists, who, in theorizing an essentialist, ahistoric woman, had simply imposed their ideas of feminism on women worldwide—practicing a form of intellectual colonization, not unlike the political and economic colonialism of the past (Scholz 2010, 133–57). After all, what was feminism in rural India? What was oppression? Liberation?

Literary theorist Gayatri Chakravorty Spivak's 1988 article "Can the Subaltern Speak?" was one of the first to connect postcolonial ideas to feminism, and, like Said's, her work became a central postcolonial text. She writes, "Both as object of colonialist historiography and as subject of insurgency, the ideological construction keeps the male dominant. If, in the context of colonial production, the subaltern has no history and cannot speak, the subaltern as female is even more deeply in shadow" (28).[8]

Queer Theory

Another important area of research that arose early in the third wave was queer theory. Although it began as an extension of lesbian, gay, bisexual, and transgender (LGBT) studies, queer theory is less about homosexual identity practices and politics than about all sexual practices that diverge from heteronormativity. As David Halperin writes, "Queer is by definition whatever is at odds with the normal, the legitimate, the dominant. There is nothing in particular to which it necessarily refers. It is an identity without an essence. 'Queer,' then, demarcates not a positivity but a positionality vis-à-vis the normative" (Wikipedia n.d.c).

Queer theory is based largely on the writings of Eve Kosofsky Sedgwick (1990), Judith Butler (1990, 1993), and Teresa de Lauretis (1986, in Halperin 2005), who coined the term. Its methodology is closely related to literary criticism and, as such, has had a marked influence, especially on historical musicology and on popular music studies, largely through the work of Philip Brett, Elizabeth Wood, and Gary C. Thomas (1994); Suzanne Cusick (1994, 1999); and others. It was not, though, used heavily in the ethnomusicological research of the 1990s, as it did not generally involve fieldwork.

Feminist Anthropology

During the late 1980s and into the '90s, as anthropology began to absorb new postmodern theory, especially that of deconstruction, a profoundly self-reflexive moment occurred, and new questions began to be asked, especially about fieldwork. How could anthropologists conduct fieldwork so that the unequal power relations inherent in this process would be minimized or eliminated altogether? Further, how could an ethnographer represent a specific group of people in his or her writing without appearing to be outside the group, and thus a privileged, omniscient observer? How could the fieldworker move away from essentialist and universalizing language that shrouded the power structures philosophers and literary critics were trying to deconstruct and still write ethnographic narratives? How could anyone sustain the false self-other binary in the face of new understandings of multiple selves-others in the field? Older ideas about objectivity, outside-inside perspectives, binaries, professionalism, and the very nature of the field, and of fieldwork, were being called into question.[9]

This crisis was particularly difficult for feminist anthropologists who became more and more uncomfortable with the dual nature of their political and professional identities. In 1989 and 1990, two important articles appeared that greatly influenced my thinking and writing during that time, "The Postmodern Turn in Anthropology: Cautions from a Feminist Perspective" (Mascia-Lees, Sharpe, and Cohen 1989) and "Can There Be a Feminist Ethnography?" (Abu-Lughod 1990), both of which were foundational to a feminist challenge to postmodernism. Each in its own way articulated both a powerful critique of mainstream feminism and anthropology as well as a call for an explicitly feminist theorizing that could become central to a new, more truly honest, ethical, and self-reflexive anthropology. The critique centered on issues dealing mainly with reflexive fieldwork and its representation in ethnographic writing (the anthropological side), and the solution centered on a politically active, yet mutually reflexive, relationship between fieldworker and cultural informant (the feminist side).

Challenges and a Possible Solution

Those feminist anthropologists who became increasingly uncomfortable with their dual identities began to question their own positionality in the field and in the academy. In addition to dealing with the questions posed above, they began to ask, how could one be both a politically active feminist, fighting for women's social, economic, and political equality and, at the same time, an anthropologist, that is, a professional participant-observer of practices seen in the field that seemed to be oppressive to women? This led to an acknowledgment of discomfort with both their mainstream feminist as well as their anthropological colleagues.

Some stated, for example, that, as women, they often had more in common with the women they worked with in the field than with their male colleagues in anthropology. Further, as feminism was largely (until the 1990s) a Western enterprise, many politically active feminists, especially of the second wave in the United States, saw women's oppression and the reasons for it in terms of Western definitions and concerns. Turning to feminist anthropologists mainly to help them find the origins of gender inequality or lost matriarchies, mainstream historical and cultural feminists were largely ignorant of contemporary cultural differences outside the West and how these could and did affect basic notions of man, woman, personhood, and gender.

Mainstream anthropologists also seemed to relegate their feminist colleagues' work to a marginal category—filling in the gaps, or of evening the score—not central to theorizing. For example, in response to postmodern issues of representation and the unequal power relations inherent in fieldwork and writing, many anthropologists began, as we saw earlier in the 1980s, to develop new styles of writing where self-reflexivity and fragmentation became more prominent, calling it the new ethnography. Many turned to current discussions in literary and cultural criticism that attempted to expose privileged readings of narrative forms in an effort to move away from an authorial voice.[10]

The new ethnography relied on creative, sometimes playful, writing styles that allowed for multiple voices to be heard in dialogue and for authors to position themselves in their own writing. The work of Clifford (1988), Clifford and Marcus (1986), Geertz (1988), Marcus and Fischer (1986), and Marcus and Cushman (1982) laid out a new theoretical framework for ethnographic writing that would expose the constructed nature of cultural texts and act, more or less, as a critique of Western hegemonic culture and literary criticism. Further, recognizing the constructedness of texts allowed the new ethnographers to ally themselves with fiction, or with the "partial truths" of cultural accounts, where no one perspective could ever be the whole truth (Clifford 1988).

Feminist anthropologists began to critique the new ethnography early on, first pointing out that when confronted with challenges to Western male authority, mainstream anthropology had turned to poststructuralist ideas of deconstruction and *différance* rather than to feminist theory for answers. Feminist theory, they argued, had long-held notions of multiple voices and perspectives, of dialoguing with others through various forms of political activism, and of recognizing the privilege of Western (white) cultural understandings.

As Frances Mascia-Lees, Patricia Sharpe, and Colleen Ballerino Cohen wrote, new narrative devices borrowed from literary discourse, rather than exposing authorial control and embracing difference, "erase difference, implying that all stories are really about one experience: the decentering and fragmentation that is the current experience of Western white males" (1989, 29). Further, literary theory and analytic techniques "constitute a masking and empowering of Western bias rather than a diffusing of it. . . . These narrative devices potentially structure and control as surely as does the narrator of classic works, whether literary, historical, or ethnographic" (ibid., 30–31).[11]

This criticism stemmed partly from the feminist belief, especially of Marxist feminists, that the roots of oppression lay primarily in the material world and partly from the anthropological belief that oppression always had to be carefully defined and contextualized within a specific cultural framework. Both mainstream feminism and anthropology's new ethnography, in their urge to decenter authority, to find multiple voices, and to fragment selves and others, had erased real women and their common concerns within specific (mainly non-Western) cultural contexts.

Further, although mainstream feminism and feminist anthropology both focused primarily on gender and more and more on gender, race, and ethnicity and were both rooted in "historically constituted self/other distinctions, they come at it from different places within the structure of difference" (Abu-Lughod 1990, 24). According to Abu-Lughod, "Anthropology is the discourse of the self, which defines itself primarily as the study of the other, which means that selfhood [is] not problematic. . . . Feminist discourse . . . begins from the opposite side in the other great system of difference in our society: gender. Feminists could never have any illusions with regard to the power of a binary like self/other" (ibid.).

These ideas had been elaborated previously in an important article published in 1987, by Marilyn Strathern, "An Awkward Relationship: The Case of Feminism and Anthropology," where Strathern suggests that mainstream anthropology and feminism differed mainly on the central (and supposed shared) paradigm of self-other relations, as well as on the very notion of a paradigm.[12] She states that while anthropology is the study of the experience of the other, the other can exist only in relation to a self, and the self of anthropology remains largely unexamined. Further, the self is assumed to use core models (i.e., Marxism, structural anthropology, and so on) that are shared and commonly understood among all anthropologists—an essentialist argument of a different kind. Anthropology's stated aim, according to its feminist critics, is collaboration, finding common ground, sharing experiences between a largely unexamined self and a closely examined, presumed-to-be-stable other. Feminist theory, however, is based on ever-changing models, on collaborative discourses between many selves-others in constant debate. And, among feminist anthropologists, there is no one current model or theory shared by all its practitioners.

Some feminist anthropologists, such as Mascia-Lees, Sharpe, and Cohen (1989), Abu-Lughod (1990), Micaela di Leonardo (1991), and Elizabeth Enslin (1994), among others, began to theorize a new anthropology, informed by a kind of gentle feminist activism that would come closer to the experience of women's and men's lives, both in Western and in non-Western cultural settings. First, they took on various postmodern themes, such as the dismantling of the self-other divide; the theme of multiple, intersecting selves and others (even within the same person); an acknowledgment of one's own gender in relation to one's work; and a grounded positionality based in the material and real worlds of women in different cultural settings.

One especially important concept, borrowed from science historian Donna Haraway (1988), defines this positionality as situated knowledge. Responding to early feminists' tendency to define science as a masculinized tradition, thereby polarizing scientific practice as either a "contestable text and a power field" (Code 2000, 461–62) or a strictly empirical discipline based on "objectivity," Haraway suggests a new feminist positioning that would collapse and merge these poles. (See also Harding 1986.) She draws upon feminist standpoint theory, which takes into account the multiple positions of both the investigator and the investigated within any work, thereby creating a more equal and ethical exchange of knowledges. A feminist standpoint is not a woman's perspective, per se, but, rather, a political space of resistance against unequal power relations (Code 2000, 461–62).

As the 1990s came to an end, feminist anthropologists had clearly adopted many of the ideas of mainstream postmodern anthropology, while, at the same time, adapting them to use as the foundation of a new activist anthropology, one that was sensitive to those in the field as well as to those in the academy. This form of feminist anthropology, they hoped, would help collapse the feminist-anthropologist divide and create a more ethical fieldwork process, ultimately resulting in truer ethnographic narratives.

Feminist Ethnomusicology

As postmodern ideas and new research paradigms spread through the sciences and humanities, ethnomusicology responded with a burgeoning literature examining gender and music cross-culturally. Indeed, the decade of the 1990s marks an early peak in the number of publications devoted to these discussions and many feminist musicologies developed that led down different paths. Here are a few sources that particularly interested and helped me in that they not only opened my eyes to different genres seen through the lens of gender, but also helped me coalesce some ideas concerning a critique of historical and critical musicology and its preference, like that of mainstream anthropology, for postmodern literary and cultural criticism over that of an ethnographically based feminist method and theory.

During the 1990s, the field of new musicology seemed to discover ethnomusicology, with its growing focus on musical systems in living musical cultures and its attention to different cultural settings, especially those of gender, race, ethnicity, and class. New things began to happen: collections of articles formerly limited to historical Euro-American art musics began to expand to include at least one contribution from an ethnomusicologist.[13] Some of these focused on gender issues, but other disciplinary boundaries also began to blur: many of these same collections also included articles on contemporary Western popular musics, genres that had previously been addressed largely by ethnomusicologists, or scholars of American music.[14]

Thus, divisions between old and new musicology and between historical and ethnomusicology seemed to be coming to an end through a multiple focus primarily on gender and class.

Entries on women and music also began to appear in large canonic encyclopedias and journals. In 1991, for example, Charlotte Frisbie published an essay in *Ethnomusicology* (the journal of the Society for Ethnomusicology), chronicling the history of women in the early, formative period of the society; other texts, including *Ethnomusicology: An Introduction* (Sarkissian 1992) and volume 9 of the *Garland Encyclopedia of World Music, Australia and the Pacific Islands* (Kaeppler et al. 1998), continued this trend; and in 2001, the first entry ever published on women and music in the *Grove's Dictionary of Music and Musicians* (Tick and Koskoff 2001) appeared.

The first Feminist Theory and Music Conference was held in 1991, hosted by the University of Minnesota, under the leadership of Susan McClary and Lydia Hamessley. McClary's book *Feminine Endings: Music, Gender, and Sexuality* (1991), now a foundational text in historical musicology, had just been published and had already caused a stir. Equally fluent in the gender and sexual politics of Western art music (Monteverdi and Bach) and contemporary popular music (Madonna, Laurie Anderson), McClary addressed a wide range of issues that crossed musical periods and genres. Near the end of the decade (1997), *Woman and Music: A Journal of Gender and Music* arose, dedicated to publishing new, cutting-edge articles exploring gender and music issues from the perspective of all music disciplines.

A Parting of the Ways

It was precisely at this moment that I began to feel, like the feminist anthropologists described above who had responded to the new ethnography, that something was off here, and it was at this moment that I realized how deep the methodological differences between historical and ethnomusicology were. My feminist side was happy for the moment, but my anthropology side was beginning to squirm. Whereas the new musicology had developed a new sensitivity to class and race issues (at least in the United States) by taking popular music more seriously, and had responded to gendered identity issues via cultural criticism and queer theory, it was still not dealing with issues of contemporary, cross-cultural difference. The West was still the best, but the best now included popular music and queer readings of all musics. Granted, the opening up of the new musicology to the ideas of postmodernism, as filtered mainly through literary and cultural criticism, represented perhaps an unprecedented decentering and democratizing moment—but these ideas, fitting so beautifully with analyses and interpretations of Western art and popular musics, did not seem to help ethnomusicologists with their issues of close interpersonal fieldwork and cross-cultural ethnographic research and writing.

On the other hand, mainstream ethnomusicology, like mainstream anthropology, also seemed to turn away from the more general potential of a feminist theory by moving toward the new paradigms of self-reflexive writing and to the more abstract issues of globalism and musical movement (i.e., diasporic and migrating musical cultures). Thus, ethnomusicologists interested in gender issues continued to struggle with a feminist theory that did not seem to apply outside the West, with an anthropological theory that did not often address music, and with an ethnomusicology that did not see its true potential. Where was a feminist theory for ethnomusicology, one that would be sensitive both to cultural difference and to feminist political action, one that would be taken seriously as a more general theory? Feminist ethnomusicologists, like their anthropological sisters, seemed caught in a gap.

An important early critique of historical and ethnomusicological literature on gender was published by Anne Dhu Shapiro in 1991, where she clearly outlined six issues that she believed had been problematic in the recent new scholarship of the 1980s[15] and that she thought had contributed to the marginalization of feminist theory in music studies generally:

> (1) The study of music and gender is most often [labeled] as [the study of] women's music and is done most often by women; (2) the women seen as most worth studying are those who hold equivalent status to the professional males in a culture; (3) a corollary to #2: if their cultures do not give talented female performers equal status . . . then this is deemed wrong [by the scholars writing the articles—my clarification]; (4) the expression of femaleness is found in the texts or contexts of performance, rather than in the music, itself; (5) the granting of "non-music" status to a woman's performance genre is constructed [by insiders] as a degradation; and, (6) perhaps most important, the gender makeup of the performing and composing forces of music is [often] studied in separation from other "non-musical" aspects of culture. (1991, 8)

Shapiro's critique of this literature centers on its underlying ethnocentric assumptions, made invisible by the "zeal to right old wrongs" (ibid., 15); she urges us to become more sensitive to insider positions of all kinds. As the decade progressed, many scholars in both historical musicology and ethnomusicology took up this challenge, and more self-reflexive and intersubjective work on music and gender began to appear in both fields.

Some of us began to hope that the new common interest in gender would bring historical and ethnomusicologists together in ways that had been impossible before. However, by the mid-1990s, when more abstract theorizing was developing, various musics began to become separated from real women in real-life situations and began to be seen, more or less, as persuasive fictions, or the coded texts of postmodernism; early attempts of feminist historical and ethnomusicologists at finding common ground seemed to be abandoned.

In 1997 ethnomusicologist Elizabeth Tolbert presented a paper at the third Feminist Theory and Music Conference, titled "Negotiating the Fault Lines: Ethnomusicology, Feminist Theory, and Cultural Difference," where she lamented that gender studies, rather than bringing historical and ethnomusicology together over common feminist ground, had created a substantial fault line between them. Ethnomusicologists, unlike their historical musicology colleagues, had been slow to take up feminist criticism as an analytic paradigm. Unlike historical musicology and other disciplines dealing primarily with Western cultural forms, she said, ethnomusicology had already had "a long-standing engagement with difference—not gender difference, to be sure, but cultural difference" (6), an engagement that had, for a long time, forced ethnomusicologists to deal with the ethical and moral problems inherent in the representations of cultural difference within Western academic discourse.

Further, this long-standing engagement with difference, seen and experienced in the field and in fieldwork, had caused ethnomusicologists to see that "tidy one-to-one referential meanings between musical forms and cultural ideologies did not correspond to the realities of the complex and contested nature of culture" (ibid.). Notions of the supremacy of the text and the decentered self, while seemingly well suited to the study of Western musics, did not seem to fit comfortably with non-Western music cultures, especially those based on oral traditions. In short, feminist ethnomusicologists tended to avoid current trends in literary and cultural criticism, while feminist historical musicologists tended to avoid anthropological understandings of cultural difference based on intersubjective fieldwork.

Four Significant Works in Feminist Ethnomusicology

As in chapter 1, I will avoid here simply listing the many works that appeared during this time and focus, instead, on four that beautifully captured, for me, the moment when feminist ethnomusicologists truly began to fill in the theoretical gap between their feminist and ethnographer selves. Below I discuss one collection, *Music, Gender, and Culture,* edited by Marcia Herndon and Susanne Ziegler, that appeared in 1990, just as the new decade began; two monographs, *The Voice of Egypt: Umm Kulthum, Arabic Song, and Egyptian Society in the Twentieth Century,* by Virginia Danielson (1997) and *Engendering Song: Singing and Subjectivity at Prespa Albanian Weddings,* by Jane

Sugarman (1997); and, finally, Pirkko Moisala's article "Musical Gender in Performance" that appeared in 1999, just as the decade and millennium were closing. All of them were important to me at the time and continue to be inspiring. They were chosen to be discussed here because not only are they wonderful examples of feminist ethnomusicology, but each tells the story of music and feminism differently, together creating their own small community of different scholarly voices within ethnomusicology itself.

Herndon's collection was the first publication to come out of the International Council on Traditional Music's Study Group on Gender and Music. Formed between 1985 and 1988, this group brought together women and men, many from Europe and elsewhere outside the United States, to "work toward a gender-balanced view of musical and dance activities" (Herndon and Ziegler 1990, 8). In her introduction, Herndon discusses the interplay between the biological and social construction of gender. Using examples drawn from her own fieldwork among Cherokee Indians in Oklahoma, Herndon points to the flexibility with which the Cherokee mediate and negotiate the relative significance of nature and nurture within specific contexts in an effort to interrogate this rigid binary. Throughout the articles to follow, another underlying theme emerges: the need for more self-reflexivity in fieldwork and a better relative positioning of researchers and their partners in the field. This attention to flexibility and self-reflexivity became a hallmark of a new feminist ethnomusicology as the decade progressed and greatly clarified for me the dangers of an unexamined self-other binary.

Virginia Danielson's engaging and intellectually rigorous book on the extraordinary Egyptian singer Umm Kulthum is not explicitly an example of feminist ethnomusicology; that is, Danielson is not interested in placing Kulthum (or herself) into a feminist theoretical framework. Rather, she is more preoccupied with the role of this singer in the political and social history of modernization in twentieth-century Egypt. This is a wonderful example of an ethnographic biography, a newish form of writing in ethnomusicology that allows the close details of an individual life to be seen and understood in a broader context. Placed at the center of a set of concentric circles, Umm Kulthum's life radiates outward to intersect with national political and aesthetic-musical issues.

Danielson begins with an initial question: "How and why an individual could sustain such popularity for so long?" (1997, 2). This question blossoms into others as the book closely traces Umm Kulthum's life and politically active times, linking them together into a satisfying whole. The beauty of this book, for me, is in how it intertwines the everyday acts of feminism (my label) into the fabric of real-time life, without self-consciously proclaiming itself a feminist text. In other words, the work of feminism is being carried out here without that being the author's explicitly stated goal.

As an outsider reading this book, however, I might (and did) interpret Umm Kulthum's success in a world of limited opportunities for Egyptian women musicians as an exemplar of a feminist life. And, in a similar way, I could construct Danielson's positioning of her in this historical biography as, in itself, a feminist act, in that it presents its readers with a successful female role model from whom to learn much about adaptive strategies (dressing as a boy, learning to recite Quranic texts, and so on). However, that is my story, not Danielson's.

Jane Sugarman's book *Engendering Song: Singing and Subjectivity at Prespa Albanian Weddings* explicitly addresses a number of issues that relate to gender (both female and male), perspective, and performativity. In addition to her close documentation of the performance contexts of Prespa Albanian weddings, Sugarman goes further by weaving these data through a variety of interdisciplinary themes to assert that the true potential of musical experience is "not merely to reinforce gender relations within other domains but to actively *engender* those individuals who participate in them" (1997, 32).

Thus, like Judith Butler and others, Sugarman suggests that genders are actively constructed in the act of musical performance through the process of performativity, where markers of gender are performed but may be invisible to the individual and to his or her "audience." Sugarman states that "highly symbolic practices such as music-making . . . have helped to inscribe and maintain these notions deep within our beings, and their very beauty and power have often distracted us from noticing the assumptions that they embody" (ibid.). Drawing upon the scholarship of Pierre Bourdieu, who theorized the nondiscursive, experiential domains as "habitus" (ibid., 28), Sugarman makes an eloquent case for a new critical theory for feminist ethnomusicology.

All of the works discussed thus far have relied on extensive fieldwork within one specific cultural setting. In short, they have not tackled the problem of theory building, of constructing more general theories that might be applied cross-culturally. In her important article, Pirkko Moisala extends Sugarman's explanation of performance and performativity by proposing an analytic concept, "musical gender," that positions music itself—not the geographical area of its performance, nor the gender of its performer, nor the specific gender ideology of its setting—as the site of gender learning, performing, contesting, and radicalizing. And although all of the issues listed between the dashes in the last sentence are crucial to an understanding of a specific musical and gendered context, the abstraction of the model she presents here, one focusing on music, moves us closer to a theory that allows for a gendered musical life, experienced in real-time flow.

Moisala presents five ontological stances to music at the beginning of her article, using data from fieldwork in four separate musical cultures: three in Finland, her home country, and one in Nepal, among the Gurung people. The five stances are as follows: (1) music is, like language, a primary modeling system, that is, a system that guides or forms our perceptions of the world or a system on which we model the world around us: (2) music is a bodily art; (3) music is most often publicly performed and is thus subject to social control; (4) music exists only in performance, even though the norms of performativity are brought to bear on the performer; and (5) music has the ability to alter one's state of mind. Using these five positions, she constructs a general and useful model in which one can examine gender in all of its performances through sounds, which are culturally and socially constructed as music.

Thus, as the 1990s came to a close, certain issues within the fields of feminist anthropology and ethnomusicology, especially those surrounding the theoretical and methodological approaches to fieldwork, had been retheorized. New models, stressing difference and multiplicity, began to appear that together helped in the 1990s to bring about a renewed interest in feminist ethnomusicological scholarship. For me, this decade marked my turn toward fieldwork as the crucial key to opening both a different understanding of subject-object positionality as well as a different, more direct form of musical and social engagement.

5   Gender, Power, and Music

✷ Introduction
   material

In the late 1980s and into the 1990s, I was still on the hunt for a usable cross-cultural model to help explain what I continued to see as the nearly universal subordination of women's musical activities. I turned again to Sherry Ortner's work, elaborating on her theme of female intermediacy and mediation and added in the work of anthropologist Peggy Reeves Sanday (1981) on ritual power. Finally, I examined music as a source of ritual power, attempting to create a threefold nexus of women, power, and music that could accommodate cross-cultural perspectives. At the time, this seemed a useful way to deal with the thorny issue of comparison.

I was beginning to see, however, that a universal, or cross-cultural, theory for gender-music ideologies, relations, and activities was not only difficult to construct (maybe impossible), but ultimately too abstract to be useful. Such a model could not explain major cultural differences between and among music cultures. Nor could it account for the fluidity of gender constructions over time. I was beginning to be uncomfortable with too many generalities and began to think more seriously about how to deal with specific differences, while still saying something meaningful about larger issues.

*   *   *

During the past two decades, sweeping changes in women's economic and political status have resulted in many new opportunities for women within the historically male-dominated Western classical music tradition. As our notions of men and women have changed, so also have our beliefs about what is considered appropriate or correct for women and men to do musically. We no longer discourage our young female musicians, for instance, from playing the cello or oboe, as western European society did in the nineteenth century, for fear that the movement of their bodies or faces would compromise their virtue. Nor do we suggest, as Carl Seashore did in 1940, that it was not only inappropriate but impossible for women to compose music because their creativity was already spent in producing and nurturing the (male) babies that would become the composers of tomorrow.

It is not, however, the purpose of this article to examine our contemporary tradition in light of its historical past, nor to highlight the considerable accomplishments of those women who achieved and continue to achieve musical success despite daunting odds. Rather, its purpose is to broaden our perspective by examining various cross-cultural beliefs about men, women, and music and to show how the interrelationship between these concepts affects the division of musical roles in many world societies, including our own.

Certain basic patterns appear to be emerging from a survey of the growing literature devoted to music and gender cross-culturally. First, like many aspects of social, political, and ritual life, musical roles in most societies still tend to be divided along gender lines. Certain activities, instruments, performing contexts, rituals, ceremonies, and so on are seen as the primary responsibility of either men or women, rarely both. It seems clear that the division of musical roles based on gender arises from the intersection of culturally held notions of sexuality and power. How is this complex interplay between gender, power, and music actually conceptualized and realized in specific social contexts? To find the answer, we must first examine more closely some recent models that have been proposed to explain the great variety of gender relations, power styles, and ideas concerning music as a communication medium.

Recent Theories of Gender Relations in Cross-Cultural Perspective

Recently, there has been considerable interest in finding a universal theory to account for gender relations cross-culturally. Many useful models have been developed over the past two decades, all of which incorporate a distinction between sex, defined here as a biological category (male-female), and gender, defined as a socially constructed category that places people within clearly delineated binary social roles (men-women). Although most societies recognize only two biological sexual categories, gender categories can be quite varied. For example, Kay M. Martin and Barbara Voorhies, in their book *Female of the Species* (1975), cite many cross-cultural examples of multiple genders. And concepts such as masculinity and femininity also vary considerably; according to George Silberbauer (1982), the G/Wi bushmen of southern Africa, for example, place little emphasis on these concepts; although they may recognize primary biological differences between males and females, there is little gender differentiation or gender-based division of labor. Further, unlike many societies that regard activities such as hunting as the province of men, Tiwi aboriginals living off the coast of Australia consider men to be responsible for food resources in the sea and women for resources on land, a division of labor that results in women hunting (Goodale 1971). Certainly, the way Western cultures have viewed the genders has also varied widely, both in the past and within contemporary societies. We need look only to our own culture to see the sweeping changes that have occurred even within the past twenty years that have affected the way we think of men and women and the interactions between them.

Evidence for the fluidity of gender categories and roles also exists in instances of cross-gender socialization, found in some Native American cultures and elsewhere. In certain American Indian societies, children of one biological sex are occasionally socialized to be the opposite gender: a female, socialized to be a man, for example, assumes all responsibilities for this gender role, including marriage to a female and hunting and warring with other males; or a young male, socialized to be a woman, marries another male and assumes major responsibility for (adoptive) children and other so-called women's duties (Allen 1986).

The term gender ideology has been used to denote the conceptual and valuative framework that underlies and structures appropriate behaviors for women and men (Ortner and Whitehead 1981; O'Kelly and Carney 1986). Gender ideologies are most often codified as religious, moral, or legal systems that justify relations between the genders. For example, for many centuries, the traditional belief in male supremacy found in many Western religious systems (Christianity, Judaism, Islam) promoted the idea that women were not suited for religious leadership. Indeed, written texts supported and validated this ideology, and it is only recently that such beliefs have been questioned by both men and women.

In spite of myriad differences in culture-specific gender ideologies, one common feature remains: in recognizing and privileging the primary biological difference between women and men—that women and not men bear and nurse children—most societies also conceptualize the gender roles of adult males and females differently. Some societies see a balance of value between men and women; others stratify the genders. But in no society do men and women have totally equal access to all cultural domains. In many societies, women are associated with nature, or natural processes, such as birth, sickness, and death, while men are more often associated with culture, technology, and warfare. In others, women, by virtue of their fertility, are seen as having a more direct, and hence a more highly valued, access to the spirit world than men and often become adept shamans. In still others, women are primarily associated with states of disorder, impurity, or immorality, while men and their activities are seen as ordered and the norm. How the biological given of one's sex is spun out into the rich social, conceptual, and symbolic webs of one's gender is as varied as culture itself, so that gender ideologies can seem quite contradictory in cross-cultural comparison.

Anthropological Models of Gender Stratification

Many models appearing recently in the anthropological literature see the instance of gender stratification as an outgrowth of the acquisition of private property and the ensuing development of various socioeconomic systems, such as capitalism. Building upon the earlier work of Karl Marx ([1867] 1967) and especially Friedrich Engels ([1942] 1972), recent scholars have developed theories that examine the degree of gender stratification noted in a given society in relation to various modes of economy. These theories propose positive correlations between the degree to which public and domestic spheres are merged and the lack, or heightened instance, of gender stratification. Such theories can be applied cross-culturally to help explain the wide variety of gender styles noted in the ethnographic literature.

Michelle Rosaldo and Louise Lamphere (1974), for example, describe societies as existing on a continuum whose poles differentiate the degree to which public and private domains are separated. Described at one end of a continuum are societies such as foragers, some horticulturalists, and pastoralists (i.e., the Sheikhanzai of western Afghanistan, the !Kung bushmen of Central and South Africa, precontact Iroquois, and others), where there is relatively little distinction between the genders or between domestic and public spheres and where activities in both spheres are fairly equally shared and valued by all. In addition, there is often little or no notion of private property, ownership, or social class in these societies, but, rather, they are more often characterized by a relative complementarity between the sexes; that is, both men and women, although performing different work, rituals, and other social activities, are seen as separately, yet equally, responsible for the balance of society. Some societies at this end of the continuum are also matrilineal or matrilocal (or both), adding to the strength of women's social and familial ties. Most important, many of these societies have had little contact with Western technology or with the value systems surrounding technology that tend to polarize male and female labor.

At the other end of the continuum are societies that demonstrate a sharp differentiation between public and domestic spheres (i.e., agrarian societies or capitalist societies with an agrarian past), such as those found in Europe, the United States, and much of Asia. Here, according to historian Joan Kelly-Gadol, women seem to "steadily lose control over property, products and themselves as surplus increases, private property develops and the communal household becomes a private economic unit" (1976, 819). Further, societies at this end tend to be patrilineal, patriarchal, and characterized by materialism, a dependency on Western technology, and class as well as gender stratification. Gender relations are often marked by a strict separation of the sexes and rigid rules governing appropriate behaviors, where women often have little access to public institutions, marriage negotiations, reproductive rights, or divorce. Accompanying such social behavior is an unequal evaluation of the sexes that places women in the subordinate position.

Unlike Rosaldo, Peggy Reeves Sanday (1981) defines societies according to their gender style—what she calls a sex-role plan. Sanday's theory relies upon an understanding of a society's basic orientation to nature and to the supernatural. She labels the two opposing poles of her continuum inner- and outer-oriented societies. Inner-oriented societies are characterized by a blurring of such categories as nature, culture, or supernatural and by a somewhat friendly orientation to nonhuman domains (perceived here as integrated with the human domain), needing mediation for the purpose of communication and cooperation, not control. Inner-oriented societies create symbolic systems supporting a spirit world that value both life giving and life taking; these societies' sacred systems are often defined by a godhead that is either female or both male and female.

In contrast, outer-oriented societies (as characterized by Sanday) show a sharp differentiation between such bounded categories as nature, culture, and the supernatural, where nature and the supernatural are perceived as chaotic, uncooperative, uncoordinated, and unfriendly, needing mediation for purposes of controlling potential danger. Although life giving is acknowledged, higher value is placed on life taking, usually in the form of hunting or warring, and such activities are supported by rich symbolic and sacred systems where the godhead is defined in masculine terms.

Ernestine Friedl (1975) suggests that age is a factor in gender roles cross-culturally and that men and women in different societies often experience status reversals when they pass through their sexually active, fertile years. Although all societies recognize various life stages, each has its own way of acknowledging sexual maturity and of placing restrictions upon male and female sexuality. Most gender ideologies prescribe different behaviors, activities, and social spheres for sexually active men and women. For example, in many societies, women upon marriage and again at menopause—when associations to fertility have passed—rise in social status. Among some forager societies, Friedl notes that men who have reached old age generally relinquish their hunting duties and often take a prominent role in child care. And in certain societies, as the distinctions between men and women lessen as they age, and as women become less like "women," they take on some of the authority of males, thus "reversing the balance of a lifetime" (85).

Although there has been considerable criticism of these theories over the years, four ideas seem valuable for our purposes. The first, central to all of the theories, is the notion that women, by virtue of their fertility and their association in many cultures to natural processes, are seen as existing (unlike men) within, or perhaps closer to, the nonhuman world, yet are also of the human world. The second idea is that which describes the degree to which societies have been influenced by Western economic systems, technology, and values. The third relates a given society's orientation to the natural and supernatural worlds. And the fourth is the view of gender-status reversal in old age.

Theories of Social Power in Cross-Cultural Perspective

At the heart of all social relations, especially those of gender, lie culturally constructed and maintained notions of power and control. Certainly, power dynamics between social classes, ethnic and racial groups, and especially men and women have profoundly affected not only the composition and performance of music in virtually all societies, but also all other social activities. But what is the nature of social power? How does it affect gender relations and, ultimately, music performance?

Over the past few years, anthropologists have dealt with concepts of social power cross-culturally and have defined it as the ability of a person or group to influence others through various forms of control—over resources, such as food, labor, and information, or over access to the spirit world. Control is maintained through language and other interactions that articulate explicit or implicit threats of withdrawal of such resources. Outward signs of control may include material wealth, large fighting forces, or other culturally agreed-upon signs of social status, such as extraordinary mental or physical capacities, age, or gender. Although the origin of social power may lie in the ways people and groups deal with primary differences in sex, age, physical, and mental abilities, or in the ability to articulate ideas, it is not the simple recognition of such differences alone that creates a power dynamic. Rather, power is an outgrowth of the ranking of such differences and in assigning value and status to particular differences over others (Adams 1977).

It is the dynamic, interactive aspect of power that is most interesting for our purposes. Richard Keesing (1981) asserts that power is not an entity in itself—one does not "have" power. Rather, power is an attribute of relation-ships between people or groups existing in specific contexts or situations. Further, it can be negotiated or overturned, through direct challenge, ritual, or other forms of social or symbolic protest. Thus, a certain ambiguity ex-ists in power interactions, an ambiguity that arises from the question of just how much control an individual or group actually has over another, whether power will be abused to the point of becoming unstable or challengeable, and whether the less powerful can succeed in challenging the more powerful. Most social relations are thus imbued with elaborate patterns of deference and reciprocity to socially articulate and define power relations, and such rules, restrictions, and consequences of social interactions are, at least tacitly, known and understood by all who share a culture.

Adams further states that a central feature of power is the manipulation of tension between polarized cultural notions of control and out-of-control states. Most societies link attributes of control and out of control with other primary dyads, forming conceptual clusters, such as human-nonhuman, young-old, order-disorder, mundane-supernatural, and male-female, where categories on the left are perceived as being essentially more in control and those on the right as more out of control. This does not necessarily mean, however, that categories on the left are perceived as controlling those on the right or that those on the right are in need of control, but rather they are seen as having the essence of "in" or "out of control–ness." Whether either of these categories is actually controlling or in need of control is more the feature of a society's power style, theoretically ranging from societies where control of other humans or nonhumans is not a major social feature, and power is kept in balance between people and domains, to societies where control is a major feature of interaction, and where power is generally out of balance between people and domains.

Sanday, in describing the power dynamic between men and women, states that "power is accorded to whichever sex is thought to embody or to be in touch with the forces upon which people depend for their perceived needs" (1981, 11). Thus, in outer-oriented societies, where the group is dependent, for example, upon large game for an adequate food supply, and where males are responsible for the killing and distribution of game, males will be accorded power. In inner-oriented societies, where women and men hunt and distribute food more or less equally, or where both men and women have equal access to the spirit world, power is more likely to be shared and kept in balance.

Before moving on, I would like to make two points clear. First, certain of these conceptual dyads are far more relevant in some societies than in oth-ers. For example, in so-called private, inner-oriented societies, distinctions between nature-culture and public-private are largely irrelevant, yet the distinction between men and women still provides the primary basis for most social divisions. Second, that women appear to link up with out-of-control states is not to be taken literally. The terms *control* and *out of control* are not to be understood as polar opposites, but as relative by degree. Further, it is not that all societies, or all individuals, perceive women (as opposed to men) as literally out of control, but rather as linked, through their fertility, with more generally out-of-control domains—that is, nature and the supernatural—and thus take on some of the essence, ambiguity, and power of these domains.

The Conceptualization of Music in Cross-Cultural Perspective

Music sound, like *women* and *power* as described above, also carries the implication of intermediacy, in that it is used virtually everywhere to communicate with other humans, with nature, and with the supernatural. Further, music is not only a link between human and nonhuman domains, but also of these domains in that it is a human creation. A general definition of music (inspired, perhaps, by Lévi-Strauss) could well be "raw" sound (natural or supernatural sound or vibration) "cooked" into human sound (efficacious, beautiful, controlled, useful sound) through the process of using a music culture (a shared ideational and material system prescribing performer, performance context, use, style, and so on).

Another notion, deriving from the intermediate position of music, concerns the power of musical performance. Often described as a channel or vehicle that transports humans between one psychological state and another, between the mundane and the spiritual, or between one social status and another, music in performance has power that is believed to be only partially controlled by humans, and its use is often limited to specialists. According to John Blacking (1976), even in societies where everyone is believed to have the potential for musical competency and is expected to perform, music, ritual, and ceremonial specialists still exist. Music, if performed correctly or efficaciously, is believed to have an often mysterious power to manipulate emotions, to challenge or protest various social arrangements, or to effect changes in one's physical or psychological state. Music or ritual specialists (composers, performers, priests, shamans, and so on), as the manipulators of sound, often take on some of the essence of this power.

To summarize the above discussion, a number of general points can now be made: many societies conceptualize certain domains as potentially in or out of control; women's fertility is frequently associated with, or seen as having the essence of, nature and the supernatural (the nonhuman, essentially out-of-control domains), yet they also exist in the realm of humans (adult males); societies deal with control and out-of-control domains by using culture-specific power styles that vary considerably, both historically and in cross-cultural comparison, and are related to other socioeconomic factors; humans use music to communicate (mediate, intervene, negotiate, and so on) with other humans, nature, and the supernatural; and music sound is almost universally conceptualized as both potentially in or out of control.

Women who perform music thus accumulate a threefold portion of potential out of control–ness: the out of control–ness associated with music as natural sound, the out of control–ness of music as a vehicle to the spirit-emotional world, and the out of control–ness associated with their fertility. Males who perform music share the first two categories of out of control–ness with their female counterparts, but it is the out of control–ness that women amass by virtue of their fertility that pushes the power dynamic out of balance. Will women's musical performance bring on social integration (control, stability) or destruction (loss of control, chaos)? Will the power of music cause women to lose control sexually? Will raw sound, in the hands of a woman, become real music? The underlying fear might be simply stated as follows: if women create or perform music, nature and the supernatural might run amok, women might become sexually insatiable or withdraw their sexuality, and, most important, sound will not turn into music and thus will not be effective in human communication or in mediating the spirit world. Therefore, sexually active, fertile women (and any other groups of women or men perceived as potentially out of control) must be restricted, as their connection to out of control–ness is seen as threatening to the social and sexual order.

A Cross-Cultural Examination of Traditional Gendered Performance Contexts

Using Sanday's model of inner- and outer-oriented societies, it is possible to present a wide array of performance possibilities and restrictions for both women and men cross-culturally.

Inner-Oriented Societies

As stated above, the general pattern in inner-oriented societies is that various cultural activities are seen as the responsibility of one gender or the other, neither dominating the other, so that rituals and other contexts for music performance are divided along gender lines that are consistent with other binary cultural divisions. Both male and female domains are seen as necessary to the balance of life, and men's and women's musical activities are more or less equally valued. Further, in inner-oriented societies, control—over other humans, sexuality, nature, the supernatural, or any other domain—is not a major social feature. Here, sexually active women and their music are defined and valued precisely because of their links to out-of-control states. Their musical responsibilities balance those of men, for both genders are regarded as equally responsible for maintaining order. Here, the division of musical and, indeed, all labor is more evenly divided, but both women and men tend to have restricted access to each other's domains. Thus, both men's and women's music serves, more or less equally, to balance the relationships between the genders and between the human and nonhuman realms. And although men and women tend to be separated during music performance, or one group may have the primary responsibility for a given performance, any restrictions imposed are present because of the general belief that both men and women have unique attributes that are especially suited to given performance contexts.

Carol Robertson's work among the Mapuche of Argentina, for example, highlights the respect given to women's connection to nature and to the supernatural in inneroriented societies. According to Robertson, the power of Mapuche women is directly linked to the power of giving birth. Thus, women have a direct path to the spirit world, and performances of *tayil* (lineage soul) accompany many ceremonies, such as female initiations, house consecrations, burials, and rites of fertility: "Tayil is central to the performance of all acts that carry potential danger or that expose humans to active supernatural energy" (1987, 236). In their intermediate position between the human world, nature, and the supernatural, women, together with *tayil,* are central to the maintenance of Mapuche order.

Marina Roseman, among the Temiar of Peninsular Malaysia, points to musical performance as providing a context for gender role reversal. Ritual singing sessions are performed by a male medium, who, in trance, contacts a female spirit guide. The medium is accompanied by a female chorus that also provides a percussive accompaniment on a pair of bamboo-tube stompers. Within the context of this ritual performance, gender is inverted: "Men, ranging extensively through the jungle during subsistence activities, are transformed into the earth-bound students of female spirit-guides during ritual singing sessions. Women, restricted daily to swidden and settlement, are the wandering teachers of the spirit-realm" (1987, 144). Roseman points to these symbolic inversions as evidence of a fundamentally egalitarian social style that pervades all of Temiar culture.

Outer-Oriented Societies

In outer-oriented societies, where control over out–of–control-ness is a major feature of power style, women can be regarded as falling within two general cultural categories that I shall call here simply "insiders" (suitable marriage partners) and "outsiders" (unsuitable, public women). It will be recalled that outer-oriented societies are usually gender and class stratified and are either actually Western or considered as having been influenced by Western technology and values through colonialism and trade. Further, they are characterized by male control, both within and across class. Therefore, restrictions placed upon women and music relate specifically to the relationship of women to men of their class, as well as to general Western gender ideologies cutting across class that support male control over both music and female sexuality.

Women within each class who eventually become suitable marriage partners, that is, women who are insiders to the social and economic system, tend to have restrictions placed upon them that prohibit public music performance, often from the time of puberty and throughout their adult sexual lives. Frequently, upon marriage, when they have become properly socialized adults, women's relationship to music performance, if any existed before, often lessens or ceases in such societies or takes highly idiosyncratic yet sometimes powerful forms. For example, although women in nineteenth-century Europe were generally discouraged from public performances, they often controlled the private salons where musical performances occurred regularly. These women were also influential in other forms of patronage and in teaching, occupations not in the public concert-performance mainstream perhaps, yet of considerable influence and power.

Women who are considered outside this system—lesbians, public women, courtesans, professional female musicians, shamans, or women who seek to cross gender class lines—tend to have restrictions lifted on their sexuality and music performance.[1] However, they are usually prohibited from gaining access to the socioeconomic system that would reward them as properly socialized adults. This breakdown seems consistent with outer-oriented societies' relationship to control and out-of-control states. Women inside the system—those who could be truly threatening—are discouraged from music or any public performance; women who are outside the system are given both musical and sexual license, because their power to control or threaten the system at large is, no matter how great locally, perceived as ultimately futile.

Many studies describing the major court traditions of Europe, Asia, the Middle East, and northern Africa suggest that public female musicians frequently functioned in dual roles as entertainers and courtesans. Generally, such women came from the rising merchant classes, and their social status often rose as a result of their association with courtly life. Thus, such women, regarded as marginal to the general class-stratified socioeconomic system, were given both musical and sexual freedom.

In private environments, such as the home, women's musical performances within the socioeconomic context of Asian and European courts were historically linked to their role as acceptable marriage partners. These women were more or less restricted in their sexual and musical display. Instruments—such as the *koto* in Japan; the piano, harp, and guitar in Europe; and the *kulingtang* in the Philippines—became associated with young middle-class women, primarily in the context of courtship, during which performers could display idealized notions of proper female behavior and "feminine accomplishments" within private settings that would not compromise their social status.

As opposed to court life, women's role in the ritual life of outer-oriented societies presents somewhat of a paradox. Despite many religious systems within such societies that stress a female principle, if not a female godhead, earthly women's participation has been quite limited in mainstream religious life. In Korea, for example, women are not generally part of public, Confucianist, or Buddhist rituals. Instead, women's ritual activities tend to be devalued and "relegated to the home." Here, women address mainly familial and household concerns: the birth of sons, the curing of illness, forecasting the marriage of a daughter, appeasing dead souls, removing evil spirits, and so on (Kendall 1985).

Ritual life in outer-oriented societies, such as those of Europe, Asia, and the Middle East, also shows a division of musical and other social roles based on gender, a division, as discussed above, that is fortified by a patriarchal, patrilocal socioeconomic system and by cultural notions of the "naturalness" of male physical strength and of women's weakness. In traditionally agrarian societies, women's primary role upon marriage is to produce children and to tend to domestic duties. The young bride is often placed into a domestic environment of extreme hardship, where she is at the bottom of a familial hierarchy of power, under the control of her father-in-law, her mother-in-law, her husband, his brothers, and other males of her generation. In eastern Europe, laments (songs of mourning usually reserved for rituals of death) are also sung at weddings, as the bride leaves the relative protection of her own household and enters the often-hostile environment of her new husband's family (see Auerbach 1987 and Sugarman 1989). When the young woman begins to produce children, her status rises, until, in old age, she assumes some of the same prestige and status of the males of her generation.

Despite sweeping economic changes during the decades since World War II, the peasant societies of eastern and southern Europe still retain in great measure traditional values and beliefs concerning the roles of the genders, especially in the arena of public performance. Men's and women's song repertoires, for example, are based almost exclusively on their social roles, where women's music is most often associated with birth, marriage, and death, and men's songs, labeled "heroic," are associated primarily with cultural history (Bartók and Lord 1951; Slobin 1984).

Music performance as both a metaphor for gender relations and an arena for the refinement of such relations has been discussed by a number of noted scholars. Louise Wrazen (1983), for example, has analyzed a complex of dances, the *goralski,* performed by young Polish women and men in traditional settings of formalized courtship. During these dances, coded movements signal the woman's acceptance or rejection of potential suitors. The movements of the young men are characterized by highly energetic jumping, leaping, and other forms of male display. The young woman's movements, in keeping with her socially defined role, are controlled and demure; her feet are generally together and do not leave the floor, and her eyes are downcast or closed.

Jane Sugarman has described a genre of wedding songs performed by Muslim men and women from the Lake Prespa district of Yugoslavia (Macedonia), now living in Albania and Canada. She has analyzed the singing styles of the men and women, noting a number of contrasting features: Men's songs tend to be performed loudly, in nonmeter, with extensive ornamentation and considerable bodily motion and interaction with other males. Texts tend to be concerned with history and heroism and are performed with high emotion, often stretched to its limits by considerable alcohol. Women, on the other hand, tend to perform using a strict meter, moderate ornamentation, and little bodily motion and interaction, and they tend to employ specialized texts and emotional displays in keeping with the wedding context and with constrained propriety.

Sugarman also examines, to some degree, the change of social status for women at the passing of fertility and the ensuing effects on music performance. First, older women begin to wear dresses of a "closed" color, such as navy blue or brown, in contrast to the more "open" (brighter) colors of their youth. Second, their singing and dancing styles may become quite boisterous, and at wedding gatherings such women can more freely express emotion and intermingle with the men. The subdued colors, combined with new, more open behaviors, provide a cultural signal that a new stage of (nonthreatening) maturity has arrived (1989, 195-203).

*   *   *

If we look at all of the examples presented here, it becomes obvior
the performance and creation of music, as well as all other human social and
expressive activities, are fundamentally dependent upon a society's understandings of men and women and the interactions between them. Conversely,
music performance can and does provide a context for understanding the
negotiation of power in intergender relations. Furthermore, tensions surrounding power and control that exist between women and men can be
exposed, challenged, or reversed within musical performance.

6 Miriam Sings Her Song

The Self and the Other in Anthropological Discourse

This article was my first attempt to deal with the idea of multiple, simultaneous voices. And it also marked a return to my work on Lubavitcher music and gender ideologies, most clearly realized in the law of *kol isha* (a woman's voice). Here, I present three different interpretations of the same event, attempting to uncover the situated perspective of different readers. This article, its structure loosely based on that of two very different works that were inspiring to me in the 1990s—Japanese director Akira Kurosawa's 1950 film, *Rashomon*, depicting four different versions of a sexual encounter and murder, and feminist anthropologist Margery Wolf's *Thrice-Told Tale: Feminism, Postmodernism, and Ethnographic Responsibility* (1992), three different accounts of a rural Taiwanese woman's "unusual" behavior, used as the basis of a serious critique of postcolonial feminism—explores the power of different underlying assumptions and biases embedded, and largely invisible, in any perspective.

＊   ＊   ＊

It is Friday evening, and Miriam is alone in her apartment waiting for her husband to return from work. As she lights the candles for the Sabbath, she begins to sing a *nigun,* one she has composed herself. She loves to sing and is pleased to be able to offer such a gift to the Sabbath queen who will soon descend. Miriam is observed by a married male neighbor, who retreats into his own apartment next door, observing the law of *kol isha.* Miriam hears her neighbor's door close and continues singing.

Scenes such as this, and countless others noted by anthropologists in the field, constitute the raw data from which convincing cultural pictures and analyses will later be derived. The anthropologist, seen essentially as a transla-tor between—or an analyst of—cultures, interweaves the bits and pieces of others' lives into stories and collages, often of immense power and integrity.

Two common perspectives found in the anthropological literature result in what will be called here *descriptive* and *analytic* ethnography. In descriptive ethnography, which is usually limited to portraits of one culture, all of the parts seem to be uniquely and correctly connected, much like a completed, intricate jigsaw puzzle. They are written ostensibly from an insider's perspec-tive, yet the reader understands that this is a fiction; it is the ethnographer who, in selecting and thereby privileging some bits of data over others, has constructed a convincing story. Such ethnographies are essentially distil-lations, presenting no individual view, yet somehow representative of the whole.

Analytic ethnography, by contrast, often attempts to expose and change systems that oppress or dominate. In this sense, it is openly political in its purpose. Recent feminist anthropology, for example, often comparative and clearly written from an outsider perspective, points to deeper social structures that have been obscured or mystified (in the Marxist sense) by political or religious ideology.

Although it can be an occupational hazard of anthropology to portray cultures either as neat ethnographic packages or as evidence for a particu-lar political viewpoint, it is clear that the resulting portraits are essentially outsider perspectives. But what of the insider, the person actually living the culture, the so-called other of ethnographic presentation? This essay explores the differences in presentation that result when cultures and their musical systems are presented from these very different perspectives. The ethnographic data come from many years of observing and participating in the musical practices of a group of Hasidic Jews (Lubavitchers) living in Brooklyn, New York.

I first don the describer's hat (perspective 1): I present, as in a monograph, the Lubavitcher religious and philosophical belief system and the resulting social roles that Lubavitchers adopt to create and maintain a sense of social order and balance. Next, I move to a more openly analytic perspective (per-spective 2), as in a feminist political text, examining gender roles within this society, using Jewish laws pertaining to gender differences and musical per-formance as evidence for the asymmetry of value between Lubavitcher men and women. Third, I offer the insider's viewpoint (perspective 3), as in a diary, based on direct quotations taken from field notes and from conversations with Lubavitchers during which they expressed to me their misgivings about outsider perspectives. Finally, I offer a way to understand these perspectives, by introducing the dynamic of power that exists between the observer self and the observed other. In doing this, I hope to clarify both the voice that is speaking in these cultural presentations and the end to which it speaks.

Perspective 1: The Describer, Looking In

The Ethnographic Setting

> In Hasidism, one of the most important things is the happiness of the heart, and the adherence of the heart to the worshipping of our God. The Hasid can only allow his soul expression through melody. Only melody has the strength to elevate the soul. Woman's body reflects more of the aspect of G-d's essence than does man's, as Chassidus [*sic*] explains. For woman has the ability to create within herself new life, a new creature, a "something from nothing," and this parallels, and derives from the power of the essence of G-d to create ex nihilo, to create from utter nothing. This is one of the ways in which woman is in a more sensitive spiritual position than man. (Zalmanoff 1947, 19)

Hasidism is an orthodox and mystical Jewish movement, the modern phase of which was begun by the seventeenth-century Polish rabbi Israel ben Eliezer, the Ba'al Shem Tov (1698–1760) (Handelman 1981, 25). The Lubavitcher court was founded in the late eighteenth century by Rabbi Schneur Zalman of Liadi (1745–1813), a Lithuanian rabbi who codified his essential philosophy in the *Tanya,* a four-volume collection of writings and commentaries upon Talmudic and mystical texts. At the core of Schneur Zalman's philosophy is the concept of the *benoni,* or the intermediate, that is, any Jew who stands between opposing souls, expressed metaphorically as the animal and the divine soul. The status of *benoni* is within the grasp of anyone who succeeds in living his or her life without intentionally committing an evil act (Zalman 1969, 77–83). Lubavitchers today often speak of the polarization of animal and divine souls, of the process of moving upward and inward from the animal to the divine realm, and of the considerable tension between these two equally powerful forces in everyday life.

Rabbi Schneur Zalman's form of Hasidism came to be called Habad, an acronym based on three Hebrew words: *hochma* (conceptualization), *binah* (cognition), and *da'at* (understanding). After the death of Schneur Zalman, his followers moved the center of Habad Hasidism to the town of Lubavitch, from which the community has since derived its name. The contemporary Lubavitcher court is led by Rabbi Menachem Mendel Schneerson, known as Rebbe, or Tzaddik (Holy One), who emigrated to the United States in 1941 and settled in Brooklyn, New York. There are roughly 250,000 Lubavitchers worldwide, the majority of whom live in Crown Heights.

Lubavitchers, unlike other Orthodox Jews, practice a mystical form of Judaism that focuses on the concept of *devekut,* or adhesion to God ("oneness," or unity with the divine). The process of achieving *devekut* is described as moving from the animal to the divine soul (or, often, from the "heel of the foot to the top of the head"); when the divine soul is reached, the animal "falls away." The metaphor of heel and head is further expressed through the Lubavitcher notion that as the generations pass, they move "upward" in spirituality. For example, Moses, Rabbi Schneur Zalman, and other ancestral males are often referred to as existing at the "top of the head," and people living today are in the realm of the "heel to the foot." Finally, the animal, or mundane, soul is conceptualized as disordered, often needing restricting laws or codes, whereas the divine soul is seen as ordered, or having the capability of ordering. One's spiritual quest for *devekut,* then, is regarded as a movement away from disorder toward order (ibid., 22–30).

Devekut is brought about by adhering to the laws of Orthodox Judaism and by living all aspects of one's life with the proper godly intention (*kavannah*). *Kavannah* is prepared for ("awakened") by the expression of two essential emotional states: *simhah* (joy) and *hitlahavut* (enthusiasm). Lubavitchers regard their melodies, or *nigunim* (singular *nigun*), as essential vehicles for expressing *simhah* and *hitlahavut,* as *nigunim* are believed to hold traces of these properties that are "freed" through active performance.

Nigun *and Its Performance*

Nigunim (plural of *nigun*) are paraliturgical melodies, often borrowed from, or newly composed to resemble, both Jewish and non-Jewish eastern European folk melodies. They are performed on a variety of occasions, including the rebbe's *farbrengens* (Hasidic gatherings where the rebbe speaks), the Sabbath or other festive meals, or during private moments of prayer and contemplation. Lubavitchers believe that performances of *nigunim* ready them for divine communication, enabling them to communicate with God and with their spiritually elevated ancestors. *Nigun* performances, especially during *farbrengens,* are often marked by an intense, at times frenzied, singing style that can temporarily render the performers emotionally or physically out of control.

The dichotomy between the animal and divine souls discussed above also appears in the Lubavitcher distinction between texts and melodies in music: text is connected to the mundane or animal soul, music to the spiritual or divine. Thus, many *nigunim* are wordless, sung to vocables, which occupy an intermediate spiritual position between the mundane and the spiritual.

Furthermore, *nigun* tunes are frequently borrowed from the music of the host culture, as this music is regarded as especially mundane, needing freeing from its mundane setting by Lubavitcher intervention. Borrowed *nigunim,* then, are tunes that are considered to be raw but to contain trapped properties of *simhah* and *hitlahavut* and therefore to be worthy of adoption and adaptation by Lubavitchers. In order to be incorporated into the repertoire, however, *nigunim* must be performed in the presence of the rebbe in a socially sanctioned context such as a *farbrengen.*

Two primary factors affect the performance, composition, and acceptance of *nigunim*: the spiritual lineage of the performer and the performer's gender. Many Lubavitchers now living in Crown Heights were born into Hasidism, and many come from powerful Hasidic lineages that extend back to eastern Europe and to the seventeenth century. In this country, in the late 1960s and the 1970s, Hasidism, especially Habad Hasidism, saw the growth of the Ba'al Teshuvah,[1] or "returnee" movement, which resulted in a heavy influx of new, predominantly American-born, non-Orthodox Jews who wished to return to orthodoxy. Ba'alei Teshuvah often describe themselves as being on a perpetual journey toward spirituality. This journey takes years of study and contemplation and parallels, if on a different plane, the spiritual journey of Lubavitchers who have been Orthodox (or observant) since birth. Many Ba'alei Teshuvah, however, are regarded as slightly suspect by lifetime Lubavitchers, as their roots are in the mundane world of contemporary U.S. culture. It is usually only with marriage—often to another Ba'al Teshuvah—and the birth of children that they are truly accepted.

The second factor that affects the performance, creation, and acceptance of *nigunim* is gender. In Orthodox Judaism, men and women are prohibited from praying, singing, or otherwise engaging together in social activities that offer a danger of unacceptable sexual behavior. Restrictions upon males prohibit them from hearing women singing and from talking freely to women who might cause them to become *ervah,* or sexually stimulated in a prohibited way.

In Orthodox and Hasidic Judaism, women are believed to be inherently closer to spirituality than men. As is noted in the quotation cited above, their fertility—their ability to create, like God, something from nothing—puts them closer to God, and thus makes them more naturally and powerfully holy. This natural superiority is reflected in many ways, one of the most important of which concerns women's exemption from many of the 613 commandments that Orthodox Jews follow.[2] For example, women are exempt from commandments that are linked to time and place (going to the synagogue at a specific time for prayers and so forth) because their duties in the home are seen as already fulfilling a commandment of greater spiritual value. But a woman's voice, especially in singing, is problematic in that it can lead to promiscuity. The singing voice of a woman has the potential to connect the body to prohibited sexuality, and thus to the mundane world and the animal soul.

Kol Isha

An entire body of Jewish law, known as *kol isha* (the voice of a woman), addresses the issue of illicit sexual stimulation, with specific reference to musical performance. The question of *kol isha* centers on the interpretation of a small passage in the Bible from the Song of Songs, "Let me see thy countenance, let me hear thy voice, for sweet is thy voice and thy countenance is comely." The first to comment on this passage was the sixth-century Talmudic scholar Samuel, whose interpretation firmly linked women's voices to prohibited sexuality. Commenting on the above passage from the Song of Songs, he wrote, "*Kol b'isha ervah*" ("The voice of a woman is a sexual incitement") (Cherney 1985, 24a: 57). During the tenth century, another scholar, Rabbi Joseph, added a refinement: "When men sing and women join in, it is licentiousness; when women sing and men answer, it is like a raging fire in flax" (ibid., 58).

Later scholars debated other issues, such as whether *kol isha* referred to the speaking as well as to the singing voice, or whether a woman's voice was sexually stimulating all of the time, only when one (male) was reciting the *Shema* (the holiest of Hebrew prayers), only when one was engaged in religious study, or only when one was nude. One commentator, Rabbi Judah He-Hasid (d. 1217), anticipating a feminist argument that would not surface for another 750 years, proposed the notion of *kol ish* (the voice of a man) as constituting the same sexual problems for women as *kol isha* for men.

Perhaps the most important commentary for our purposes, for it is the one that is followed today by most Orthodox and Hasidic Jews, is that of the great philosopher Moses ben Maimon (Maimonides, 1135–1204). He saw the word *ervah* as referring to the woman and to the performance context, not specifically to the woman's voice. He preceded the word *ervah* by the definite article *ha*. To Maimonides, the original commentary by Samuel read, "*Kol b'isha ha-ervah*," or, "The voice of an illicit woman is prohibited."[3] He states in the fifth book of his *Code,* in the section titled "Forbidden Intercourse,"

> Whoever indulges in [having intercourse with an illicit woman] lays himself open to the suspicion of forbidden unions. A man is forbidden to make suggestive gestures with his hands or legs or wink at a woman within the forbidden unions, or to jest or act frivolously with her. It is forbidden even to inhale her perfume or

gaze at her beauty. Whosoever directs his mind toward these things is liable to
the flogging prescribed for disobedience. He who stares even at a woman's little
finger with the intention of deriving pleasure from it, is considered as though
he had looked at her secret parts. It is forbidden even to listen to the singing of a
woman within the forbidden unions, or to look at her hair. (1965, 133)

The word *ervah* in Maimonides's interpretation referred only to a woman
of the "forbidden unions"—that is, one who was not likely to become a
marriage partner, one with whom a man might establish an illicit relationship. Maimonides in effect shifted the emphasis from the inherent sexuality
of women and their voices to the context of a potential illicit relationship
between a man and a prohibited woman within a nonsanctioned context.
Sexual stimulation in itself was not prohibited; rather, it was the potential to
create a context of sexual stimulation that was restricted.

Thus, in theory, men may listen to their wives and premenstrual daughters—in the first case because the couple is already married, and in the second
because it is unlikely that an illicit relationship will develop between two close
relatives, especially when one is a child. In addition, unmarried women (with
whom a marital relationship could be possible) and one's wife while she is
a *niddah*, a menstruant (because sexual intercourse will soon be possible),
are also excluded from this prohibition.

Although *kol isha* prohibits men from hearing women sing, it does not
prevent women from singing. Thus, women, especially Ba'alot Teshuvah and
young, unmarried women, when not in the presence of males, freely engage
in many of the same musical activities as their male counterparts. It is not
uncommon, for example, to hear women singing *nigunim* in the home while
lighting Sabbath candles. One particular event, the *forshpil*—a party given
for a young woman on the Sabbath before her wedding—rivals the musical
and spiritual intensity of the predominantly male *farbrengen*.

Thus, Orthodox and Hasidic Jews make a distinction between the natural
spirituality and positive sexuality of sanctioned women and the perhaps unintentional, yet powerful and potentially destructive, sexuality of prohibited
women. This destructive sexuality, symbolized by the speaking and singing
voice, can create the context for illicit sexual relations that can threaten the
very existence of the group and hence must be restricted.

From the Lubavitcher point of view, then, *kol isha* and many other laws
of Orthodox Judaism are socially agreed-upon rules for various forms of
interaction between men and women that guard against their loss of sexual
and physical control. In controlling women's voices, Lubavitchers (both men
and women) believe that they are balancing out the shift of power that might
result in group disintegration if women were permitted true freedom, for in

such a case the animal soul would dominate. Such laws are thus necessary to Lubavitcher life, for they preserve the essential binary contrasts that lie at the heart of Lubavitcher identity and form the underlying structure of Lubavitcher social relations.

Perspective 2: The Analyst, Looking In

Hierarchies of Value in Lubavitcher Life

> The cultural celestialization of the sources and nature of male power over women and juniors has an important consequence. Those who are subordinated are locked into the system not by a political and legal superstructure of state power but by their encapsulation within a closed universe of cosmic power.... If rules, such as pollution rules that exclude women from religious and political realms, were visibly the creations of men, they could be challenged. But if they are imposed by ancestors, who hold powers of life and death over the living, they are beyond challenge. (Keesing 1981, 299)

If we examine Lubavitcher gender relations in terms of the relative value between men and women, a different picture emerges. Let us move beyond the restrictions of *kol isha,* as outlined in the Talmudic writings above, and observe what happens in everyday practice, for in doing so we can expose the hierarchy of value that underlies Lubavitcher gender relations. Although in theory *kol isha* does not restrict men from hearing their wives sing, in practice married women almost never sing in the presence of their husbands, for they might inadvertently be overheard by a close male neighbor, relative, or one of their husband's students. Living in the close quarters characteristic of large urban centers, with the risk of being heard, even inadvertently, women have been effectively silenced. The restriction of *kol isha,* for all practical purposes, affects not only prohibited women (however defined), but virtually *all* adult (menstruating) women.

In contrast, all males are encouraged to sing, especially at *farbrengens* in the validating presence of the rebbe. Indeed, some of the most highly regarded males are those who act as the rebbe's musical assistants, suggesting specific songs and initiating the long, intense singing sessions that are so much a part of these gatherings. For Ba'alei Teshuvah, singing is especially important. Such a high value is placed on "correct" *nigun* performance that many Ba'alei Teshuvah gain a measure of social and spiritual acceptance through intense and heartfelt singing styles displayed during *farbrengens.*

Women, especially married women, do not usually attend the rebbe's *farbrengens* or, for that matter, Sabbath or other religious services, as their exemption from commandments of time and place has freed them to fulfill commandments in the home that have a higher spiritual value. Women who do come to the main Lubavitcher synagogue in Crown Heights sit in the women's gallery, a balcony high above the area occupied by the men, to ensure strict separation of the sexes. The gallery is enclosed by darkened sheets of plastic, so women's view of, and participation in, the proceedings below is quite limited.

In practice, then, a sharp social division arises for women, but not for men, in regard to musical performance: the division by marital status. Thus, if we ranked the various subgroups within Lubavitcher society, we might end up with a hierarchy of value that places the rebbe and all males who have been Lubavitchers from birth (as well as all male ancestors) at the top and all adult married lifetime Lubavitcher women slightly beneath them. Unmarried Ba'alot Teshuvah tend to be the least valued, but also the most active musically and the most adventurous concerning their musical practices, often singing under their breath during the rebbe's *farbrengens* or religious services, composing their own tunes, calling their own *farbrengens,* and, at times, listening to current popular music. Thus, it appears that the status hierarchy for women is in inverse proportion to their musical activity. Women in the most valued social and religious position, achieved through "correct" origins and marriage, tend to have the least active connection with music.[4]

Using the model of a hierarchy of value to analyze Lubavitcher society can bring us closer to an understanding of the underlying complexity of Lubavitcher social interactions surrounding gender and of their implications for musical performance. The rebbe, as the spiritual and symbolic head of this group, controls its fate through his spiritual lineage, personal holiness, and, most important, his access to the divine realm. That he is also male and elderly tends not only to validate his spirituality but also to reinforce the relatively high value that this group places on gender and age.

Members of the group of least value, unmarried Ba'alot Teshuvah, are believed to be still somewhat connected to the mundane world and are relatively out of control in that they have not yet married and produced children. This belief is borne out in everyday Lubavitcher life, for of all the social groups within Lubavitcher society, it is unmarried Ba'alot Teshuvah who are most encouraged to continue on their spiritual path not only by hard study and close observance of traditional laws, but, more important, by marrying and producing children. Ba'alot Teshuvah, the least valued group, are exploited in a pure Marxist sense, as the group at the top (older, lifetime Lubavitcher males) controls, through the ideology of spirituality, the fruit of their labor— their children. Ba'alot Teshuvah could be called collaborative, in that they work within the system and seem not to be oppressed by it.

Returning now to the binary contrasts represented in the Lubavitcher worldview, we see that they seem to line up as follows: the mundane domain consists of, among other things, the animal soul, Ba'alei Teshuvah (especially females), contemporary U.S. culture, non-Lubavitcher music, texted music, and women's voices. The spiritual realm consists of the divine soul, all adult lifetime Lubavitchers, eastern European Jewish culture, *nigunim,* and male voices. Things perceived as mundane have the potential to go out of control—accumulate too much animal soul—and must therefore be restricted, controlled, or otherwise limited for the protection of the group.

Women, especially Ba'alot Teshuvah who perform music, accumulate a threefold dose of potential out of control–ness: that associated with music, with their fertility, and with their sexuality. It is the accumulation of too much potential out of control–ness that creates tension. The tension relates to whether women's musical performance will bring on social integration or destruction, whether the power of music will cause women and men to lose control sexually or withdraw their fertility, and whether raw sound, in the hands of a woman, will really become music (*nigun*).

From the feminist perspective, then, the laws pertaining to *kol isha* indicate part of a carefully constructed and historically validated ideology that explains, rationalizes, or otherwise obscures the asymmetrical relationship of Lubavitcher men and women as social groups. *Kol isha,* in its effective silencing of women's literal and figurative voices, is at its core a strategy of males to deny women their sexuality, hence their power over group survival. *Kol isha,* like many of the restrictive codes of Orthodox Judaism, is a complex elaboration upon a theme of male dominance within a strongly patriarchal system that, in spite of protestations to the contrary, values the actions and behaviors of men over those of women.[5]

Perspective 3: Miriam, Looking Out

The idea is that a woman's voice is beautiful. It has a lot of qualities that would be enticing to a man. This is a fact known everywhere. It's been looked over a lot because "liberated" woman is pushing away all her ideas about being different. [For us] the facts are taken as they really are. Woman is woman and man is man. Now, one of the considerations is that when woman sings, it has a very appealing aspect to another man, and it should not. (Rosenblum 1975)

Over the years, in my work with Lubavitchers, I have often discussed my portraits of their culture with them. Hopeful that I have presented a true picture of their lives, I ask them to comment on my interpretations, to tell me whether "I've got it right." The consensus is that I often come close but that I cannot really understand the true nature of Lubavitcher life while I still remain on the outside.

For example, they say that I make too much of the artificial distinction between lifetime Lubavitchers and Ba'alei Teshuvah. Worse, I completely reverse the status hierarchy: lifetime Lubavitchers say that Ba'alei Teshuvah are *more* spiritual, *more* intense, *more* connected to the divine than they. After all, look at all they have given up to become Orthodox! Everyone does *teshuvah* (repentance), they say, but to be called a Ba'al Teshuvah is a tremendous honor. Many lifetimers say they long to have this title. Of course, there are those who look down on the Ba'alei Teshuvah, seeing them as still part of the "secular" world, but they are not in the majority.

Concerning *kol isha,* I am told that I have understood the legalities but have missed the real point by inadequately portraying the positive and vital power of women's sexuality. This is the reason, women say, that the restrictions of *kol isha* are so necessary. *Kol isha* protects them not only against prohibited men, but also against their own sexual power. Furthermore, I have not adequately described the sense of relief that obeying the laws of *kol isha* (and all other laws and codes) has provided for the community at large in its struggle to maintain balance. I have not successfully captured the real and constant combat between animal and divine souls.

Finally, they say, my analysis of their gender roles and statuses is simply wrong. Don't I know how important women are to maintaining Jewish continuity and how central home life is to Jewish culture? How can I suggest that women are a subordinated social group or that individual women are pawns, manipulated by powerful social forces beyond their control—at best, unconscious of their subordinated position; at worst, victims of a dominant male hierarchy that seeks to deny them their powerful sexuality? It is easy, they say, simply to dismiss this description; it is too secular, too much a part of the outside.

Is it possible that I have been mistaken in my descriptions and analyses? Have I not observed carefully enough? Have I allowed my biases to creep in and to skew what I have seen? Or, worse, are my informants not being truthful with me? Are they, tired of being misinterpreted by researchers and the press, expressing a party line to the latest outsider, however well intentioned she may be?

Out and In Together

Lately, in these self-reflexive days of postmodernism, there has been an attempt in anthropology to integrate inside and outside perspectives better by interweaving the voices of informants and ethnographers into a more convincing picture that represents cultural collaboration rather than presentation. Known as the new or reflexive ethnography, this style has perhaps been best represented in works by James Clifford and George E. Marcus (1986) and by Marjorie Shostak (1981), among others.[6] In allowing the other to speak, the new ethnography attempts to equalize the traditional power relationship between the observer self and the observed other by reversing, or at least minimizing, the differences between these perspectives. On the surface, this goal appears laudable, in that the ethnographer no longer appears to speak for the informant, and the insider perspective is apparently integrated into the analysis. Even the new ethnography, however, is still somewhat encumbered by the voice of the ethnographer, who, in openly attempting to acknowledge and minimize the power differential between self and other, can actually highlight it.

How, then, can we uncover the separate, often competing voices that inform cultural descriptions? First, we must make clear whose voice is really speaking and to what purpose. In the spirit of the new ethnography, I suggest that we examine more closely the dynamic of power, not only within the societies we study, but also as it affects cultural representation.

The Dynamics of Social Power

Underlying all social relations are cultural notions of power that are continuously enacted in everyday and ritual behaviors. According to Roger Keesing, in an analysis of power relations, we need to "look *through* cultural conceptualizations as well as *at* them. . . . We need to see the realities of power: who has it, who uses it, in what ways, to what ends" (1981, 298–99).

In an important article devoted to modeling the dynamics of social power, Richard Adams argues that power is "the ability of a person or social unit to influence the conduct and decision-making of another through the control over energetic forms in the latter's environment" (1977, 388). Control over valued resources is maintained through elaborate interactions that articulate explicit or implicit threats of withdrawal. Simple control over resources, though, does not necessarily create a dynamic of power. Rather, power is an outgrowth of the *ranking* of differences and the assignment of value and status to certain differences over others. A central feature of power, according to Adams, is the manipulation of tensions between cultural notions of control and out of control–ness. Adams cites the tendency in many cultures to associate elements of relative control in their world and to place them in binary opposition to elements that are relatively out of control.

Developing Adams's model, let us distinguish between states of in control and out of control—states of differing degrees of order or balance, based on culture-specific notions of those states—and controlling, that is, exercising a degree of constraint upon another. Second, let us place this system within a specific context. Power, in a general sense, can be seen as part of a larger closed system involving culture-specific (or idiosyncratic) notions of states of in control and out of control, belief systems of tremendous complexity that help to define and give validity to these notions, and controlling behaviors of various styles (ranging from influence to coercion) that are brought into play for the purpose of stabilizing the system. The system itself is embedded in a context that defines the specific people or social units and their long-term or immediate interests.

We have not yet introduced specific people (or social units) into the model. Doing so will isolate and crystallize the relevant dynamic of power. Carefully defining in-control, out-of-control, controlling behaviors or laws, and the context of their interaction by inserting specific people, groups, and behaviors into these categories helps to clarify the voice that is speaking and to what end it speaks.

We can now isolate at least two general kinds of power relationships that exist simultaneously and are embedded in any portrait of a culture: dynamics that exist between the people or social groups being described or analyzed and the power dynamic between the ethnographer and the informant, each with his or her own agenda. In this essay, we have been concerned primarily with describing and analyzing the first set of power relationships: those within Lubavitcher culture. Let us now focus on the second dynamic, through which the first dynamic is filtered: that between the narrating self and the carefully constructed other. To illustrate, let us return to the scene with which we began, of Miriam singing her song as she lights Sabbath candles. Using the model I have been developing, I will show how differing power dynamics between the presenter and the presented create the widely different portraits seen above.

In perspective 1, the so-called descriptive portrait, the ethnographer is primarily interested in portraying a convincing picture of a culture largely foreign or exotic to his or her anticipated audience. This observer sees the system as a whole as in balance; individual differences are smoothed over, possibly seen as irrelevant or even problematic. This observer is not making an explicit judgment about either the validity of Miriam's actions or their value.[7] What is highlighted is the balance of life in the big picture. To give authenticity to this portrait, the ethnographer may give the impression that Miriam herself is speaking. However, we know this is a fiction, that it is really the ethnographer who has recorded the event and fitted this piece together with others, locking them into a satisfying whole.

Miriam, for her part, wishes to present her culture carefully and truthfully. She knows that the researcher (possibly a professor from a major university) has access to the larger world outside, and if the description is "right," many people will be affected by the beauty and strength of Lubavitcher philosophy. Both she and the researcher need each other: their relationship must be kept in balance, or the chance for her truth to reach the secular world will be lost.

Now we move to perspective 2. Here the outsider analyst's agenda is to expose the underlying structures that govern Miriam's life and, by implication, those of all Lubavitcher women. There is no pretense of an insider's perspective here. Miriam is not even presented as an individual. What are highlighted are the potential instabilities of the system and the controlling factors, in the form of codes of behavior imposed by one social group on another for the purpose of maintaining a status quo of male dominance. Miriam will no doubt be offended by this portrait. She will see it as simply wrong; it will be of no use to her. She may attribute this skewed analysis to the dominance of the animal soul in the researcher and will dismiss this picture of her world.

Finally, in perspective 3, Miriam's agenda (the word seems odd here) is to light the candles and to greet the Sabbath joyously. She is simply acting, not observing herself act. There is no audience for her actions (except perhaps God). She understands, without really thinking about it, the need for *kol isha,* because she has internalized the Lubavitcher worldview that sees her as more inherently spiritual than a man. *Kol isha* validates her spirituality and sexuality and links her to other women in a positive way. Miriam is empowered by this, secure in the knowledge that she occupies a structurally superior and more powerful position than her male counterpart. However, she is also aware of the threatening potential of her voice and understands that for the moment, the animal soul has the potential to dominate. Here the animal and divine souls and the controlling code of *kol isha* are not in balance but are widely fluctuating, their outcome uncertain.

The ethnographers, for their part, might or might not be aware of or sensitive to Miriam's ideas. They may feel that they have the right to present her as they wish, for their main goal is not to please Miriam or to become like her but, rather, to present their own picture for a different audience. Their audience is not God or other Lubavitchers but, most probably, other academics—historians, ethnomusicologists, and feminists—who form part of a larger scholarly and political community.

I do not wish to imply that observers of any stripe are simply a bunch of insensitive louts, constructing fictitious accounts of others' lives to serve a malevolent colonialist or political purpose, much less that they do not care about or that they demean the people with whom they work. Nor do I wish to suggest that cultural informants are always politically motivated, purposefully untruthful, or eager to trick ethnographers—although there are certainly such cases. Rather, I simply wish, in this small academic exercise, to call attention to the many intentional or unintentional biases through which all so-called raw data, whether currently ethnographic or historic, are filtered, and to suggest that we begin to integrate perspectives so that we may better portray the wholeness of cultures, both observed and lived, rather than remain content telling stories that are less about the other than about ourselves.

7 The Language of the Heart
Music in Lubavitcher Life

I was asked to write this article for a book examining contemporary Hasidic culture in the United States. This collection, *New World Hasidim: Ethnographic Studies of Hasidic Jews in America*, edited by Janet S. Belcove-Shalin, appeared in 1995 and contained perhaps the first collection of articles about Hasidic culture based on the ethnographic method of fieldwork. My article was the only one addressing music and its role in Hasidic ritual and spiritual life, and it was perhaps the first published discussion of Hasidic musical culture that integrated women's musical practices with those of men.

This volume strove to move the previous historical study of Hasidic culture in two new directions: toward the anthropology of religion and toward feminist theory. Also to appear in this volume were two articles, one by Debra Kaufman, "Engendering Orthodoxy: Newly Orthodox Women and Hasidism," and the other by Bonnie Morris, "Agents or Victims of Religious Ideology: Approaches to Locating Hasidic Women in Feminist Studies," both of which used recent feminist anthropological theories surrounding individual agency and autonomy to argue that within the constraints of orthodoxy, women were actively and successfully negotiating new positions of social and ritual power. Some of the material presented here was used later in my book *Music in Lubavitcher Life* (2001).

*   *   *

As a small child growing up in Pittsburgh, Pennsylvania, in the late 1940s, I was often drawn to the sounds I heard when, on my way to school each day, I passed the Lubavitcher yeshiva (school) at my corner. I was struck by the spirit and intensity both of the singing and of the radiant faces of the men and boys I could see through the window on Hobart Street. I would often stop to listen, attracted by the sense of purpose that the singing seemed to have and by the sometimes joyful, sometimes yearning, quality of the music. Coming from a secular Jewish family where I was expected to become a classical musician, I could not fully understand the relationship these people had to Judaism or to their music. Later, as an ethnomusicologist—a trained outside observer—I came not only to better understand this relationship, but also to develop a high regard for the musicianship and musical creativity of the men and women with whom I worked.

This article examines the traditional music of Lubavitcher Hasidism (*nigun*), its meaning and use in Lubavitcher life, and its role in the ongoing negotiation between traditional Lubavitcher values and those of the U.S. urban mainstream. I regard *nigun* as a musical expression of essential Lubavitcher religious and philosophical beliefs and its performance as an articulation of these beliefs within the realm of social and musical action. "Making a *nigun*" is not simply a joyous activity for Lubavitchers; it is a religious act, carrying with it the same awesome responsibility as prayer.

The Contemporary Setting

The contemporary Lubavitcher court, led by the late rabbi Menachem Mendel Schneerson (1902–94), is the largest of the modern Hasidic courts, its members numbering around 250,000 worldwide. The Brooklyn community of Crown Heights (approximately 100,000), according to Lis Harris, encompasses an area "whose borders are loosely defined by their synagogue [770 Eastern Parkway], schools, kosher shops, and the last Hasidic family on a block" (1985, 13).

Contemporary Lubavitchers in Brooklyn live in many ways much as their eastern European counterparts did in the eighteenth and nineteenth centuries. Strictly adhering to the laws of Orthodox Judaism, wearing specific garments of piety that mark their identity, and joyously, often loudly, participating in frequent gatherings (*farbrengens*) with their rebbe (religious leader), Lubavitchers seem anachronistic to their New York neighbors. Moreover, their activities are often a point of curiosity, sometimes ridicule, for fellow less observant Jews from Manhattan and elsewhere.

Although they may resemble their eastern European ancestors, contemporary Lubavitchers do recognize considerable differences in class and economic opportunity in America that would have been impossible in Europe. For example, some hold jobs outside the community, many live quite comfortably on the tree-lined streets of residential Brooklyn, and some women even continue to work, most often within the community as teachers, after children begin to arrive. Lubavitchers feel that this increase in social and economic access is primarily the result of an unprecedented tolerance of Jews in today's America. Such tolerance, though, also represents a potential threat—the lure of the secular, with its life of spiritual impoverishment. For women, especially, the threat of the secular presents a special challenge. As one woman states:

> Years ago, the role of the woman was to sit at home and to learn within her home all that she needed to know to prepare her for a later life as a wife and mother. . . . But, in this day and age, when we are such a part of our society, there is no such thing as living in your home anymore. By way of the media, the neighborhood, where you walk, where you move, what you hear, what you read, you are by your very nature so affected by the world you live in. . . . The Jewish woman must, if anything, prepare herself even more so, by going out. It has become the thing to work, for economical or emotional reasons. . . . I would say that the trend is so strong now, I hardly know of any of my contemporaries who just stay at home—very few. (Rosenblum 1975)

In spite of the ever-present dangers of contamination and assimilation, one of the most interesting features of contemporary Lubavitcher society is its willingness (and its administrative ability) to forge links with the surrounding modern, urban, non-Hasidic society. For example, Lubavitchers run an extensive outreach program that reaches local, often non-Jewish communities and educational institutions, where Lubavitcher "mitzvah mobiles"—large vans, often wired with loudspeakers blaring music—seek out less observant Jews and invite them to learn more about their *Yiddishkeit.* Men are encouraged to don yarmulkes (skullcaps) and tefillin (phylacteries) and women to light Sabbath candles.

Over the past twenty years or so, these activities have resulted in a heavy influx of new, predominantly American-born, non-Orthodox Jews who wished to return to Orthodoxy, the Ba'alei Teshuvah (newly Orthodox, returnees). The contemporary community now counts more Ba'alei Teshuvah among its members than those who have been observant from birth.[1] Ba'alei Teshuvah often describe themselves as being on a perpetual journey toward spirituality. This journey takes years of study and contemplation and parallels, if on a different plane, the spiritual journey of Lubavitchers who have been Orthodox from birth. Many Ba'alei Teshuvah, however, are regarded as slightly suspect by their lifetime counterparts, as their roots are in the mundane world of contemporary U.S. culture. It is usually with marriage (often to another Ba'al Teshuvah) and the birth of children that they are truly accepted.[2]

Lubavitcher Spiritual Heritage

Like all modern Hasidim, Lubavitchers trace their spiritual lineage to the great seventeenth-century *Zaddiq* (holy man) Israel ben Eliezer, the Ba'al Shem Tov (d. 1760), and like other groups, their philosophy borrows heavily from the Lurianic kabbalist tradition, the Zohar, and other mystical and halachic (Jewish legal) works. Unlike other Hasidim, though, Lubavitchers adhere to a philosophy developed by their founder, Rabbi Schneur Zalman (1745–1813) of Liadi, a philosophy known as Habad, an acronym based on three Hebrew words: *hochma* (conceptualization, where an idea is first conceived), *binah* (the cognitive faculty, where an idea is analyzed), and *da'at* (the final state in which an idea attains comprehension) (Mindel 1969, 33).

Schneur Zalman codified his essential philosophy in the *Tanya*, a four-volume collection of writings and commentaries upon Talmudic and mystical texts. At the core of Habad is the concept of the *benoni*, or the "intermediate" man—a category of Jew who stands between two opposing souls, expressed metaphorically as the animal and divine souls. The *benoni* status is within the grasp of any person who succeeds in living his or her life without intentionally committing an evil act. This can be accomplished if the Hasid strives continuously to achieve *devekut*, or adhesion to God (i.e., "oneness," or unity with the divine). *Devekut* is brought about by adhering to the laws of Orthodox Judaism and by living all aspects of one's life with the proper intention (*kavannah*). *Kavannah* is often activated by the expression of two essential emotional states: *simhah* (joy) and *hitlahavut* (enthusiasm).

The process of achieving *devekut* is described as moving from the animal to the divine soul, so that when the divine soul is reached, the animal "falls away." The animal, or mundane, soul is conceptualized as neutral, yet potentially out of control, often needing restricting laws or codes, whereas the divine soul is seen as being ordered, or having the capability of ordering. One's spiritual quest for *devekut*, then, is regarded as a movement away from disorder toward order. Lubavitchers thus speak at once of the binary polarizations of animal and divine souls, of the ongoing process of moving from animal to divine, and of the difficulties of accomplishing this process in everyday life.

Achieving *devekut* is conceived, though, not as a onetime goal, but rather as an ongoing process, one that is repeated daily throughout one's life. The divine and earthly realms, often referred to metaphorically as the head (associated directionally with the right) and the heel (associated with the left), are to be in constant communication through the heart (central and inward), which is the seat of emotion. It is precisely the energetic repetition of religious precepts and rituals—that is, the endless, intensely felt reinforcement of the bond between God, who is always pure, and human, who is daily tainted by impure influences—that promotes *devekut.* Thus, Lubavitchers conceive their religious philosophy somewhat as a three-dimensional, fluid model, endlessly moving in both an upward-downward and an inward-outward movement through a centralized node of emotion.

The Role of Music in Lubavitcher Life

Lubavitchers often refer to their music as the language of the heart. Words, they say, are from the brain—they express the mundanities of life; they are connected to the material, everyday, "on-the-surface" aspects of existence. But music, especially a *nigun,* is able to go far beyond that—it expresses the essence of the godly soul that lies in the heart of every Jew. Music, unlike words, can carry one to the highest spiritual levels, can bring forth the spirit of a longed-for ancestor, or can directly communicate with the divine.

Lubavitchers regard their melodies, or *nigunim,* as essential vehicles for expressing *simhah* and *hitlahavut,* as *nigunim* are believed to hold traces of these properties, or "sparks," that are "freed" through active performance. Music is thus a primary link to the divine realm, and the performance of *nigunim* is regarded as an essential activity of Lubavitcher life. Further, Lubavitchers make a distinction between texts, even those taken from biblical sources or prayers, and pure music. Musical sound itself exists at a higher and deeper spiritual level than words; it can communicate more directly and more powerfully with one's own godly soul and with the divine. Thus, many Lubavitcher *nigunim* are performed using vocables, or syllables without referents in spoken language.

Musically, *nigunim* resemble other Jewish and non-Jewish eastern European folk songs, marches, or dance tunes. Although Lubavitchers themselves categorize *nigunim* into many different groupings according to their use (e.g., Sabbath *nigunim,* High Holiday *nigunim,* dance tunes, and so on), I will broadly define two categories based on musical style: *nigunim simhah* (happy tunes) and *nigunim devekut* (yearning songs). Generally, *nigunim simhah* are those tunes with a regularly recurring duple meter (often highly emphasized in performance), without extensive ornamentation, occasionally in the major mode, and most often performed by large groups, especially in the context of a rebbe's *farbrengen,* a gathering of the entire community where the rebbe speaks and there is much singing throughout the night.

Figure 1, "Nigun Rikud," is a dance tune performed frequently at *farbrengens* and other gatherings. Before death, the rebbe came to favor *simhah* over *nigunim devekut,* as he wished to infuse the souls of his following with enthusiasm, not to bring them down into despair in the face of their difficult task of Jewish redemption in the modern world. It is an excellent example

Figure 1: "Nigun Rikud," performed by Habad Choir on Nichoach, 1969. Transcription by the author.

of a *nigun simhah* and is often performed with much stamping, clapping, and increase of tempo. Its scale employs a lowered second and raised sixth degree, giving it the quality of a southern European or Arab musical mode.

Figure 2 is a *nigun devekut*, "Nigun Shalosh Tenuot" ("Nigun of the Three Parts"), part 1 of which is attributed to the Ba'al Shem Tov; part 2 to the Maggid of Mezeritch, his disciple; and part 3 to Rabbi Schneur Zalman, the Maggid's disciple and founder of Habad. This particular *nigun* is greatly revered among Lubavitchers, as its three composers, linked together, form a musical chain of holiness.

Senza Misura

Yi ya --- ma ma ------- ya -- ma ma   a   ma ma ma ya --- ma ma ----

A - ma a - ma ma ---- ya-ma ma ma ma   a --- yim ma ma ma ---- a -----------

yoi ma ma ma mam.   Ya ma mamam ya yin na na --a nam,

a na na na   ya -------- yin na nam   a ma ma ma ma -----------

ya ma ma ma mam   a   yin na na ma ----------- ya oi yi--- ma mam.

Ti ya   ma   ma ma ---------- -ya ---- yi-na na -----   a ma ma ma ma

ya --- yi na nam   a ma ma ma yoi   ya ma ma ma moi

a a-yin na na   na ------- i ---- a ye ai yi -------- nai nam.

Figure 2: "Nigun Shalosh Tenuot," performed by R. Ephraim Rosenblum, April 1976. Transcription by author.

Lubavitcher Social Structure and Music Performance

We have seen now how *nigun* acts to communicate with the divine realm. But the performance of *nigunim* also acts to delineate internal social divisions within Lubavitcher society itself.

The Hierarchy of Spiritual Lineage

Observing the seating pattern at the late rebbe's *farbrengen* beautifully underscores the social and musical hierarchy that exists within Lubavitcher society. The men and women are, of course, separated, with the women above in their own gallery and the men below near the Torah scrolls and the rebbe. Seated at the rebbe's table are his closest associates—his secretary, perhaps a visiting dignitary, and others who will assist him during the course of the hours-long event. Radiating outward from the rebbe in row after row of bleacher-style seats are the rest of the men, arranged in almost perfect correspondence to their relationship to the rebbe and to Lubavitch. The most recent Ba'alei Teshuvah are found, most often, in the last, highest bleacher row, at the same level as the Plexiglas screen, shielding the women from view.

Close to the rebbe, in addition to his associates, are various men who act as the rebbe's "musical assistants," starting specific *nigunim* or urging their fellows during a performance. In a sense, they are extensions of the rebbe, and they carry the responsibility of choosing the appropriate *nigun*—one that corresponds to the basic theme of the *sicha* (the rebbe's talk)—and of making sure that its performance is spirited, energetic, and effective. The musical assistants sit close to the rebbe, either at his table with the others or in the front rows of the large synagogue at 770 Eastern Parkway.

These men are also responsible for another important musical task—choosing an appropriate *nigun* for the rebbe's birthday. Each year, as the rebbe's birthday approaches, various Lubavitcher composers begin setting the words to the psalm that corresponds to the rebbe's new year. A committee, made up of the same musical assistants who help the rebbe at a *farbrengen*, chooses the best song. The winning song is introduced at the *farbrengen* held closest to the rebbe's birthday and is immediately learned by the entire community, spreading quickly throughout Crown Heights.

Who are these men? How have they been chosen to carry out these musical responsibilities? At first, I assumed that they were chosen on the basis of their musical ability—yet not all of them were musically active or had what we might consider "beautiful" voices. Perhaps they had been selected on the basis of age—yet not all were elderly. Later, I came to realize that the main criterion was one of spiritual lineage; all of the rebbe's close associates were

Lubavitchers from birth, who learned the *nigun* repertoire from their fathers and, most important, could trace their lineage back through many, if not all, of the seven generations from the present rebbe to Schneur Zalman, the founder of Lubavitch. Thus, it was their connection to the holy men and holy music of the past, ultimately validating their own spirituality, that accounted for their special musical status.

Gender

Various Orthodox Jewish laws prohibit men and women from praying, singing, or otherwise engaging in social activities together where there is a danger of unacceptable sexual behavior between them or when unwarranted sexual stimulation (*ervah*) might occur between people who are, for various reasons, prohibited from marrying. Eschewing the values of contemporary feminists and the exhortations of other Orthodox Jewish women who have begun to fight for more equality—especially in areas of public ritual observance—Lubavitcher women adhere strictly to such laws, even though they clearly separate them from the domain of men, stating, "The Torah's restrictions are the Jewish woman's safeguard. For where the Torah restricts, it does not demean—it protects and sanctifies. . . . Any hint of inferior status [is] not a result of Torah law, but a reflection of the times and culture" (Lubavitch Foundation of Great Britain 1970, 219).[3]

The voice of a woman (*kol isha*) has long been seen as a source of male sexual stimulation, and various prohibitions have developed, limiting men's interactions with singing, and at times speaking, women.[4] Briefly, the question of *kol isha* centers on the many interpretations of a small passage in the Bible from the Song of Songs (2:14), "Let me see thy countenance, let me hear thy voice, for sweet is thy voice and thy countenance is comely." The first to comment on this passage was the sixth-century Talmudic scholar Samuel, whose interpretation first linked women's voices to prohibited sexuality. Samuel proclaimed, "*Kol b'isha ervah*" (The voice of a woman is a sexual incitement) (Cherney 1985, 24a: 57).

Later, the great philosopher Moses ben Maimon (Maimonides, 1135–1204) added a refinement. He saw the word *ervah* as referring to the woman and to the performance context, not specifically to the woman's voice. He preceded the word *ervah* by the definite article *ha,* or *the.* The original commentary by Samuel now read, "*Kol b'isha ha-ervah*," or "The voice of an illicit woman is prohibited."[5] Maimonides, in effect, shifted the emphasis from the inherent sexuality of women and their voices to the context of a potential illicit relationship between a man and a prohibited woman. Sexual stimulation, in itself, was not prohibited; rather, it was the potential to create a context of sexual stimulation between a Jewish male and a forbidden partner, especially a "public woman" (i.e., a non-Jewish courtesan, or prostitute, who sang and danced in the context of clubs or other public meeting places), that was restricted.

Although *kol isha* prohibits men from hearing women sing, it does not prevent women from singing. Thus, women, when not in the presence of males, freely engage in many of the same musical activities as their male counterparts. It is not uncommon, for example, to hear women singing *nigunim* in the home while lighting Sabbath candles. One particular event, the *forshpil*—a party given for a young woman on the Sabbath before her wedding—rivals the musical and spiritual intensity of the predominantly male *farbrengen*.

More recently, women have begun to form their own choirs and to hold their own *farbrengen* complete with storytelling, personal reminiscences, and much spirited singing. In addition to traditional *nigunim,* one particular song, "Dvorah Leah's Song" (figure 3), is frequently sung at women's *farbrengens*.

Figure 3: "Dvorah Leah's Song," performed by Leah Namdar, December 1990. Transcription by author.

Based on a contemporary Israeli tune, "Har Ha-Gilboa," the text, composed by Miriam Bela Nadoff,[6] tells the story of Dvorah Leah, the daughter of Schneur Zalman, who, fearing that her father's imprisonment on charges of treason and his resulting depression would kill him, sacrifices her life so that his teachings can continue. She leaves behind her small son, whom she gives to her father to raise. That virtually every woman I interviewed knew this song attests not only to its popularity but also to its salient and idealized message of women's sacrificial love.

Traditional Uses of *Nigun*

Central to the expression of Lubavitcher philosophical and religious beliefs, *nigun* holds a special status within Lubavitcher life, acting in many ways to articulate these values. First, *nigun* is a supreme vehicle of communication. In performance, the individual comes to "know himself," to transcend himself, and, ultimately, to enter the realm where divine communication is possible. Thus, *nigun* provides the Lubavitcher with a key to self and divine knowledge. Second, the performance of *nigun* validates and reinforces Hasidic beliefs and thus acts not only to ease divine communication but also to bind people together in this effort. Finally, *nigun* acts as a group signifier, defining the boundaries of the Lubavitcher worldview, and is thus used as a primary means of communicating Lubavitcher values to other Hasidim and of negotiating Hasidic values with other, non-Hasidic, groups.

Many stories attest to the power of music in performance, especially as a vehicle for self-knowledge. For example, a story is told of Menachem Mendel (the Zemach Zeddik), who came questioning his grandfather Schneur Zalman as to the essence of the Jew:

> When the Zemach Zeddik was still a child, he asked his grandfather, "What is a Jew?" His grandfather answered that a Jew is a person who can reveal the root of his soul. A Hasid must know himself and do something good for himself. But he may study Torah and the ideas of Hasidism and still not be complete. It is the responsibility of the Hasid to know himself—and he can only do this with a *nigun*. A *nigun* shows him who he is, where he has to be, and where he can be. A *nigun* is a gate through which he must pass in order to know what he is to be. A *nigun* is not only a melody—it is a melody of yourself. (Zalmanoff 1948, 41)

Another story shows the power of *nigun* to achieve a spiritual union with holy men of previous generations, who are said to live at a higher spiritual level, closer to the divine "head." Here, *nigun* becomes the agent through which the singer and those present achieve *devekut* and are thus bound to each other and united with earlier, more holy, Zaddiqim:

Everyone stood up and joined the singing. When they got to the place, where the words are "Happy are they who will not forget Thee," everyone became ecstatic—so much so that their faces became inflamed and on their cheeks tears began to flow. You could see that these people were reliving [a] holy moment. There was no shadow of a doubt that everyone there knew and felt that he [Menachem Mendel, the Zemach Zeddik] was standing near the Rebbe and was seeing and hearing how the Rebbe prayed. (Zalmanoff 1950, 25)

Another important use of music is expressed in this story of Schneur Zalman and an old man who had come to him to study Torah. Here, a *nigun* communicated where words failed:

The Ladier [Schneur Zalman] noticed an old man among his listeners who obviously did not understand the meaning of his discourse. He summoned him to his side and said: "I perceive that my sermon is unclear to you. Listen to this melody, and it will teach you how to cleave unto the Lord." The Ladier began to sing a song without words. It was a song of Torah, of trust in God, of longing for the Lord, and of love for Him. "I understand now what you wish to teach," exclaimed the old man. "I feel an intense longing to be united with the Lord." (Newman 1944, 283)

Although Lubavitchers compose some of their own music, the majority of *nigunim* are either older melodies that have been retexted (or have had their texts removed and vocables added), tunes whose texts have been reinterpreted, or those that have been borrowed from other, often secular, sources, such as Russian drinking songs or, today, musical comedies or television commercials. Indeed, according to the Zohar, the sparks of godliness resulting from the breaking of the *kelipot,* or holy vessels at the time of Creation, are deeply hidden, often in the most mundane places, and only a person with the proper holiness and intention can free the sparks from their bondage. The following story of the organ grinder clearly illustrates this spiritual need to rescue the holy sparks perceived as trapped in a simple peasant tune:

Rabbi Schneur Zalman once heard an organ grinder sing a song which he thought was beautiful, and he asked him to sing the song again. He paid him a couple of coins and he asked him to sing it again until he learned it. And after the Alter Rebbe [Schneur Zalman] learned it, he asked the organ grinder to play it again, but he wasn't able to. He had forgotten it completely. It seems that there are profound songs which are somewhere else, too . . . like one can speak of a lost soul, one can also speak of a lost piece of music. So, the Hasidim have adapted and adopted it because they feel there's something in it. (Rosenblum 1975)

This story also illustrates a traditional strategy used by Lubavitchers to negotiate with the non-Hasidic environment. In redeeming the holy spark within the (originally non-Hasidic) tune, it was transformed into a *nigun*. The (non-Hasidic) organ grinder was also transformed—he forgot the tune, that is, he no longer had the power to use the tune toward an unholy end (i.e., as mere entertainment). Thus, the borrowing and transformation of the tune effectively neutralized the power both of the mundane, earthly music and of its user, the organ grinder.

Music as Emissary

Over the past two decades, as various music technologies, such as digital re-cordings, synthesizers, and computers, have become more and more sophis-ticated in mainstream society, so, too, have the means by which Lubavitchers have preserved and disseminated their music. When I first began visiting the Crown Heights community in 1973, for example, one of the local stores, Drimmer's, carried a few LP recordings produced by the Nichoach Society, a music publishing house established in the 1940s by the previous Lubavitcher rebbe, Joseph Isaac Schneersohn (1880–1950). Now a visit to Drimmer's in-cludes sampling a variety of audio and videocassettes, CDs, and movies aimed at both adults and children for home use. The rebbe has recently stated that the new technology is not, in itself, harmful to an observant life—if it transmits a divine message. Thus, today's Lubavitcher home may include a radio, VCR, and an occasional synthesizer, in addition to the more standard piano or accordion.

Because of music's importance as a vehicle for self-knowledge and spiritual attainment, Lubavitchers have begun to use a variety of musics as "emissar-ies" to attract new adherents to the group as pedagogical tools to introduce Habadic concepts to those just entering the community. Performed frequently at Lubavitcher-run schools, camps, small home gatherings, and other meet-ing places, both in and outside the Crown Heights community, these tunes not only enliven and inspire a gathering, but also, in the Lubavitcher view, reach the heart of even the most stubbornly nonobservant Jew. The popular Jewish song "Ufaratzto" (see figure 4) has become, in recent years, somewhat of a rallying cry for Lubavitchers in that its text, taken from Genesis 28:14, enthusiastically urges one to "go forth" and spread *Hasidut* to the West, East, North, and South. It is frequently sung at camps, school, and other gatherings for the Ba'alei Teshuvah.

Although Lubavitchers who have been Orthodox from birth, especially the younger, unmarried ones, often participate in musical activities, it is the Ba'alei Teshuvah who excel as teachers of new members. Older Lubavitchers say that the Ba'alei Teshuvah still have the drive and energy to accomplish the

Figure 4: "Ufaratzto," performed by the Habad Choir on Nichoach, 1969. Transcription by author.

difficult task of translating Habadic concepts to those unfamiliar with such ideas and that they are especially well suited to the task because their own transformation is still occurring. After all, a Ba'al Teshuvah understands, perhaps better than a lifetime Lubavitcher, how much of the mundane, modern world one must give up to lead a truly observant life. That is why, in fact, they have been given the honorific title Ba'al Teshuvah—every Jew does Teshuvah, but only one who has given up everything to do so is truly a master.

Many of the Ba'alei Teshuvah who have recently entered the community have had considerable experience with music. As is true for most of the American white middle class, many Ba'alei Teshuvah have had piano or other instrumental lessons, either privately or in public school. Some, such as Chaim Burston or Moshe Antelis, were professional rock musicians in their youth and now perform both standard *nigunim* and newer songs, based on rock models, for a variety of audiences. Another Ba'alat Teshuvah, Ruth Dvorah Shatkin, a conservatory-trained classical musician, uses her talents as a composer and arranger of *nigunim* for various women's gatherings.

Thus, a new repertoire of music, never officially sanctioned by the rebbe but used as a means of reaching a contemporary Jewish audience, has developed, often bearing a striking resemblance to rock, heavy metal, classical, and other forms of historical and contemporary music. Two examples will suffice to illustrate how new concepts and uses of music, combined with new musical forms and technologies, have produced music that is at once accessible to a wide range of Jewish audiences and still adheres to basic tenets of Jewish orthodox life.

The first example is Yisroel Lamm's "Philharmonic Experience," typical of a growing number of recordings of Hasidic medleys performed by classical symphony orchestras. The accompanying cassette literature states: "The emanations of the symphony orchestra affect the heart and the mind. From euphoria to melancholia. From ecstasy to misery. The intrinsic value of music is profound. . . . Music is understanding. Music is unity" (Lamm 1988). The tape includes various arrangements of Hasidic *nigunim,* including "Carlebach Medley," arranged by Lamm from *nigunim* composed by Rabbi Shlomo Carlebach, a man considered by some Lubavitchers to have "fallen away" from Hasidic beliefs and by others to have followed in the footsteps of the great Ba'al Shem Tov by creating a new Hasidic court in California. The music is performed by members of the Jerusalem Symphony and has the quality of any superbly produced classical music recording.

The second example is a recording known as *Radical Rappin' Rebbes,* arranged by Moshe Antelis from raps composed and performed by three skilled Lubavitcher rock musicians, Solomon Bitton, Michael Herman, and Yosef Kilimick. Some of the selections include "Aleph Beis," "Funky Dreidle," "Being

Jewish," "Radical Rappin' Rebbe Rap," and an arrangement of Sam Kinison's extraordinarily erotic "Wild Thing," called "Shabbes Thing," performed with undulating synthesized guitar and bass. Below is the text of the opening verse:

> Let's do it!
> Shabbes thing—I like to do the Shabbes thing.
> Shabbes thing—I like to do the Shabbes thing.
> Shabbes thing—I like to do the Shabbes thing.
> (Words unclear) Workin' all week six days for my dough
> So when Shabbes comes, I can go take it slow.
> I can't do no work, because it's the day of rest.
> We take a shower, all dress up, and try to look our best.
> Do it every Friday night, when the sun don't shine.
> The ladies do the candles and the guys do the wine.
> After we pray to God, we come home, eat and sing—
> And welcome the Shabbes Queen (if you know what I mean),
> And we call it the Shabbes thing.
> Shabbes thing—let me do the Shabbes thing. (Antelis 1990)

Although most of the older, lifetime Lubavitchers regard this sort of thing as highly suspect, they do recognize its effectiveness in attracting otherwise unapproachable Jews to Hasidic life. Indeed, it was in the house of the renowned Lubavitcher musician Rabbi and Cantor Eli Lipsker that I first heard about *Radical Rappin' Rebbes*. His son, who was watching the interview, confessed that he had recently purchased the tape, more or less as a joke. His father shrugged this off with some embarrassment, reassuring me that this was *not* Lubavitcher music—although if it reached a Jewish soul, it would have accomplished its purpose (Lipsker 1990).

Conclusion

Music, especially *nigun*, functions in Lubavitcher society as a sound expression of essential beliefs and values. Its use as a vehicle for self and divine knowledge, as a channel connecting the heel of the foot with the divine head, and as a tool for spreading and teaching Hasidic values to others cannot be underestimated, for it is precisely the performance of *nigun* that ensures, like prayer, that the constant dialogue between God and man will continue. And although local communities change, incorporating new members and adjusting to new social environments, the basic tenets and values of Lubavitcher life do not.

To Lubavitchers of past generations, the performance of music has always been regarded as a profoundly effective means of connecting the inherent godly soul of every Jew with its divine source. In today's America, with its many lures, both attractive and dangerous, music still functions not only as an essential expression of Hasidic beliefs, but also as a statement of positive social values. The captive, holy sparks of both the secular, nonobservant Jew and the mundane ditty can still be freed to perform their divine service through the performance of a heartfelt *nigun,* and its beauty and spirituality can bring even the most unlikely people together. As Rabbi Lipsker remarked to me—with considerable ironic amusement—"What *else* would have ever brought *us* together, but a *nigun*?"

8 When Women Play

The Relationship between Musical Instruments and Gender Style

Having for some time noticed that various accounts of women participating in musical activity did so primarily as singers and dancers, I began to wonder in the mid-1990s why this was the case. Why did so few women play musical instruments, and when they did, why did their activities seem to be so undervalued? In researching this article, I sought literature from both ethnographic and historical sources available in the 1980s and early 1990s, but the pickings were slim—only about 10 percent of the total literature I surveyed mentioned women instrumentalists. Photographs of actual women playing instruments (not artwork depicting women playing, which were plentiful) were even scarcer. Was this actually a true picture, or more evidence for bias in music scholarship and publishing?

In this article, I examine four contexts, each with its own gender style, that is, an inherited and practiced set of gendered expectations and behaviors embedded in musical activity, and then survey relevant literature describing women as instrumentalists in those contexts. In doing so, of course, I also dipped back into my desire for a comparative, cross-cultural theory—still an elusive goal. The four contexts are as follows: the court, courtship, ritual practice, and the context of everyday life. These four general contexts proved useful, so I used them again in my part of the entry "Women and Music," written with Judith Tick and Margaret Ericson for *The New Grove Dictionary of Music and Musicians* (2000).

* * *

In many societies, musical roles are divided along gender lines: women sing and men play. Of course, men also sing, and women sometimes play; yet, unlike men, women who play often do so in contexts of sexual and social marginality.

This essay surveys the literature on women playing musical instruments in a variety of social and cultural contexts. It then presents some recent anthropological theories regarding the interrelation between social structure and gender stratification that can be useful in understanding these data in the broader perspective of gender relations. I will, for now, regard women's performance on musical instruments, or lack thereof, as an indicator of the gender style of a given society, for although all performance may be regarded as a locus of power, performance on musical instruments is often bound up with cultural notions of gender and control in ways that vocal performance is not.

First, some preliminary remarks concerning gender, musical instruments, and cross-cultural surveys. The term *gender* is being used here to define a socially constructed category (man and woman) and is distinguished here from sex, the biological category of one's birth (male and female). Further, although most societies recognize a relative difference between the two sexes and often use these as the primary bases for the division of labor in economic, ritual, and other domains, gender categories are often quite fluid, with so-called masculine or feminine behaviors appearing to a certain degree in both sexes.[1]

The term *gender ideology* has been used by Ortner and Whitehead (1981), among others, to denote a conceptual and valuative framework that underlies and structures behaviors for women and men. Ideologies may be codified as religious, moral, or legal justifications for gender relations. Although gender roles are based to a certain degree on biological categories, it is the value given to one gender over the other that promotes a certain gender style, theoretically ranging from relatively equal autonomy and value for both men and women (complementarity) to a lack of equality in both autonomy and value (gender stratification).

Musical instruments are defined here simply as material objects for the most part outside the body, or connected to the body, that are used in performances of music, dance, ritual, and ceremony, however culturally defined. Clapping, slapping one's thighs, snapping fingers, or other rhythmic accompaniment that uses one's own body as a musical instrument will not be considered here.

Concerning cross-cultural studies, it goes without saying that social contexts for performance vary widely across cultures and time, as do the relative distribution and significance of musical instruments and instrumental performance. Asserting generalizations about gender and musical roles is therefore fraught with difficulties. Native perspectives, individual exceptions, and the complexities of everyday life tend to be glossed over or ignored in such generalizations, and they can often veer toward the glib. Yet there is value in the cross-cultural survey, for certain broad patterns emerge from this perspective that can help us clarify relationships between men, women, and music and the relative value given to those who engage in musical activity.

Contexts for Performance

Descriptions of women performing musical instruments are relatively rare in the literature. Indeed, in a rough survey of various ethnomusicological journals and encyclopedias, I could find no more than 10 percent of the total literature referring to women instrumentalists. Here, I have grouped the descriptions of women's instrumental performances into four basic (at times overlapping or related) sociomusical contexts that can serve as appropriate categories for discussion: the context of the court; the context for courtship; ritual contexts, especially those of healing, initiation, burial, or involving role reversals, where intergender relations are mediated or protested (or both); and the context of everyday life, involving musical performances accompanying food preparation, child care, or perhaps self-entertainment. Each of the contexts is structured by specific gender ideologies, so that examining them more fully can reveal much about the range of gender styles that exist cross-culturally.

The Context of the Court

Western classical music and many of the music traditions of the Middle East, Asia, and North Africa can be described as having evolved, in part, from a court tradition, where musicians for many centuries have been supported by a small, elite ruling class, dominated by males. Historically, most musicians (male and female) in this social context suffered somewhat from a low social status, yet only performances by women are described in the literature as linked to their social-sexual roles, primarily as courtesans. Generally, such women came from the rising merchant classes, and their social status often rose as a result of their association with courtly life. Thus, such women, regarded as marginal to the general class-stratified socioeconomic system, were given both musical and sexual license in these contexts.

There are many passing references to instrumental performances attached to the great courts of Europe and Asia; notable among them are descriptions of the *devadasi* in India (Post 1987), the *qaina* in Tunisia (L. Jones 1991), the geisha in Japan (Malm 1959), the all-female *mahori* ensemble in Thailand (Morton 1976), and an especially full treatment of women's music in Sudan (DjeDje 1987). Within the Western art music tradition, Anthony Newcomb traces the growth of the *concerti di donne,* the all-female performing ensembles of both singers and instrumentalists attached to the northern Italian courts of the late sixteenth and early seventeenth centuries. Newcomb suggests that over a period of thirty years (1580–1610), the status of these performing women rose from that of courtesan to professional performer. These women, he notes, were often musically gifted as children and received musical training from male family members. Although skirting the issue of their sexual role, Newcomb fully documents their musical careers with many (often droll) references to their frequent marriages or to their single status, which marked them as "remarkable renegade(s) to be looked at, applauded, but not included in polite society" (1986, 103). Such women, although not technically courtesans, were nevertheless associated with courtly life, seen as a "neo-pagan world [where] physical beauty was regarded as divine, and sensuality came not far behind" (ibid., 105).

The term *courtesan* is similar in meaning to *geisha* in Japan (derived from *gei,* meaning "art"), *devadasi* in India, and *qaina* in the Middle East and arose as a label in fifteenth-century Italy. Courtesans were usually dependent economically and socially on men—often one patron—yet, unlike their less privileged counterparts, many were highly educated, especially in music and literature, and were thought of as witty and intelligent. Some even achieved a remarkable degree of economic and sexual freedom.

The Context for Courtship

A second context, related to that of the first, provided other women of the upper and middle classes with some opportunities for instrumental as well as vocal performance. Certainly, from the eighteenth century to the present, again in the areas of the world that supported a court system, the home, a semiprivate, protected environment, became the most important context for women performers as noted in the literature. Unmarried women, often viewed as property to be transferred from father to husband, perfected skills there that would make them desirable to potential mates; males, in positions of economic and social power (relative to women of their class), on the other hand, generally had access to musical training and to public, even professional, environments for musical performance.

Though the literature here is scanty, musical instruments such as the *koto* and *biwa* in Japan, the piano, harp, and guitar in Europe, and the *kulintang* in the Philippines became associated with women, especially in the context of courtship during which the performers could display idealized notions of proper female behavior and "feminine accomplishments" within private settings that would not compromise their social status. Judith Tick, for example, describes nineteenth-century parlor performances as flourishing in western Europe and the United States, where such performances, especially on the piano and harp, were deemed proper for domestic female entertainment, as they "required no facial exertions or body movements that interfered with the portrait of grace that the lady musician was to emanate" (1986, 327). And in Japan, William Malm states that in contrast to the *shamisen,* with its association to the "turbulent excitement which the entertainment districts of Edo represent, the koto entered the home as an accomplishment for the daughters of the rising commercial class as well as those of the nobility" (1959, 165).

Perhaps one of the best descriptions of a female instrumental performance tradition in the context of courtship is that found in Usopay Cadar's article "The Role of Kulintang Music in Maranao Society." The *kulintang,* a set of tuned gongs, is both a traditional instrument in the Philippines, as well as the name given to the ensemble that employs it as the main elaborating melody instrument. It is traditionally played by young, unmarried women: "Men are considered too masculine, too expressive, and too stiff to be able to play the melody part. Nevertheless, there are a few men who play the kulintang, but they are either feminized or regarded as people endowed with extramusicality" (1973, 239). Normally, men accompany the female performer on a drum, considered a proper male instrument.

According to Cadar, *kulintang* performances usually take place in the home during a gathering of friends, relatives, or guests, and everyone is expected to perform at some time during the evening, although elaborate social rules exist as to the order of performances according to age, experience, and ability. Cadar beautifully describes the entrance of the *kulintang* performer: after having waited a proper interval of time, so as not to appear impatient or greedy for attention, "the kulintang player stands, leaves the section for women and walks toward the instrument. On her way to the instrument she may execute the Maranao traditional walk, using her left arm to hold the *malong* (loose tubular skirt) while her right arm freely and gracefully swings" (ibid., 243). But even more interesting is Cadar's suggestion that the elaborating melodies she plays are encodings of intergender relations during courtship, marked by the teasing, yet discrete, flirtation characteristic of Philippine courtship practices. Cadar's description of interplay, both musical and sexual, between the *kulintang* player and her accompanying male drummer makes this connection clear.

Ritual Contexts

Ritual contexts, especially those surrounding shamanism, burial, initiation, and rituals where role reversal is a major theme, provide other, if limited, opportunities for women performers. Consider, for example, the prominent role of men in the major religions and medical institutions of the world—as musicians, priests, cantors, or doctors. Women's ritual activities usually take place outside of these contexts, and women often play musical instruments not usually available to them. Gilbert Rouget, for example, in his *Music and Trance* (1985), describes a female shaman tradition among the Araucan of southern Chile, where participants induce trance through dancing and drumming. Martha Binford in Mozambique (1980, in Falk and Gross 1980), Jacqueline DjeDje in Sudanic Africa (1987), and Laurel Kendall in Korea (1985) state that shamans commonly use drums and cymbals attached to their bodies to induce trance.

Barbara Hampton describes a genre of song, *adowa*, performed solely by Ga women of Ghana. The songs are accompanied by rattles and bells and by bamboo tubes used in place of the traditional drums found in other ensembles. Hampton states that this single-sex grouping and substitution of a musical instrument is a social fact reflected in a musical practice and grounded in the cultural belief in the contamination of ritual objects, if touched by menstruating women: "Drums belong to this category of ritual objects and are not performed by . . . women" (1982, 76).

The literature describing gender role reversal is fairly large, and women's ritual practices in those contexts are well documented.[2] One vivid example will suffice here. In an article describing women's love rituals (*yilpinji*) in central Australia, Diane Bell (1981) states that their performance is linked to aboriginal notions of women's control of the land and of human emotions. Songs and dances performed in these rituals are frankly sexual, with women enacting both roles. Intercourse is often described textually or simulated in dance, where the participants use musical instruments (rhythm sticks and so on) as mock penises.

The Context of Everyday Life

Outside the ritual domain, opportunities for performances on musical instruments exist in everyday life for a variety of reasons, including self-amusement. Ken A. Gourlay, for example, among the Kagoro of Nigeria (1970), describes female performance genres used for this purpose, and Margaret Kartomi in Java (1973) describes women's rice-stamping music, performed with hollow tubes, which eases the tedium of food preparation. Finally, Lorraine Sakata in Afghanistan describes the *chang*, a jaw harp usually performed on by women, noting, however, that when played by a woman, it is not considered a "real" instrument, and when played by a man, the performer is usually old, that is, not culturally considered a "real man" (1989, 86–87).

The Symbolism of Musical Instruments

One cannot help but notice that women's opportunities to perform on musical instruments are limited, relative to those of men, across cultures and time. Of course, it may be that ethnographers have ignored women performers or have been denied access to their performances. Nevertheless, it appears that women simply do not play musical instruments to the same degree as do men. If this is so, why? Some clues lie in the symbolic content of musical instruments and in the use of metaphors for musical sound, as expressed by native informants that conceptually link music to other cultural domains. Unfortunately, many of the works cited above make only passing references to women performers and do not provide adequate information on the symbolic content of the instruments described, so that generalization is somewhat inhibited here.

The symbolic content of musical instruments, often expressed through gender-based metaphors, frequently discloses complicated and ever-changing interrelationships between women and men that can help to mitigate power imbalances. Two examples: John Blacking gives us clues as to the sexual and gendered symbolism of male drumming during the *domba* (girls' initiation ceremony) among the Venda of South Africa: "The heartbeat of the baby is represented by the beat of the drumstick on the centre of the skin of the bass drum: the drum represents the head of a child and the centre of its skin, the baby's fontanel. Each performance of the domba in the morning and late at night symbolizes both in movement and in music the mother's womb and the sacred act of love [sexual intercourse] whose repetition is believed to build up the fetus" (1976, 23). And Marina Roseman in her discussion of the Temiar of Peninsular Malaysia discusses gendered metaphors for the sounds made by the women's bamboo stamping tubes, stating that the lower-pitched, larger tubes and their combined sounds constitute a "father," whose sounds decay naturally, and the shorter, higher-pitched tubes constitute a "mother," whose sounds are of short duration. Similarly, a rain tube is said to have a "short whitish section near the ground (the mother) and an arching, colored midsection (the father)" (1987, 142).

Perhaps another way to approach the question of why women appear not to play is to examine the use of musical instruments as instruments of power, sometimes used by men to intimidate women and children, who are frequently prohibited from playing or even seeing instruments and where threats of extreme punishment, such as gang rape or death by insect sting, are common.[3] In these instances, the instruments and sounds they produce are agents of control that one group of people (adult males) uses to subordinate all others (uninitiated males and all females).

Toward a Theory of Gendered Instrumental Perfoi

What appears to be central to all of the descriptions presented
notion that musical instruments are generally linked to gende
however culturally constructed and maintained. Such ideolog
and prescribe who can and cannot play and under what circumstances performances will occur. Thus, on the one hand, it appears that the instruments
and sounds associated with men and with masculinity (however defined) are
frequently linked to economic, ritual, and sexual power. Such instruments
are often used by men to limit, control, or coerce women (or to heighten
their own sexuality, as in rock performances). For men, this constellation of
music and power may take an extreme form, such as that described above,
or the form of simple lack of access, as when a young girl, for example, is
discouraged from performing on a trombone or drum. Women who protest their socially accepted roles and perform, especially on male-associated
musical instruments, risk punishment and social ostracism or, conversely,
may be elevated to the status of a feminist icon. Instruments, their sounds,
and performance contexts associated with women tend to be devalued in
many societies, often seen as amateur or associated with children. These are
most frequently linked to women's marginal social and sexual status, and
performances by males on these instruments can result in similar social
punishments as for women.

A deeper understanding of the unequal division of musical roles results
when one examines the complex interrelationships between these symbolic
associations, a given society's gender ideologies, and their social structures.
Much recent feminist scholarship has adopted a perspective that regards
gender stratification as an outgrowth of patriarchy, notions of private property, and capitalism. Recent scholars, such as Michelle Rosaldo and Louise
Lamphere (1974), Joan Kelly-Gadol (1976), Peggy Reeves Sanday (1981), and
Gerda Lerner (1986), have developed theories that examine the degree of
gender stratification in relation to various modes of economy. They show
positive correlations between the degree to which public and private spheres
are merged and the lack, or heightened instance, of gender stratification. Such
a theory can be applied cross-culturally to help explain the wide variety of
gender styles noted in the ethnographic literature.

At one end of the economic continuum are forager or horticultural societies,
where there is little distinction between domestic and public spheres. However
those domains are conceptualized by insiders, activities in both spheres are
fairly equally shared by both men and women. Here, there is little or no notion
of private property, ownership, or social class. Such societies are characterized
by a complementarity between men and women; that is, although they may

perform different work, rituals, and other social activities, they are more or less equally and mutually valued, and power is shared. Some societies at this end of the continuum are matrilineal or matrilocal, adding to the strength of women's social and familial ties. In addition, many of these societies have had little contact with Western technology or with the value systems surrounding that technology that tend to polarize male and female labor.

Toward the other end of the continuum are agrarian or those recently developed capitalist societies with an agrarian past, where there is a sharp differentiation between public and domestic spheres. In these economies, women "steadily lose control over property, products, and themselves as surplus increases, private property develops and the more communal household becomes a private economic unit" (Kelly-Gadol 1976, 819). Societies at this end tend to be patrilineal, patriarchal, and characterized by a high degree of technology, materialism, and class stratification. Gender relations are marked by a strict separation of the sexes and rigid rules governing appropriate behaviors, where women, seen (at least historically) as property, have less or no access to public institutions, marriage negotiation, reproductive rights, or divorce. Accompanying such social behavior is an unequal evaluation of the sexes that places women in the subordinate position.[4]

The literature cited above suggests a theory that relates women's use of musical instruments to broader issues of social and gender structure. In societies where public and domestic spheres are relatively merged, there appears to be a higher degree of, and more value for, women's instrumental performances than in those societies where these spheres are more highly differentiated. This is not surprising, as in such societies women, in general, have more economic and political power, as well as sexual freedom, and gender ideologies tend to support and value women's social position to a relatively greater degree. Therefore, in such societies, rituals surrounding initiation, healing, and those of gender reversal, where women's power is most evident and effective, provide the most opportunities for women's instrumental performance. In societies characterized by a heightened gender stratification, contexts for women's instrumental performances are most often linked to their potential as sexual partners, either as wives or as courtesans, and even access to musical instruments, considered, like women themselves, as property, is severely limited. Descriptions cited here seem to bear out both of these scenarios.

Two caveats: The first concerns the gap between the idealization of gender roles, often stated or acted out in ritual or in metaphorical language, and the reality of everyday existence, where relations between men and women are far more interactive and contested. For example, in the literature on the male use of musical instruments as tools for asserting power over women, cultural informants often state that these stereotyped behaviors are seldom acted out in everyday life. Similarly, in the literature on the courtesan tradition, it is often suggested that individual women were in positions of considerable power and that environments that fostered women's musical performance not only reflected the subordinate sexual and economic status of women, but were also real everyday environments that encouraged female bonding and the development of political power.

The second qualification concerns the issue of age and its relation to women as instrumental performers. Young unmarried, uninitiated girls and older women are thought of in many societies as existing in a marginal state. Premenstrual women, who are not yet settled in their adult status, and postmenopausal women, who are no longer believed to be sexually active, cannot be threatening to the social and sexual order. Frequently, restrictions regarding instrumental performance are lifted for these females. For example, much of the literature on female shamans describes their accumulation of power as they grow older. This is linked not only to their advancing age and to the acquisition of knowledge, but also to their passing out of a polluted or contaminated state, where their power may be able to disrupt the social order.[5] Similarly, in the court context, where sexually active women are the main performers, their sexual status is heightened, and performance can be regarded as a metaphor for sexual relations. These women, though, often lose their social status and power whether they are upper-middle-class maidens or courtesans.

This theory also provides the possibility for change. If changes in the economic structure of a society occur, will these be reflected in gender ideology and ultimately in access and contexts for women instrumental performers? Has this, in fact, occurred? Some final examples of newly emerging performance contexts for women do support this notion. Jennifer Post, for example, in her article "Professional Women in Indian Music: The Death of the Courtesan Tradition" (1987), describes the end of the courtesan tradition that had flourished in India for centuries. By the late nineteenth century, British notions of proper gender relations had effectively destroyed this tradition, yet at the same time had opened new opportunities for women's instrumental performance within the more highly regarded genres of Indian classical music. Thus, early in the twentieth century, it became fashionable for women, especially of the upper classes, to study musical instruments, such as the *vina* or *sarod,* previously performed exclusively by men. Sarah Weiss (1993) also notes recent changes among Javanese women, who have formed all-female gamelan groups called *ibu-ibu* (older women) that regularly perform today on the radio.

Carol Neuls-Bates (1982) discusses similar developments in Western classical music, especially in the United States during the period 1925–45. Postwar prosperity and changing roles for women created more performing opportunities. She traces the growth of the all-female orchestras (often conducted by men) to the "mixed" orchestras of the forties, where women, although somewhat accepted, still faced powerful discrimination that was eased only with the advent of screened auditions in the 1960s.[6] Certainly, today, we see many more female performers in major orchestras, although the percentages seem to correlate rather well with the status of the professional orchestra.

Changes are also occurring in the United States among Native American groups, most notably Northwest plains Grass Dance performers. Both Orin Hatton (1986) and Judith Vander (1988) have described these changes as having been motivated, in part, by the need to revitalize this tradition and return it to its former status. Hatton traces the history of women drummers, showing a three-stage development: the late nineteenth century, when women merely assisted male drummers; the early twentieth century, when women danced the traditional male dances in men's costumes, imitating men's dance style; and the present, when women now perform as drummers in all-female as well as mixed groups containing family members. Hatton suggests that the family orientation of the mixed groups not only solves certain economic problems associated with powwow performance, but also keeps the older tradition alive through direct oral transmission. It seems clear, then, that social changes, with corresponding changes in what is culturally defined as appropriate gendered behavior, do affect instrumental musical performance for both women and men.

Finally, although I have concentrated on women's instrumental performance here, I would like to stress that women, like men, are active participants in their social lives and engage with men in many varied activities where issues of power, authority, and control are negotiated on a daily basis. Whether the potential power in human musical performance is perceived as ultimately benign or malevolent, it is how individual societies, or individual people, use this potential that reveals much about the quality of their lives, in relation to each other and to the world around them. Thus, the future of gender studies in music cross-culturally depends not only on an understanding of men's and women's musical practices, per se, but also on understanding the ongoing and infinitely varied interactions, interrelationships, and interdependences of men and women and how these are enacted musically.

9 "Well, That's Why We Won't Take You, Okay?"

Women, Representation,
and the Myth of the Unitary Self

Having finally had my fill of the generalities of cross-cultural surveys, I jumped to the opposite pole of abstraction here, examining one small portion of a longer conversation with one of my Lubavitcher informants, Miriam Rosenblum, whom you met in chapter 6, "Miriam Sings Her Song." I hope here to deconstruct our dialogue and uncover, as Bonnie Morris writes, "conflicting approaches to the subject of [Jewish] womanhood" (1995, 161).

This article also marked a turning point in my thinking about gender and music more generally. First, it signaled the end of my attempts to find viable answers to questions of unequal power relations in cross-cultural comparisons. Second, I began with this article to more fully understand the usefulness of deconstructing language to uncover the rhetorical interactions and negotiations between multiple voices in real-time conversation. Here, I was greatly influenced by the earlier work of anthropological linguists and performance studies scholars Dell Hymes (1974), Edward L. Schieffelin (1985), and Richard Bauman and Charles L. Briggs (1990).

Most important, however, I began here to work out what I saw as the deep significance of fieldwork and to more fully distinguish data-gathering, analytic, and interpretive methods of ethnomusicology from those of historical and critical musicology. These issues are framed here by some of the ethical implications of these different disciplinary methods and their scholarly lineages. (This issue is explored further in chapter 12.)

I decided to write the article in somewhat of an experimental form, as a sort of play, or conversation between the multiple voices of the many Ellens and Miriams who emerge as the conversation goes on. These different versions of my selves (and my others) seemed to uncover the less visible assumptions and agendas that drove the conversation, as I played with the notion that there are not only many different kinds of women, but also many different performative versions of one single woman. This article was written in the mid-1990s, but not published until now.

*   *   *

This article examines some of the ethical issues inherent in ethnographic and historical research on music and its social context. Speaking through the filter or lens of a feminist analysis, I assert that the fieldwork process, that quintessential method of data collection that most distinguishes ethnomusicologists from historical musicologists, creates tensions for the ethnographer that are different in kind from those of the historian, tensions that must be resolved on an ongoing basis within real-life contexts and cannot be neatly modeled using a feminist epistemology, as it is now defined.

Ethnomusicologists, whose subjects are living people with whom they form real relationships, differ from historical musicologists, whose subjects, no matter how vital they may appear from their works, are historical, and therefore unable to counter contemporary interpretations of their lives. Feminist analysis, essentially drawn from a Western political ideology, does not always work outside that context, and indeed the feminist ethnographer may find her- or himself quite at odds with an informant who argues back. To illustrate these issues, I draw examples from my own fieldwork, analyzing the tensions that can result from competing agendas in the field.

The first half of the title of this paper comes from an actual statement made by Miriam Rosenblum, a Lubavitcher Hasid, mother of six, teacher, and the wife of Rabbi Ephraim Rosenblum, a prominent Lubavitcher musician with whom I worked over many years. It was made a few days after a conversation between Miriam and me, when I first learned about the intricacies of the Orthodox Jewish position concerning men hearing women's voices, the so-called dictum of *kol isha,* about which I have written extensively elsewhere (Koskoff 2001).

I present the scene between us below, but first I would like to situate it within the context of recent trends in postmodern scholarship that have dealt with two interrelated issues of great importance to the study of music in its social context: the twin issues of representation and the myth of the unified self-other. To do so, I take a short journey backward into the history of the culture concept to show how culture has come to mean very different things in its modern usage within cultural studies and cultural anthropology.

Actually, the subject of this article was motivated by a series of mostly e-mail conversations between historical musicologist Suzanne Cusick and me, as we were fleshing out ideas we might present at a conference on feminist theory and music a few years ago, concerning the ethical nature of our two disciplines. Always the champion of ethnomusicology over historical musicology, I maintained that in doing fieldwork, the ethnomusicologist faced far more immediate and pressing ethical concerns of representation, especially in dealing with gender issues, than did historical musicologists. What fieldwork afforded the ethnographer and not the historian, methodologically, I argued, was live dialogue—real face-to-face conversations between living people in specific social and cultural settings. That we tended to call these people collaborators, colleagues, or friends attested to the real and living relationships we formed during the fieldwork process, relationships that were different, in kind, from those formed by historians with dead people, no matter how alive they may seem in their works or printed words.

I wrote an e-mail message to Suzanne outlining these thoughts, and in her response to me, she explicitly addressed the ethical problem common to both of our disciplines, asking, "Is the theoretical use of 'others' so different, morally, from capitalism's use of their labor and land?" and ending this question by acknowledging my underlying premise that it was certainly "much easier to do this with the dead" (Cusick 1995). Yes, I acknowledged, although ethnomusicologists deal primarily with the living, we are not so naive as to be totally unaware of our use of these living others for our own personal gain, a subject to which I will return later. Thus, this article initially focuses on the ethical problems of representation inherent in musicological and ethnomusicological dialoging, not with each other, but with our so-called informants, living or dead, in an effort to represent them in a coherent and meaningful way that maintains the integrity of their and our own situated lives.

Different Methods, Different Data

What are some of the differences between historical and ethnomusicological methods of dialoguing? Although these differences may seem obvious, they nonetheless need to be stated here: In a dialogue that one might have with a person who is no longer alive, the living partner constructs the total context for the conversation, framing all of the questions and answers, perhaps making sure that the course of the conversation moves in a way that will suit his or her agenda or motivation for doing the work. In a dialogue between two living people, each must listen to and consider what the other is saying, in a form of real-time improvisation. In doing so, questions and their answers cannot always be anticipated, but they can, and often do, follow a certain unexpected course that does not necessarily suit the agenda of either participant. Thus, doing fieldwork requires negotiation and collaboration between real people, each of whom has a stake in, and can affect, the outcome.

But who are the people actually involved in this negotiation? In the course of even a small conversation during a fieldwork experience, many different voices emerge, voices that constantly reposition both the ethnographer and the informant in changing, often conflicting, stances toward each other, ultimately directing much of the course of fieldwork itself. So the main questions I ask are the following: Who is speaking? To what end? And exactly what or who is being represented?

Miriam and Ellen Play

Using data drawn from my work with Lubavitcher women in Crown Heights (New York), Pittsburgh (Pennsylvania), and St. Paul (Minnesota), I present one small snippet of conversation that took place between Miriam Rosenblum and me that I jotted down in my diary along with my thoughts.[1] Afterward, I point to the changing voices that emerged in our conversation as it moved along, somewhat like the entrance of a cast of characters in a play. I hope more fundamental questions concerning various political and ethical problems inherent in representation will emerge.

It is 1974, and I have been invited to a Shabbos dinner with the Rosenblums.[2] We have just finished dinner, and the singing has begun, with Rabbi Rosenblum and his six children (all under the age of ten) shouting out the Lubavitcher *nigunim* I have come to hear.

Soon a familiar tune pops up. Miriam is humming. I begin to sing along.

"Shh," Miriam leans over and whispers in my ear. "Stop singing."

"Why?" I whisper back.

"I'll tell you later. Just be quiet."

The singing continues into the night. Rabbi Rosenblum has a beautiful baritone voice and sings with tremendous feeling and gusto. He and the kids are really enjoying themselves.

"So, why can't I sing?" I prod Miriam later. "I know women and men can't sing together in the synagogue, but does that extend to the home as well?"

"The idea is that a woman's voice is beautiful. It has a lot of qualities that would be enticing to a man. This is a fact known anywhere. So, it's better that you don't sing. It would distract my husband."

"Hmm . . .," I think. "Am I really that attractive?" I try another tack. "Wait a minute," I suggest. "I might think that the sound of your husband's voice is enticing, so why is he allowed to sing in front of me?" I can see by her face that I have missed the point. She turns to her husband.

"Ephraim, Ellen wants to know why she can't sing in front of you, but you can sing in front of her." They both smile patiently at me as though I am a willful but lovable child. "Because the Torah forbids it, that's why," says Rabbi Rosenblum, expecting me to simply accept this. "And the Torah is the will of God."

I am not happy with this explanation and begin, once again, to argue.

Miriam says, "Ellen, this is the way it is. It's been looked over a lot because liberated women are pushing away all of their ideas about being different. But for us in the Torah way, it is like this. Woman is woman and man is man. Women have certain aspects, which are appealing to men, and they cannot be taken away. Now, one of the halachic (legal) considerations is that when a women sings, it has a very appealing aspect to a man who is not her own husband." She finishes with a look that says this conversation is closed.

I am annoyed. These people look so reasonable! How can they believe this? Two days later, I am talking with Miriam about this incident:

EK: I knew I shouldn't have done it (sing), and I remember turning to you and saying, "I know I shouldn't be singing, but I don't know why," and then you explained it, and then I said . . .

MR: You got on the defensive.

EK: No, I didn't. I said that a man's voice is just as enticing.

MR: "You're not gonna make me religious," you said [laughing].

EK: No, no, that's not what I said.

MR: It came around through what you said, I think [still laughing].

EK: I said to you, "But a man's voice is just as enticing," and you laughed.

MR: I guess it's not.

EK: Oh, it is to me.

MR: Yes, I guess that's—well, that's why we won't take you, okay?

Who is speaking in this dialogue? At one level, it is simply Miriam and Ellen, but who are we and why are we having this conversation? Analyzing this bit of dialogue closely, within the context in which it occurred, reveals a multitude of voices performed through subtle changes of tone, attitude, body position, and so on that reorient the perspective of the speakers, creating new dialogues between new actors.

Just who are the characters that I play in this scene? First, it is 1974, and I am at the beginning of fieldwork. I am carrying into the field all of my assumptions and stereotypes about Hasidic Jews and about Hasidic women learned from my parents, my Reform Jewish community, the society at large, and the many books I have read (written primarily by male authors), most of which are pretty grim. One thing I have already learned about Lubavitchers, though, one of the behaviors that separates them from other Hasidic groups, is that they proselytize—a real no-no in mainstream Jewish culture—and they have already started on me. So, part of my beginning fieldwork personality includes a person with tremendous resistance to becoming "Lubavitch."

Next, I am a musician—in fact, it was the sound of music that originally attracted me to Hasidic culture. And as a musician, I can perhaps cut across other social boundaries, such as being a woman, that might better position me vis-à-vis Hasidic culture, which seems to greatly value music. The musician is my least problematic personality. But I am also a feminist, in the very early stages of seeing the big picture of sexism in my own cultural context. I am set to be angry, looking for confrontation, and ready to save my Jewish sisters. This is my most openly problematic voice.

But perhaps the most fundamental Ellen is also here: the trickster, the comedian, the little devil girl, who will do almost anything to get a laugh. She is the oldest of the identities present, formed from countless interactions with scary and out-of-control situations starting in her youth. She is perhaps the most entertaining and likable, but also the most deeply problematic (and at the time largely invisible to that Ellen) in this fieldwork situation—the most subtly frightened, angry, and most controlling. I am, of course, many other people here: a young white person, a poor graduate student, a dog lover, an African violet enthusiast—in short, many other identities that are totally irrelevant to this particular context. These are other Ellens that may emerge in their own time and place.

What cast of characters does Miriam play?[3] Miriam is the quintessential Lubavitcher handler for young female newcomers to the community. She is the one who takes young women under her wing, teaching them the half-forgotten prayers, the laws of *tzniut* (modesty) and *kol isha* (a woman's voice)—anything one will need to know as a woman entering the community; obviously, that is what I am doing from her perspective, at least. Miriam is also a protector of her husband and children. She is protecting them from me, a secularized Jew, who has entered her house to work on music with her husband. Although fairly certain that he will not be tempted to follow me to ruin, she is nonetheless cautious and worried about my motives.

Miriam is also confrontational and, in this context, slightly annoyed with me. She accuses me of being defensive, and perhaps I am, given my distaste for proselytizing. But she is also annoyed at my resistance—she has seen this for a number of years with other young women, many of whom are dealing with new social and sexual freedoms and are either questioning their more traditional Jewish values or running toward a more conservative environment to escape such freedoms.

As our conversation goes on, it becomes clear that Miriam cannot understand why I do not plainly see the truth of the Hasidic way of life. Why doesn't Ellen understand that women have a profound and holy obligation to maintain sexual boundaries and to act correctly according to the laws of modesty? Even if Ellen *is* sexually stimulated by my husband's singing, she had better control it!

I, for my part, simply become more resistant and rebellious as I plod on. After all, my new feminist consciousness says I have the right to express my sexuality, although I may choose not to under these circumstances. I am not going to let a religious law tell me what to do! Why doesn't Miriam understand that religious systems like hers are simply cultural rationalizations for white male hegemony? Uh-oh! I have radically switched positions here, from neutral-observer-ethnomusicologist to political-advocate-for-Lubavitcher-social-change.

Now, although none of these thoughts is actually conscious or articulated in our dialogue, they serve, nonetheless, to direct the course of this conversation, under the surface, acting to subtly reorient us or to solidify a political position, because neither Miriam nor I is simply one voice—we are each a cast of characters called up in real time as a response to the other. But how do I ultimately present this scene or its content in my own scholarly writing? The job of a scholar is to be able to find a way to represent these multiple voices coherently and with integrity to an audience largely unfamiliar with the actors or context, and in this way he or she is somewhat like the director of a play. Should this scene be presented at all? If so, what should be highlighted? Well—what, exactly, is the underlying agenda, the motivation for doing the work in the first place? It is here that the real ethical trouble begins for me, but perhaps less so for my historical musicologist sister. How do I (or even can I) represent Miriam as a real-life person in such a way that she simultaneously represents all Lubavitcher women and her own multiple selves?

Methodological Histories

The ethical problem presented here goes beyond simple methodology (fieldwork versus document work). It is connected to two fundamentally different understandings of the term *culture,* as inherited by the disciplines that have led to gender-based historical musicology and ethnomusicology. Much feminist historical musicology today is heavily influenced by cultural studies—that newly formed postmodern discipline that has nothing and everything as its subject. Although I recognize that the following explanation is brief, even simplistic, I feel that it does get to the heart of the differences between historical and ethnomusicology's understanding of *culture* as an analytic term.

The field of cultural studies has the critique of culture as its underlying premise: critique of racism, sexism, classicism, and other noxious isms that perpetuate systems of power that privilege some over others. Students of cultural studies have inherited the idea of culture mainly from French literary criticism and English sociology, especially through the work of Matthew Arnold, who regarded culture as the "development of humanity's highest faculties" (in Handler 1998, 451) and saw England's working class as not having any.

Cultural studies attacks this idea by critiquing "hegemony and the relationship of culture to social stratification in modern societies along axes of class, race, and gender" (ibid., 458). In doing so, however, it perpetuates the model, initially set up by Arnold, that culture is something valuable that some groups "have" and others do not. It is the job of cultural studies to even the playing field, especially within those parts of society with which they themselves identify (i.e., mass or popular culture) and show their worthiness vis-à-vis elite culture.

Ethnomusicology, on the other hand, is historically linked to anthropology and to its own very different understanding of the culture concept. Anthropologists generally trace their view of culture back to the work of E. B. Tylor, who, in his *Primitive Culture* (1871), defined *culture* as the study of the complex whole of human life. Anthropology, unlike cultural studies, is motivated primarily by the need to understand human diversity, not to critique or change it. In anthropology culture is not a thing that certain groups do or do not have, but is rather a universal process of interactive learning, using, and passing on the sum total of knowledge about who you (and others) are in a given time and place.

Most anthropologists, then, are not primarily interested in exposing or eradicating unbalanced power systems *within the cultures they study* (i.e., those cultures with which they do not primarily self-identify); some are, however, interested in doing this *within their own Western-centric academic or intellectual contexts.* Thus, it is not merely the methodology that separates historical musicology from ethnomusicology, but also a distinctly different historical and intellectual lineage, complete with differing positions vis-à-vis the object of study.

So, in the spirit of Lila Abu-Lughod (1990), I ask, is being a feminist ethnomusicologist a contradiction in terms? Is it necessary for me to be political with Miriam? Is she less valued than a man within her own cultural setting? Does she need saving? As a feminist, I would say yes, but as an anthropologist, listening closely to Miriam, I would say no. Is it necessary to overthrow traditional male-dominated Jewish culture? Is it oppressing Jewish women like Miriam? As a feminist, I might say yes, but as an anthropologist, listening to Miriam, I would say no. But who am I, really? And who is Miriam?

In doing feminist analysis, I will violate Miriam's Lubavitcher voice. In doing anthropology, I will violate my own feminist voice. But these are only some of the voices—and maybe not even the most interesting ones—that emerged in our dialogue. Privileging them to highlight over the others might be neat and easy, and will certainly produce an academic paper, but it will give a skewed picture of what really happened. If I put all of the voices together in my play, casting it with multiple postmodern characters, will I come closer to the truth of what actually occurred between Miriam and me? Perhaps, but my play will be so fragmented, no one will understand it, or even want to see it, for not only do Miriam and I not represent a single unified female Lubavitcher or ethnomusicologist-feminist position, but we do not even represent a single unified Miriam or Ellen position. We and our positions are fluid and changing as the conversation is changing, calling upon our vast repertoire of Miriams and Ellens to perform in this specific context.

Perhaps being a feminist ethnomusicologist is a contradiction in terms, but being both a feminist and an ethnomusicologist (among many other identities) simultaneously is not. As an ethnomusicologist, I am interested in understanding the whole of the Lubavitcher musical world, not for the purpose of comparing it to any other, or in undermining or critiquing it, but to understand it on its own terms. As a feminist, I am interested in what Miriam has to say about her own world and in maintaining the integrity of her words and her position in my writing, and, in a broader political way, in impressing on my colleagues that Miriam's words should be heard, if only to expose the underlying gender and class inequalities inherent not in Miriam's world, but in my world of work and family.

And finally, the ethical problem raised by Suzanne in her e-mail message— am I using Miriam for my own gain? Yes, but unlike using the words or works of people no longer with us, who have not given us permission to do so, and who cannot truly negotiate with us about this process, Miriam and I have together made a bargain that benefits us both: she, for her part, is happy that she has used me to communicate her world, and her specific position in it, to a broader audience; I, for my part, am happy that I have used her words, through my own academic writing and talking, to fight my own, not her, feminist battles. Neither of us agrees with the other's position. We both recognize how different our worlds are and have come to accept these differences, but, ultimately, it has been a fair exchange, one that could only happen between two people who had both an equal part in the process and an equal stake in its outcome.

PART III

2000–2012

10   Unresolved Issues

In the late 1990s, I began to feel a sense of frustration with mainstream eth-nomusicology. Wonderful new monographs and anthologies were appearing, as well as countless articles documenting various gendered musical practices cross-culturally. Why, then, had this literature remained largely on the mar-gins of the field? Why had the obvious (to me) benefits of feminist music scholarship based on fieldwork been so slow to integrate into mainstream discourses? Growing interest in new technologies, diasporas, and global-ism, to name just a few shifting paradigms, seemed to lead away not only from feminist theory, but also, as in anthropology, toward a reevaluation of ethnographic fieldwork as a basic method of gathering data.

Further, although third-wave feminism, which privileged individuality, was helpful in understanding the real-time flow of gendered musical per-formances, it also seemed to be fragmenting itself out of political usefulness. And I could barely see a feminist consciousness among the younger genera-tion of students I taught. Their understanding and use of gendered politics seemed to have shifted to such a degree that I no longer recognized it as such. In short, I was getting cranky and began to look at other, larger, underlying issues that could account for these problems.

Here is a story describing an incident that occurred in 2002, at the East-man School of Music where I teach, that gives a sense of my growing unease (perhaps disappointment?) in what I saw then as the younger generation's lack of interest in current unequal gender relations, coupled with a certain attitude of disdain (perhaps ungratefulness?) for all they had inherited—in short, the usual feelings of a parent toward a recalcitrant child.

October 2002

It is the new millennium, and I am teaching a course called Music, Gender, and the Body. One day before class, I go to the second-floor reserve area in the library to retrieve some readings. There, the head of Reserves and Recordings has placed an LP record jacket on display for all to see. He is a young man in his thirties and, along with most of the students at the Eastman School, regards much of the older recording technology and marketing as amusing and the stuff of parody.

I am beginning to see a change in my relationship with the students I am teaching. Sometimes, when I tell a joke, it goes completely over their heads. They no longer seem to get my references and are so concerned about what I think about them that they are afraid to laugh. Was that a joke? They just look at me oddly while keeping their faces arranged and controlled. I am worried that I can no longer relate to them—our worlds and worldviews are simply too different.

I have been noticing such differences for a long time now. My stepdaughter, Rebecca, who is an artist, became rather well known in the early 1990s through her parody oil paintings—beautifully executed portraits of the Pillsbury Doughboy (from the perspective of a number of artistic periods) and of plastic creatures built from Legos and the Barbie Doll franchises. This is Art, I thought? And it was! I just wasn't understanding it as such. I talked with her about this. She said, "Oh, Ellen, this is just my generation's way of dealing with irony and cynicism. Your generation ['60s hippies] never did fulfill the dream. This is how we answer you."

Even my own son, an actor, would frequently entertain me with what I thought of as unconscionably sexist and racist humor, poking fun indiscriminately at all groups without any regard to their history or social context. Yes, I would laugh—he was funny! But I was also uncomfortable. "David," I would say, "you'd better not say this stuff in public—it's not only hurtful, but you can get into trouble for this out there. And it really is upsetting to me personally—you know, women still get paid only seventy-eight cents to the dollar men get, and most African Americans in Rochester live below the poverty line!" "Oh, Mom," he would say. "Get real! Everyone does this now, and no one gets upset anymore!"

It was clear that I no longer "got it," that I did not relate to this generation's values or to their idea of humor.

Okay, so I show up at the library on that fall afternoon. I see the current LP record jacket in its clear plastic holder: a beautiful African American woman straddling a cardboard mock-up of a very white quarter-moon—about the size of a large man—with the bottom curved point of the moon coming out of her behind, as though it has pierced her and is holding her, like a stick-pinned butterfly on a display board. Her face is a parody of ecstasy—she seems to love this, while she looks outward to an imagined audience of (male, white?) consumers.

I am horrified! I say to the young woman behind the desk, "Well . . . that's a double whammy! That's not only racist—it's sexist! It's disgusting—take it down." She gives me the exaggerated eye roll that her generation has perfected, no doubt thinking Professor Koskoff must be in a bad mood today.

"What do you mean?" she asks sweetly.

"I find that record jacket really offensive! Please take it down!"

"This?" she asks innocently, pointing to the display. "Don't you think it's funny?"

"No, I don't think it's funny!"

"It's just a picture of the way it used to be in the old days. You know—lounge-lizard music? We don't think that way anymore. We don't think about racism and sexism like your generation did. Those problems are over. We just see this as funny."

"Funny?" I say. "Well, I lived through those good old days, and they weren't so funny. And they're not funny today, either! Just wait until you get out there—you'll see what it's really like. I bet you'll just be laughing your head off!"

"Whatever," she says, with another eye roll.

Feminism's Third Wave?

By the turn of the millennium, as noted earlier, many different feminisms existed, and various critiques of the third wave were growing. Here, I discuss those strands that were the most useful to me and helped explain the conflict of worldviews presented in the vignette above. If postfeminists had declared the movement over, then it was becoming clear to me that feminism, at least as I understood it, was over, too.

In the late 1990s, newer forms of feminism began to proliferate: younger third-wave feminists, such as Rebecca Walker (1995) and Jennifer Baumgardner and Amy Richards (2000), continued to advocate for a new feminist political action, but this energy had been transferred mainly to young girls. Other scholars and activists continued to form collaborative alliances, such as Walker's Third Wave Direct Action Corporation and the Feminist Majority Foundation, as well as scholarly communities such as the Global Feminisms Collaborative at Vanderbilt University.

New Critiques of Third-Wave Feminism

Criticism of the third wave, as discussed in chapter 4, started early and came first from feminists of the second wave, who saw this new incarnation of feminism as too diffuse, lacking a core mission or unifying theory. Third-wavers responded by asserting that issues such as a core mission or even an overall theory were too universalizing. Growing tensions between second- and third-wavers became quite public when Rebecca Walker, daughter of Pulitzer Prize–winning writer Alice Walker, stated in an interview that Alice had "resigned" from being her mother when she (Rebecca) had chosen to have a baby (Driscoll 2008). Alice Walker (1983), a staunch second-wave feminist and proponent of "womanism"—a theological feminism practiced from the perspective of women of color—had become so upset that her daughter had become pregnant that she cut off all communication with her and her soon-to-be-born grandson.

Critiques of the third wave, by third-wavers themselves, also grew as the decade progressed, especially around the term *postfeminism*. The term itself had been and continues to be variously defined, but the use of *postfeminism* to describe the belief that feminist political action is no longer needed, as sexism has been successfully eradicated, is the one that most interests and troubles me.[1] Stacy Gillis et al., in the introduction to their book, *Third Wave Feminism: A Critical Exploration,* outlines some of the issues concerning postfeminism. First, they posit that feminism still remains a largely white, middle-class, heterosexual Euro-American venture, although they do acknowledge the work of black, transnational, global, and lesbian feminists. They also flatly assert that the third wave is most definitely not (post)feminist (2007, xxvii). Quoting from one of the articles in their collection, they write, "In the perpetual battle of representation and definitional clout, the slippage from 'third wave feminism' to 'postfeminism' is important, because many of us working in the 'third wave' by no means define our feminism as a groovier alternative to an over-and-done-with feminist movement" (Heywood and

Drake in ibid., xxvii). Gillis et al. also take earlier third-wavers to task for constructing and reifying a false binary between the second- and third-wave philosophies and actions and for paying too much attention to individuality, which inevitably falls into solipsism. Further, they ask whether all the attention paid to young women and "girlie culture" is true liberation or merely a sell-out to commercialism.

For me, the most significant issue raised by Gillis et al. concerns the split between so-called feminist activists, those on the streets advocating for social change through mostly local political action, and feminist academics, some of whom rely on global materialist-poverty and commodification systems without taking into consideration individual situated lives and local contingencies. (Of course, feminist action and scholarship can also be done by the same person.)

Further, many third-wavers, especially those influenced by Walker's Third Wave Foundation and Baumgardner and Richards's *Manifesta* (2000), see the activist feminist as the true feminist. So-called academic feminists, they say, must universalize issues and lump various people together to construct theories; they are thus violating the primary expansionist values of the third wave: difference and the multiplicity of voices. This effectively aligns academic third-wavers with the activists of the second wave, not with their activist third-wave colleagues who focus on smaller local issues, such as registering rural women to vote, electing women to public office, and organizing small-scale, localized resistance to continuing feminist social issues. Thus, as the decade progressed, fault lines were forming within the third wave itself.

Feminist Anthropology

Around 2002 I began, as mentioned earlier, to sense a lessening of interest by colleagues in feminist anthropology and, by extension, in feminist ethnomusicology. Somehow, the promises of previous decades had not been fulfilled, and many scholars (including me) seemed to be losing focus and energy. Mainstream anthropology had more or less normalized the inclusion of women and gender into its cultural accounts, but using consciously feminist theories to critique large issues of gender relations, both within the societies discussed and within anthropology and ethnomusicology itself, seemed to be waning. I wondered if a new activist feminist anthropology, in its effort to include differing and multiple voices, no longer served a coherent purpose.

Henrietta Moore addressed this last issue by asking some basic questions in an important article, "The Future of Gender or the End of a Brilliant Career?"

(2006). She asks, what is the basis for a feminist politics if women are no longer a group? If gender can no longer be separated from other identity markers, such as race and class, how can it be used successfully for political action? Should gender still be an important category of analysis in academic theorizing, and, if so, what should be its link to feminist politics? Do multiplicity and ambiguity solve the problems either of analysis or of politics? Moore cautions that truly giving up women as a group and gender as an analytic category will weaken the new feminism's potential for political action.

Further, the journal *Anthropology in Action* recently published a special issue also devoted to this topic (18, no. 1 [2011]), where the authors locate the source of the problem in endless debates between the politically engaged and the analytic deconstruction camps (Whitaker and Downe 2011, 3). Attempting to reconcile and merge the activist-academic divide, Robin Whitaker and Pamela J. Downe write in their introduction, "Far from undermining the prospects for politics or critique, a political and categorical deconstruction-ist stance can give rise to clear and defined moments of activist engagement and critical insight" (ibid.). And in addressing debates over global and locally situated approaches, the authors make clear that the work of a new feminism must be done locally, in collaboration between fieldworkers and cultural informants, with as much seamlessness and flexibility as possible.

Performativity and Embodiment

For me, the two most significant and useful threads of anthropological scholarship to grow in the first decade of the new millennium were those that further developed earlier theories of performance-performativity and embodiment. These themes, linked together by their common focus on the body, were first formulated in the 1990s and introduced even earlier, but began to take on new life in the ethnographic work of the 2000s, especially within ethnomusicology. They seemed to have a natural kinship with music and its performance; after all, music both is performed and provides a space for all kinds of identity performativity. Indeed, performances of music and body are always embedded within each other, in that music is carried in, brought out by, and received through the human body.

The literature on these topics is large and complicated, with various inter-twined strands of thought emanating from different scholarly lineages, such as cultural studies, psychology, and philosophy, in addition to anthropology.[2] Further, one of the hallmarks of third-wave feminism and its presence within feminist anthropological scholarship has been its dialogic and multivocal nature. It is not my intent or purpose here to trace all of these intertwined arguments, but, rather, to show again my own path through this wonderfully intricate intellectual and disciplinary maze.

I begin with some basic terms that I needed to understand at the time, as I continued to think and rethink the interrelationship between gender and music in the new millennial decade. I am well aware, though, that younger readers of this text will most likely already be familiar with at least some of these strands, as Deborah Wong has stated: "My generation of ethnomusicologists experienced two things: the arrival of multiculturalism in the academy and the ascendance of cultural studies in the humanities" (2006, 259).[3] My generation, however, experienced these things in adulthood, so my learning curve was steep. Here, I pass along my understandings of these two central themes and how they informed my work.

The term *performativity,* I learned early on, was distinct from *performance,* largely on the basis of conscious awareness and intention. Thus, cultural performances, such as rituals, political events, and concerts, are largely symbolic yet intentional expressive reenactments and validations of cultural values, where performers and their audiences collectively understand them as specially marked and intentional events. Performativity, on the other hand, describes often small, generally unmarked, and expressive gestures of the human body and voice that are performed as we move along in our daily lives. They are largely unconscious acts learned over a lifetime of reiteration and practice that legitimize and reproduce social and cultural norms. They are performed, but unmarked as a performance, and are largely invisible to "performer" or "audience," simply regarded (if noticed at all) as "normal."

Earlier work of anthropologist Edward L. Schieffelin (1985, 1998) was important to me as I began to connect the concept of performativity to musical and gender performances. Citing the even earlier work of Irving Goffman on discourse analysis, Schieffelin states:

> I believe that there is something fundamentally performative about human being-in-the-world. As Goffman has suggested (1959), human intentionality, culture, and social reality are fundamentally articulated in the world through performative activity. . . . The focus here is not on a type of event but rather on performativity itself: the expressive processes of strategic impression management and structured improvisation through which human beings normally articulate their purposes, situations, and relationships in everyday life. (1998, 195)

These ideas resonated with the work of French sociologist and anthropologist Pierre Bourdieu (1977), who had developed and extended the notion of performativity through practice theory. This theory posited that individuals learn and practice throughout their lives (largely unconsciously, seamlessly) certain bodily gestures, tones of voice, and the like that are seen as typical, or normal, in their specific social contexts, thus legitimizing and ultimately reproducing them as socially constructed norms. Bourdieu's work differed from that of earlier scholars in its focus on the body, not on verbal discourse. These performance schemas, labeled by Bourdieu as *habitus,* were not dependent upon language, but rather were experienced, known, and performed solely through the body (i.e., embodiment).

Influenced by the work of Bourdieu, Derrida, and J. L. Austin (1975), Judith Butler (1990, 1993) further developed these ideas by focusing specifically on the bodily experience and knowledge of gender, combining with it the notion of reiteration—repetitive acts of performativity that subtly construct, legitimize, and reproduce (in real time) socially and sexually normalized men and women and continue to do so throughout a lifetime, responding to various life changes. Butler writes:

> It is important to distinguish performance from performativity: the former presumes a subject, but the latter contests the very notion of the subject. . . . What I'm trying to do is think about performativity as that aspect of discourse that has the capacity to produce what it names. Then I take a further step, through the Derridean rewriting of Austin, and suggest that this production actually always happens through a certain kind of repetition and recitation. So, if you want the ontology of this, I guess performativity is the vehicle through which ontological effects are established. Performativity is the discursive mode by which ontological effects are installed. (1996, 111–12)

Resistance to these norms is possible, but can come about only through a conscious awareness of their performative power.

In the late 1990s and into the 2000s, feminist anthropologists began to use new theories of the body, producing much scholarship on both performativity and embodiment within different cultural settings. Various collections, such as those of Elizabeth Grosz (1994), Katie Conboy et al. (1997), and Janet Price and Margrit Shildrick (1999), focused their attention on the body and its performance of lived and sensed knowledge. Much of this work centered on medical issues, on rape and other violent abuses (especially in times of war), as well as on menstruation and childbirth.

Also appearing at this time were studies of young girls and new constructions of the "legible sexual body,"[4] as learned through various new media and their concentration on "grrrl power."[5] Another important stream (for me) came from anthropologists outside the West, who sought to position women's bodies and their performative acts within contexts that did not necessarily share Western notions of gender equality or feminism, or even, sometimes, body or woman.[6]

Feminist Ethnomusicology

In 1977 anthropologist and ethnomusicologist John Blacking published the first collection of articles devoted to the anthropology of the body. Although it is largely concerned with dance and ritual performance, I nonetheless present it here because it foreshadowed a growing concern in ethnomusicology with how the body performs socially constructed and gendered norms through musical performance. This collection mainly focused on the thought-to-be a priori givens of male and female bodies, as seen in various cultural performances, and less on issues of real-time, improvised gender construction and performance, or on seeing the body as a site of political constraints and systems of power, ideas that were to blossom in the decades to come.

As in previous chapters, I will not list here the many significant works in ethnomusicology that emerged in the millennial decade, but will again concentrate on four that were important to my understanding of performativity, embodiment, and other new trends in feminist scholarship and ethnographic writing. Here, I discuss one collection, Pirkko Moisala and Beverley Diamond's *Music and Gender* (2000), and three monographs, *Listening to an Earlier Java: Aesthetics, Gender, and the Music of Wayang in Central Java* (2006), by Sarah Weiss; Tomie Hahn's *Sensational Knowledge: Embodying Culture through Japanese Dance* (2007); and *Songs in Black and Lavender: Race, Sexual Politics, and Women's Music* (2010), by Eileen Hayes. Each of these, in its own way, does the work of contemporary feminist scholarship, borrowing and adapting new paradigms and writing styles that reflect recent developments.

Moisala and Diamond's collection is valuable from a number of different perspectives: it not only presents fourteen carefully grounded case studies, using a variety of theoretical methods (ethnography, biography, history, and so forth), but is also a beautifully "self"-conscious literary performance of the essence of fieldwork and collaboration. Moisala and Diamond take an unusual and creative step: in addition to the case studies, they present real conversations between and among the authors, who argue, joke, and ruminate on their own and others' essays. In doing so, they provide a true multileveled multivocality in this work, stating, "The subjects represented here are culturally plural not only in relation to one another but within themselves. Musical communities are depicted as intercultural, interactive, and responsive to the sweeping changes currently affecting every human society" (2000, 3). It is perhaps this presentation of intersubjectivity during fieldwork that most helped me later crystallize my ideas concerning the rich potential of fieldwork as a site for doing feminist work. Finally, the epilogue, written by Marcia Herndon, who died during the completion of this work, provides a creative set of questions that help us move forward in the persistent problem of, what she calls, tertiary analysis, which attempts to "create conceptual frameworks for the examination of comparative data" (ibid., 351), something that still piques my interest, but remains an elusive goal.

In *Listening to an Earlier Java*, Sarah Weiss skillfully brings together changing and always contested notions of male and female power and potency, as realized within the central Javanese court tradition of "old-style" (sometimes called "village-style") *wayang*. Specifically focusing on the musical form *grimingan*, where a female *gendér* player traditionally accompanies her husband, the *dhalang*, Weiss extends present-day performance practice of this form backward through the lens of Javanese literature, myth, and epic. Contemporary old-style playing, still performed by and associated with females, thus provides "an aural bridge between the performance styles of today and a style of performance that reaches as far back as the middle of the nineteenth century in terms of musical continuity . . . [and] also resonates with Javanese aesthetic traditions that can be rediscovered in the first written Javanese interpretation of the [twelfth-century] Bharatayuddha" (2006, 7).

What was especially rewarding for me when I first read this book was Weiss's assertion that the familiar structure of the male-female binary, and its linking up with other relevant binaries, such as order-chaos and so on, has proved in modern Java to be less rigid than in many other places colonized by the West. This, Weiss suggests, is due in part to an older, underlying Hindu aesthetic, showing instead a "less static, more interactive, and more plural model of gender and power relations . . . one that makes more sense when we listen to grimingan in old-style wayang" (ibid., 54).

She regards the male-female binary as still existing within the Javanese belief system, but not in its common value structure of contrast or even of complementarity, but rather in an interactive exchange structure, where males and females both emerge as powerful at different times and in different places, what Bourdieu (1977) refers to as circulations of symbolic power. What was also rewarding here was the presentation of a large body of feminist literature previously done by Western and Javanese scholars on gender relations—a bountiful gift we rarely have an opportunity to open. And again, the potential of fieldwork comes through this text, here used to take us seamlessly back through an older, gendered musical history.

Tomie Hahn's monograph on the embodiment of the Japanese dance genre *nihon buyo*, like Virginia Danielson's work on Umm Kulthum, is not a self-consciously feminist work, that is, it is not obviously positioned within feminist theoretic scholarship. But, also like Danielson's, Hahn's book smoothly and elegantly does the work of feminism by focusing on the body as a field

site and by presenting the learning and performing of the dance as an embodied process transferred back and forth between two women over many
years. Hahn states that one of the main reasons for writing this book was
her wish to take back certain symbols of Japanese femaleness that she felt
had been appropriated through media stereotyping. She writes, "Though this
book is not solely about gender, one of my aims has been to re-appropriate
the fan, *kimono*, and hair ornaments to tell a very different story of Japanese
performing women" (2007, 15).

The creative visual and literary aspects of this book mark it as one of
the first in ethnomusicology not only to tell a story through a phenomenological, bodily lens, but also to tell it in a visually beautiful way. Hahn
carefully mirrors the grace of the dance she has learned with her own
literary performing style, visually orienting the reader to unusual place-
ments of field conversations, curving margins of texts to soften their usual
brusque squareness, and judiciously using metaphor to help translate her
understandings of the embodied dance into a text that looks and reads
more like music and movement. Basing her work on the anthropology of
the senses, Hahn is able to go way beyond the usual ways of describing
dance, music, and gender into a how-does-it-feel to dance, to musick, to
be a female self, answering the question of how the body communicates
and passes on cultural and social knowledge. Thus, this work captures a
new sensibility for feminist ethnomusicology and does so in a particularly
creative and beautiful way.

The third monograph to be discussed here, Eileen Hayes's *Songs in Black
and Lavender: Race, Sexual Politics, and Women's Music,* is a close examination of women's music festivals as sites of representation, construction, and
validation of gender, race, sexual orientations, and other identities. I concentrate here mainly on the gender aspects of this book, remaining true to my
scholarly choices outlined in the introduction to this collection. Of course,
one of the strengths of Hayes's work is that it reminds us that gender, race,
and sexuality (among other identities) are embedded within each other and
position both researcher and researched.[7]

I have to admit that one of my favorite parts of this book is its dedication,
the first I have ever read that actually made me laugh out loud. I quote it here
in full, so you can enjoy its wonderful blend of humor and irony:

> Some say feminism is dead. Others say black feminism stopped by but left in
> a hurry. A few claim that "women's music" is dull; "Besides," they say, "Bessie
> Smith is *so* last century." Others don't know any lesbians and would rather
> watch them on TV. It was chic to be lesbian—last year. They say you can't be
> black, lesbian, and musical at the same time. Maybe you can be black, lesbian,

and love music—but if so, you probably can't dance, and if you can, you don't
care about social change.

> Lots of folks say all these things.
> This book is not dedicated to them. (Hayes 2010, v)

The no-nonsense, on-the-ground language of this book, interspersed with
cogent description and theoretical analysis of the fluidity of gender and sexuality construction, and often hilarious diary and field-note entries, does an
excellent job of documenting not only the presence of a black lesbian feminism in the United States, but also the presence of the safe space of women's
music festivals as sites for the performance of these identities. Like Hahn's
book dealing with gendered stereotypes, Hayes examines, plays with, and
reappropriates stereotypes of women and their bodies, of lesbians, and of
women's music, showing how women's music festivals also provide a space
to promote and encourage a new political feminist consciousness.

Further, Hayes traces the tensions between the generations spanning sec-
ond- and third-wave feminisms in the United States, showing how newer
ideas have been adapted by current performers. She also provides a sorely
needed discography of the "dream girls"—the black lesbian singers who have
helped to keep feminism alive within the black community while also en-
couraging it forward.

*   *   *

Thus, the first decade of the new millennium marked major changes within
a new multivocal and younger feminism and within a new feminist anthropological and ethnomusicological scholarship. For some, these changes,
characterized by a focus on the empowerment of girls, on reading legible
bodies, and on local politics, have effectively separated the political efforts
of second-wave feminists from those of their third-wave counterparts; for
others, these changes have been met with a certain frustration, perhaps sad-
ness, that the ultimate goal of forever dismantling unequal power relations
between the genders has yet to be met.

11 The Ins and Outs
   on In and Out

This article marks my first attempt to uncover what I had begun to see as underlying stumbling blocks to answering certain political questions concerning anthropology and ethnomusicology as scholarly disciplines. I continued asking myself, why had mainstream anthropology and ethnomusicology largely ignored the insights of feminist music analysis and theory and moved on instead to larger, more global, interests? What had happened to real women and men in real-life gendered musical contexts? Why had the revolutionary attempts of feminist poststructuralists to dismantle the rigidity of the self-other binary not yet completely revolutionized our ways of thinking and talking about women, men, and musics? And why weren't more scholars seeing the nonmediated, face-to-face (as opposed to virtual) fieldwork itself as part of the answer?

This article has an unusual history but highlights the frustrations I had been feeling for a long time. I first wrote it in the early 1990s and delivered it as a paper at an annual Society for Ethnomusicology conference. In the ensuing years, I reworked and updated it, using it as the basis of various discussions on the relative usefulness of the self-other binary and on fieldwork as a profitable context for teasing out ways that scholars had discovered to minimize the power differential in this method. I never worked it into a publishable article, though, and it still reads more like a paper than an article, using a more colloquial, intimate voice.

I decided, nonetheless, to leave it that way here, because it comes closer to the way I think and might speak in a conversation with a like-minded friend or colleague. And because I had been reworking it on and off until around 2000, I took that year as the year of its "writing." That is why it is in this section of the book, but may seem somewhat dated, especially to younger readers. The article, in its later stages, was greatly influenced by Gregory Barz and Timothy Cooley's collection *Shadows in the Field: New Perspectives in Fieldwork in Ethnomusicology* (1997 [2008]), and especially by Michelle Kisliuk's "(Un)doing Fieldwork: Sharing Songs, Sharing Lives" (2008). Finally, although not explicitly concerned with gender or feminist issues, this article presents a working out of certain issues that I began to see as stumbling blocks to the acceptance of a feminist ethnomusicology more broadly.

*   *   *

One day, when I was about six years old and in the second grade, our class was introduced to maps. The teacher passed out maps of the United States and gave everyone a new box of crayons. She asked us to find Pennsylvania, our state, and to color it. I opened my box of crayons and selected my favorite, the red one. I admired its vividness and shiny pointedness and eagerly set to my task. But something stopped me. I simply could not color Pennsylvania red, not because I disliked the color or the assignment, but because I had this creepy feeling that if I colored Pennsylvania red, I would be coloring the people who lived there red, their houses, their cars, their dogs, their yards—even my own house, my own yard, even myself—literally everything, red!

I was, for an instant, simultaneously outside the map, a giant with the power to obliterate the varied colors of Pennsylvania with one stroke, and inside the map, an unsuspecting victim of my own red crayon. I froze. Fear took over. I could not do the assignment. As I got older, of course, I learned better to distinguish real topography from its symbolic map, but I never forgot that overpowering and frightening feeling I experienced when I first realized that I could simultaneously exist both inside and outside—and could not always tell the difference between the two.

Etics and Emics

I would like to examine some assumptions underlying the analytical categories we used to call "emic" and "etic"—now defined in ethnomusicology and elsewhere as "inside-outside," or "self-other"—and to reexamine its early history as a analytical model in anthropology, from its first appearance in the work of linguist Kenneth L. Pike (1947). I then look more closely at this model and its usefulness for ethnomusicology; finally, I play with some different understandings of this model and suggest methods for its use. To illustrate, I draw upon my own fieldwork among Lubavitcher Hasidim conducted in

Crown Heights, Brooklyn, among other places, on and off over a period of about twenty years. To get to the heart of the matter, I will share some of my more uncertain, shall we say disorienting, moments of fieldwork, moments when the boundaries between my construction of myself and my informants were breached, when the feelings of blurring or turning inside out were most powerful, and therefore most useful. And in doing so, I wish to explore the emotional quality of these moments in a phenomenological sense, as well as my reactions to them, in order to better understand their somewhat chaotic essence.

I am sure most of you have also had such experiences, whether or not you have ever conducted fieldwork. They are a part of everyday life and occur often when we are confronted with a radically different view, value, or propriety. I propose that before we throw these moments away as irreconcilable anomalies of life, or as bizarre out-of-body experiences, we use them more productively to better understand the usefulness of the in-out relationship.

Certainly, the past twenty years or so have revolutionized our thinking about these analytical categories. Indeed, the major project of deconstructionists has been to interrogate, subvert, or dismantle binary oppositions of all kinds. French philosophers, such as Jacques Derrida and Michel Foucault, and feminist writers, such as Judith Butler and Diana Fuss, among many others, have attempted to deconstruct the notion of in and out almost to the point of collapse. What I propose here is to resurrect this structure and to suggest a more improvisatory model for its use.

To get started, I would like to briefly trace the history of the original terms *etic* and *emic,* as proposed by Pike in his 1947 work, *Phonemics: A Technique for Reducing Language to Writing,* and later developed into a theory that he called tagmemics, in *Language in Relation to a Unified Theory of Human Behavior* (1964). This model set the stage in many of the social sciences, including anthropology, and by extension ethnomusicology, for an understanding of distinct and contrasting units of culture, those seen by an "objective" outsider-observer-fieldworker (etic) and those, possibly internal, mental units held by a "subjective" insider-informant (emic).

According to Pike, both emic and etic referred to a method of deriving information about related binary contrasts in language, what he called "situated language units." Initially developed to distinguish contrasting linguistic units, Pike's reworked model later became a theory of tagmemic discourse whose basic tenet was to show the situatedness of human communication. To Pike, *etics* referred to the physical description of sets of verbal, and later nonverbal, behaviors gathered by an outsider or fieldworker; *emics* referred to the so-called cultural analyses of these units by an insider—a practitioner of the language who could assign meaning to the units, explain their function in the language, and show their relatedness. Each plane was complementary to the other; both were needed for a complete analysis. In Pike's view, etic and emic were never conceived of as opposing binary contrasts, especially when used to model nonverbal behavior, but rather seen as two ends of a continuum. Indeed, the whole motivation behind tagmemic discourse theory was to bridge the gaps between these equally valuable poles, with one informing the other in a two-way relationship.

It was the further reworking of Pike's ideas by cultural anthropologist Marvin Harris (1964) that began the now more than forty-year in-out controversy in anthropology. Harris's position, outlined in his book *The Nature of Cultural Things,* posited a materialist view of culture, one that could never account for internal, mental, or so-called insider positions. In Harris's view, the etic-outsider approach was to be favored over the emic-insider position, because it was simply impossible to correctly determine just what another person was thinking. In Harris's view, the outsider used an objective discourse of analysis, while the insider subjectively experienced the culture, with little self-consciousness or analysis.

Harris saw the etic and emic as two opposed categories, thus refashioning Pike's bidirectional, connected model into a hierarchic binary structure. In a rebuttal of Harris's position that the etic and emic planes were mutually exclusive, Pike stated in his article "On the Etics and Emics of Pike and Harris" that "to use the emics of nonverbal behavior I must act like an insider; to analyze my own acts, I must look to the outside. . . . But just as an outsider can learn to act like an insider, so the insider can learn to analyze like an outsider" (1990, 34).

Elsewhere, sociolinguists such as Dell Hymes (1974), deconstructionist philosophers, literary critics, and psychologists were also at work attempting to question the usefulness of the in-out model. Derrida, for example, in his 1976 work, *Of Grammatology,* proposed deconstruction as a method for critiquing this model, using one of the hallmarks of deconstruction—*différance.* One of the underlying assumptions of Derrida's work was the notion that in any binary contrast, one side is inevitably privileged over the other; binary contrasts could not simply be understood as value free, but must be seen as hierarchically arranged, their construction inherently driven by social power dynamics that sought to privilege those on top. Therefore, according to Derrida, the only way to deconstruct the power relations inherent in a binary contrast was to collapse the hierarchy through a three-stage process of inversion, whereby the two elements of the hierarchy are reversed, or turned upside down; reverse privilege, where the former underprivileged unit of the contrast now becomes privileged; and eventual abandonment of the model through a new, more enlightened, understanding of power dynamics.

Certainly, an important element of Derrida's project is the notion of *différance,* not precisely meaning difference or different, but rather describing a word for which there is no precise meaning; in order to define it, one must constantly defer to other words. The theoretical construct of *différance,* due to its definitional slipperiness, allows for a certain fuzziness of boundary formation, a beginning step along the road toward the eventual collapse of rigid, tightly bounded binary systems.

The work eventually trickled into anthropology and possibly fueled the so-called crisis of representation that hit this discipline in the 1980s and '90s, when anthropologists, agonizing over their own perpetuation of the very power dynamics they were trying to eliminate, began to develop new methods of fieldwork where self-reflexivity became the hallmark. Eventually, James Clifford, one of the leaders of this new movement, wrote that "it [soon] becomes clear that every version of an Other, wherever found, is also the construction of a Self" (1986, 23).

Ethnomusicology began to use the etic-emic model soon after its appearance in Pike's and Harris's work, concentrating on mapping linguistic units to musical sounds, so that one phoneme was the analog of one note. An outside fieldworker could record and transcribe all of the notes in a given musical performance, but it took an insider to determine the micro- and macrostructure of the sounds that transformed them into music. Ethnomusicologists publishing from the late 1950s through the early '80s, such as Bruno Nettl (1983) and Steven Feld (1982), among many others, including myself, attempted to relate both musical sound and nonmusical data to Pike's and Harris's models with differing success. One of the problems encountered here was the tendency of researchers to ignore the connectedness of Pike's model and to see, as Harris did, the separate and opposed nature of the etic-emic planes, transforming them into contrasting insider-outsider positions.

Five Assumptions

In my own fieldwork experiences, especially with Lubavitcher Hasidim, while I struggled to understand the "units" of their culture, their lives and music, I also struggled with the permeable, often fluid boundaries between my own outside observations and the inside meanings of my informants, as well as with my own boundaries and those of the others with whom I worked. I wondered, off and on, how truly useful these categories were, especially when they were seen as opposed to each other in a classic binary construction. My status as a nonpracticing Jew, for example, both helped and hindered me during the fieldwork process. On the one hand, even my nominally Jewish status initially made access to my chosen field site far easier. And my outsider secular Jewish status enabled me to see various connections between music and spirituality that I might have missed if I had been a Lubavitcher myself.

I have even pointed out a few such connections to my Lubavitcher friends, ones that I would like to think they would not have seen without me. They smile and nod, telling me that I am surely on to something, but we both know that I do not—nor will I ever—see it entirely their way; I will never truly understand Lubavitcher culture, much less its music, unless I become a Lubavitcher myself. And although they say I have often come close to an accurate description of their musical lives, there is still something missing. I have not become them.

Here are five underlying assumptions I have formed over the years about the etic-emic model that have directed much of my fieldwork experience. Examining these assumptions has forced me to call into question the usefulness of this model as first proposed by Pike. To illustrate the breakdown of these assumptions, I will share with you some of the uncertainties that I experienced during fieldwork and later analysis, as well as some of the questions I asked myself, and continue to ask, along the way.

Assumption 1: Inside and Outside Are Undifferentiated Categories

When first entering the field, it is tempting to see all of the people there as alike, or at least sharing a common worldview. After all, we are taught that culture is shared. Reading up on Lubavitchers, I imagined a neat cultural package, perhaps resembling the eastern European stereotypes with which I grew up. Certainly, there would be a core set of beliefs, attitudes, and practices that all Lubavitchers shared. They would all make good informants.

One of my first surprises, then, was to discover that, no more than any other group, not all Lubavitchers are alike, nor do they all believe the same things about Judaism, Lubavitcher life, music, or anything else. In fact, there was often very little correspondence between many of them except, perhaps, a core sense of being Jewish in a secularized world. The variety seemed endless: the very wealthy, the very poor; cantors, rock musicians; people from Russia or Poland who spoke no English; Israeli or Iraqi Jews attracted by the rebbe, but repelled by New York; young men, recently emerging from drug programs; young educated women, with master's degrees in psychology or sociology, seeking a spiritual home after trying the sexual revolution or feminist separatism.

Men and women descended from long, spiritual lineages stretching back to eighteenth-century eastern Europe. And there were others who, only yesterday, had decided to leave home and move to Brooklyn to be near the rebbe.

All called themselves Lubavitchers, yet what united them, save the label? What exactly did they share with each other? With all of this variety, who would make a good informant? Obviously, my work had to become focused. I could not include *everything* and *everybody*. But what to include and what to leave out? As my major project was studying Lubavitcher *nigunim,* or songs, I sought out and was directed to various singers, both male and, to my surprise, female. I had read and been told that only men performed *nigunim,* but I quickly came to see that this was a fiction: due to the laws of *kol isha,* men are forbidden to hear women sing, and as most previous scholars interested in *nigunim* had been male, having heard no women sing, they naturally assumed that women did not engage in this activity.

Furthermore, being a secular Jew—that is, not religious—I was "farmed out" to the BTs (Ba'alei Teshuvah),[1] people like me who were said to be "returning" to Judaism. Was that what I was doing? Well, I did self-identify as Jewish—both of my parents were Jewish—and that seemed to be enough for me to gain entry into the community. Certainly, it would have been harder if I had not been Jewish. But—wait a minute! Was there a bargain here? Were they giving me their music for my soul? Was I expected to "become more Jewish" in order to do this work? Whoa! Major ethical problem! I was not ready for that. And what about all of the people I was directed *away* from? Were they less "good" as informants? Weren't they Lubavitchers, too?

Assumption 2: Inside and Outside
Are Fixed and Stable Categories

Related to the first one, the second assumption assumes that the identity of an insider and that of an outsider remain fixed over time. For example, when I first began my work in the midseventies, I was unmarried, without children, and—even worse—living with a man who was not Jewish. Furthermore, I was working on my dissertation, not yet established in the academic community. Sometimes, I had trouble keeping interviews focused on music. Instead, almost everyone wanted to discuss my "lifestyle." I even got into a terrible argument one night with a woman I lived with for a time—with her screaming at me that I was not living according to "God's plan," and my screaming back that I was not interested in her assessment of me, that all I wanted to know about was *nigunim*! And, of course, this all broke down, when we both came to the same conclusion—I could not *really* know about *nigun* unless I became a Lubavitcher.

As the years went on, and I changed, so, too, did my identity change vis-à-vis the Lubavitcher community. A few years ago, after a break of many years, I revisited Crown Heights—now a married woman, with a young son and a few publications under my belt. Meeting and talking with people went like a breeze—no questions asked. Was I a different person from the student eagerly working on her dissertation? Had my status changed? Was I more of an insider now?

Assumption 3: Inside and Outside Are Bounded Categories

Anyone who has conducted fieldwork for more than five minutes knows that there is often a tremendous overlap between insiders and outsiders. Indeed, I was surprised at just how much I shared with many of my Lubavitcher friends, especially women, such as Rus Dvorah Shatkin, a Ba'alat Teshuvah, who was about my age and had a degree in voice from the Cincinnati Conservatory. After all, we were both trained musicians. We talked the same language. She would make an ideal musical informant. But wait—she was also a Ba'alat Teshuvah. And she was a woman, so she never sang at the rebbe's *farbrengen,* and she was from Buffalo, with non-Hasidic parents.

She might have overlapped with me, but how much did she overlap with her Lubavitcher neighbor Rabbi Eli Lipsker, a lifetime Lubavitcher with a long Hasidic lineage, a cantor, and a well-respected, if not formally trained, musician—one of the few of the rebbe's musical assistants? Well, she was a Lubavitcher, wasn't she? After all, she had lived in this community for more than ten years. I was beginning to see how everything overlapped—a bit here, a lot there. I began to wonder how *little* I could share and still say something significant and, conversely, how *much* I could share and not be a Lubavitcher.

Assumption 4: Inside and Outside Are Opposed Categories

One day, early in my fieldwork (mid-1970s), while I was living in the Crown Heights community, the rebbe called for a *farbrengen,* a large gathering of the Lubavitcher community where the rebbe speaks and there is a lot of singing. I was sitting up high in the women's gallery, next to a young woman with whom I had become friends. We watched the men singing below, their voices rising in volume and speed, often reaching the point of shouting. Suddenly, the rebbe began singing a new song; the others hushed themselves, straining to listen to his soft solo voice. At the time, the rebbe was already showing signs of aging: his beard was beginning to whiten, and his voice quavered a bit. He seemed to be having trouble singing this song, sometimes veering off pitch, sharping, and increasing the tempo in an effort to perform with more intensity.

My friend turned to me expectantly, eyes glowing, and asked, "What do you think of the rebbe's singing?" I was now known within the community as a musician (and from a musical family, some of whom had worked with this community in previous generations), and my opinion as an "expert" was respected. So I blurted out what I had been really thinking: "Well . . . he's not really such a great singer. I mean, he's got real problems with pitch and tempo, but I guess his intensity sort of makes up for this . . ." I trailed off as I saw the expression on my friend's face slowly recompose itself from eager expectation to cold, hostile staring. "Not such a great singer?! Ellen, this is the best performance of a *nigun* that you will *ever hear*! It is the best performance *because* it is being sung by the rebbe!" "Oh . . . ," I said, understanding, perhaps for the first time, that other factors, such as power, status, maleness, and so on, were just as crucial to musical performance as was "the music itself."

But how was I going to present this in my dissertation? Would my friend's evaluation, or mine, be right? Could they both be right, from a different perspective? Soon to come in anthropology would be the new or reflexive ethnography that would attempt to answer this question, but at the time I was unprepared for the dialogic nature of fieldwork and largely unaware of differing power relations between my informant friends and me. And as helpful as the new ethnography was in openly attempting to acknowledge and minimize the power differential between insider and outsider, we came to see that this approach could actually highlight the disparity. After all, it was still the ethnographer on the outside who enabled the insider to speak and who represented him or her to the outside world.

Assumption 5: Inside Can Be Turned Inside Out

Here are two incidents that highlight the assumption that inside can be turned inside out.

TALKING TO OTHER JEWS ABOUT HASIDIM   I frequently find myself in the position of lecturing on Lubavitcher music, usually in Reformed synagogues, to highly educated, secularized Jews, somewhat like me. My audience is often burdened with unfortunate stereotypes about Hasidim (like the ones I had when first entering the community), such as "they are all superstitious, childlike," or "they are relentless proselytizers," or "they make life difficult for other Jews, by being so flagrantly *Jewish.*" Some are even openly hostile to the Hasidic philosophy and way of life. Many fear that their children will be sucked in by the Lubavitcher "cult" or that the all-powerful rebbe is really like Jim Jones of Guyana. I am perhaps their only contact with Lubavitcher life. I am uncomfortable with this position. Am I acting ethically? After all, I am not really a Lubavitcher. I am not even an observant Jew. How much do I really understand about Hasidic life, living as I do in the "secular" world? At best, I tell myself, I am a translator, a mediator between distant cultures.

TALKING WITH HASIDIC WOMEN ABOUT THEIR MUSIC   In the early 1990s, I attended a Lubavitcher woman's *farbrengen* (gathering) and found myself in a Derrida-like moment where my status as an outside researcher observing inside informants was suddenly inverted—causing me a moment of disorientation that as I tell the story now has been processed into irony. From the very beginning of my fieldwork, I was told about a special school for women, Bais Chana (Chana's House),[2] located in St. Paul, Minnesota. I was often encouraged by my Lubavitcher friends to go there—to test out some of my ideas and to talk to other women who were interested in Lubavitcher life. In June 1991, I had an opportunity to attend a conference in Minneapolis (the first Feminist Theory and Music Conference), so one night I crossed the river and headed for Bais Chana.

There I met a group of about thirty women of all ages and of varying degrees of Lubavitcher-ness, from a few lifers to some like me, who had just dropped in for the evening. Most were long-standing Ba'alot Teshuvah, having studied Lubavitcher philosophy for some time. I told them that I was interested in music and that I enjoyed *nigunim.* I was invited back the next day to a birthday party, with a promise of a lot of singing.

When I arrived the next evening, classes had just ended, and the women were preparing for the party. Out came the candy, munchies, and a lot of vodka. We passed around the bottle and told stories. After a while, I was ready for some music. But as we sat around getting jollier and jollier, it soon became clear that many of the women did not know the *nigunim.* Then one of the lifers suggested that because I was "a *nigun* expert," I should teach them some of my favorites. I protested: "Oh, I'd feel funny doing that—I'm not a Lubavitcher," I said. "So what?" she said. "You know the music, don't you? That's good enough. *Ha-Shem* [God] will speak through the music." So there we sat, with me leading the singers at Bais Chana and feeling at once both honored and awkward.

What's Wrong Here?

Examining these five assumptions more closely, we find the first two are related in that they deal primarily with defining the actual entities, or "cultural units," within the in and out sets: number 1 assumes that all entities within each set are alike, and number 2 posits that entities do not change over time. Assumptions 3, 4, and 5 are also related to each other: they define the structural relationship between the sets, assumption number 3 examining linkage and overlap, number 4 hierarchy of value, and number 5 inversion.

Each of the vignettes I presented illustrated both the truth and the falsehood of each assumption: yes, at one level, all Lubavitchers are alike; I am still Ellen whether I am thirty or sixty; I can, if I try hard enough, pass myself off as a Lubavitcher or, at least, an "expert" in Lubavitcher music. So, at a general level of discourse, etic and emic distinctions are fine and often useful. However, at another level of analysis down the general-to-specific tree, the etic-emic distinction becomes much harder to see and maintain. Through fieldwork, and over time, of course, I found that not all Lubavitchers were alike, that I am now practically nothing like I was at thirty, and it is sometimes truly difficult to privilege either an etic or an emic view. The trick is to find the right level of discourse and the right model to fit it.

So, is the etic-emic, or any other model that structures information in binary contrasts, useful for ethnomusicology? Do such distinctions tease out a truth of the way people live? Are such tools ever satisfactory, or should we be more concerned with deconstructing them? The real problem seems to be that the cultures and people we interact with in fieldwork are far more complex than neat ethnographic models can indicate, even if they are wrapped in beautifully elegant prose. Life, like music, is experienced in real time. It is changeable, often messy, even chaotic, and it does not lend itself to modeling. Using etic-emic and other binary distinctions is not often easy or appropriate. Insides and outsides can and often do become blurred, overlapped, and inverted. All of us are inside and outside to each other and to ourselves at different times, and all of us live our lives by creatively and flexibly moving through situations of in- and outness that have no real boundaries or relationships to each other, except those that we construct in the instant of their happening.

All of the questions I have posed and the vignettes I have painted here seem to call into question the existence of inside and outside as polarized, or even bounded, categories of analysis. In fact, if inside and outside were truly opposite, they would be unknown to each other. We are all insiders and outsiders at different times and in different contexts, overlapping and intertwining in a real-time flow. And it is not always easy to tell the difference between the two. I, for one, find it no easier now than I did when I was six and sat poised and waiting before the map with my all-powerful red crayon.

12 Out in Left Field/ Left Out of the Field

Postmodern Scholarship, Feminist/Gender Studies, Musicology, and Ethnomusicology, 1990–2005

In this article, I examine the role that intellectual lineage plays in answering the question of why historical and critical musicologists seemed to publish more widely in the area of gender and music than ethnomusicologists, highlighting the major ethical issues in both fields alluded to in previous chapters. I assert here that new musicologists were in a better position in the 1990s to create a feminist theory for Western art music, and especially popular music, largely because such a theory fitted so seamlessly within already defined Western historical and cultural analytic frameworks.

Feminist ethnomusicologists, on the other hand, primarily concerned with cultural differences and depending on the method of fieldwork, were discovering and documenting very different social and cultural understandings of gender and music that could not be easily compared or universally theorized. Like their anthropological colleagues, feminist ethnomusicologists were (and still are) grappling with major cultural differences and with the ethical issues that arise from fieldwork.

Some of the material I present here is a summary of that discussed more fully in earlier chapters. This article was first published under a slightly different title that ultimately became (even to me) too confusing to be useful, so I have changed it here for clarity.

*   *   *

Since the publication of *Women and Music in Cross-Cultural Perspective* in 1987, I have watched the steady growth of feminist studies in historical musicology and ethnomusicology. Heavily influenced by postmodern theories derived from history, literary criticism, anthropology, cultural studies, queer theory, and the many "posts" of postmodernism, it is clear that recent postmodern studies have contributed much to our understandings of how both music sound and sociomusical activities are gendered.

What has been less clear, however, are the reasons behind a growing separation between the two fields of musicology and ethnomusicology with respect to this research: after a brief spurt in the late 1980s and into the '90s, work in feminist ethnomusicology seemed to slow in relation to that of musicology. Yes, certain excellent recent works stand out: Pirkko Moisala and Beverley Diamond's *Music and Gender* (2000), Tulia Magrini's *Music and Gender: Perspectives from the Mediterranean* (2003), and Jane Bernstein's *Women's Voices across Musical Worlds* (2004), among many others. Yet compared to studies in musicology, and especially in popular music studies, there seemed to be comparatively few.

I began to question, first, if this was actually the case and, second, what could explain this disparity, if it did indeed exist. To find some answers, I conducted a quick, informal search, scanning the titles of more than fifteen hundred books and articles written since 1990 on the subject of women and music, feminist theory and music, gender and music, and, most recently, men and music to see if my perceptions were correct. The book titles were culled from the Voyager Catalog on the University of Rochester's library system, and articles were taken from three prominent journals: the *Journal of the American Musicological Society, Ethnomusicology*, and the *Journal of Women and Music*.

I knew from previous searches that at least half of the works would not be scholarly, but rather trade books chronicling the lives of famous female jazz singers or rock groups. The remaining half, that is, those attempting to theorize women, men, gender, and music in some way, could be roughly divided as presented in table 1. I decided to separate musicological from ethnomusicological work on the basis of method: was the work under question derived from textwork or from fieldwork?

Table 1: Distribution of Books and Articles on Women, Gender, and Music, 1990–2004

Musicology (including Western classical and popular musics)	ca. 90 percent
Ethnomusicology (everything else, including non-Western popular and classical musics)	ca. 10 percent

Table 2: Distribution of Articles on Women, Gender,
and Music Taken from the *Journal of Women and Music*, 1997–2004

Vol. #	Number of articles	Musicology (incl. Western classical and popular musics)	Ethnomusicology (everything else, incl. non-Western popular and classical musics)
1 (1997)	7	7	0
2	8	7	1
3	6	4	2
4	4	4	0
5	6	5	1
6	4	3	1
7	4	3	1
8 (2004)	7	6	1
Total	46	39	7

The *Journal of Woman and Music,* the only music journal totally dedicated to publications on women, gender, and music, had a slightly higher percentage for ethnomusicological publications (approximately 17 percent). Table 2 shows the distribution of articles from the initial issue in 1997 to 2004.

One could partially explain the statistics shown in tables 1 and 2 as evidence for the relative numbers of musicologists and ethnomusicologists in the field today. According to the American Musicology Society and Society for Ethnomusicology websites, about thirty-three hundred people are members of the AMS, and about twelve hundred belong to the SEM. Of course, some of these are the same people, but if we accept these numbers at face value, then indeed there are almost three times the numbers of musicologists than ethnomusicologists out there, so it is easy to see why there might be comparatively fewer published works in feminist and gendered ethnomusicology.

However, this is not the complete story. In the tables, I linked Western popular music studies with musicology, not ethnomusicology, although until recently *all* music outside the Western art canon was considered the province of ethnomusicology. Western popular music studies, influenced by the newly burgeoning theories of cultural studies, brought the music of the so-called middle class into the canon—at least for some.

Until the advent of the new musicology in the 1980s, music studies were traditionally divided into three genre categories: Western classical or art, popular, and folk musics. This division, though always a fiction, has nonetheless been the defining feature of music scholarship since the late eighteenth century. German theorist Johann Gottfried von Herder (1744–1803) first coined the word *volk* (folk), thereby theorizing a structure for European musical culture divided into three class-based groups, each with its corresponding music: elites and classical music, urbanites and popular music, and folk and peasant music. Non-Western musics of all kinds were not considered in this structure. This tripart model, inherited by Guido Adler and further reified in his own model for music scholarship, "Umfang, Methode und Ziel der Musikwissenschaft" (1885 [1988]), became the basis for the division of the music disciplines we see in the academy today.[1] It is easy to map the current streams in music scholarship onto this hierarchy, "old musicology" still being mainly the study of Western classical music, using older analytic methods and interpretive models derived from late-nineteenth-century historical romanticism, with "new musicology" taking on the more recent postmodern theories and applying them to historical topics, as well as to contemporary popular music.

Today, the discipline of ethnomusicology (developed in the United States from the marriage between Adler's comparative musicology and anthropology), still sometimes defined as the study of non-Western music, is more accurately the study of all musics currently existing in the world today, using theories and methods derived mainly from folklore and cultural anthropology. In a way, the class-based hierarchy first theorized by von Herder also mirrors the underlying, implicit values of music scholarship itself, with musicological studies of the old variety still the most valued in terms of their cultural capital in the academy.

In reality, these distinctions are far more fluid and overlapping. We know that many so-called old-style musicologists have studied the popular musics of the past;[2] that new musicologists have focused on non-Western musics, especially in the guise of orientalism;[3] that old ethnomusicologists have long studied non-Western classical and popular musics;[4] and that new ethnomusicologists have become experts in Western classical and popular musics.[5] Thus, it appears that the older division that fused genre-based musics with the European social class structure no longer works well and that a new division based on theoretical and interpretive models, as well as genre, is moving forward.

Another perhaps more important distinction to be made here is between the various methods used by the two fields, both old and new. Historical musicology, from its beginnings, has based its method on the analysis and interpretation of historical music cultures with data collected from texts (both written and musical), a method derived mainly from the disciplines of European history and, more recently, literary criticism. Ethnomusicology, from its beginnings as comparative musicology, has always based its method on the analysis and interpretation of living cultures, with data collected from fieldwork, a method derived first from the discipline of folklore and, since the mid–twentieth century, anthropology. Thus, the true defining difference between historical and ethnomusicology is not the genres they study, where they study them, who studies them, or even the analytic and interpretative models they use, but, rather, their method of data collection—textwork versus fieldwork.

So why should this have implications for the relative level of interest in postmodern feminist and genderist theories as used by musicologists and ethnomusicologists? It would be beyond the scope of this article to provide a complete and up-to-date bibliographic review of the 750 or so titles I discovered—it is easily available to anyone with access to a good search engine and some time on her hands. What I would like to do instead is to trace some important moments in the recent history of feminist scholarship, as it was inherited by anthropology and passed to ethnomusicology, and then to suggest some possible reasons that ethnomusicologists seem to have been less engaged than musicologists with this work.

Recent Moments in Feminist and Gender-Based Scholarship

First, what is the difference between a feminist and a gender-based scholar? Both are people (men and women) interested in understanding unequal power relations between men and women in a variety of historical and contemporary contexts. The differences lie mainly in their approach. Feminists tend to be more politically active, perhaps more women centric; gender-studies scholars tend to be interested in holistic gender systems and are perhaps less interested in changing the cultural systems they study. The two labels also reflect a historical shift in thinking among feminist scholars, a split that continues to today (see earlier discussions in this book).

By 1990 certain central themes of postmodernism that critiqued Enlightenment truth claims and authority had emerged: the illusion of a hegemonic truth, or metanarrative; the recognition that reality is socially constructed; the deconstruction of hierarchies of power through the analysis of institutions and language; the psychological retheorizing of the body; and the role of mass culture in constructions of individual and group identities. In fact, these themes had become commonplace enough as to invite their own critique within the social sciences and humanities.

Feminist and gender-based scholars, for example, working in a variety of fields, continued to question definitions of basic terms, such as *man, woman, sex, gender,* and *sexuality,* and, more important, whether these categories of identity were biologically determined (essential) or culturally constructed (social). We were reminded that earlier works from the 1970s and 1980s first proposed "woman" as an analytic category, thus forever separating woman from the all-inclusive category "man."

A next step was a split that separated woman-centric scholarship from a broader view—so-called gender-based scholarship—that positioned men and women together in various binary constructs mapping onto unequal power relations. In the mid-1980s, notions of sex and sexuality, based on familiar binary oppositions, took a major step forward in early studies by queer theorists, such as Michel Foucault (1978) and Eve Sedgwick (1990), among others, who posited the social construction and multiple forms of both gender and sexuality.

In the early 1990s, two books appeared that were important to me, as they questioned the notion that gender could be determined on the basis of biological *or* cultural constructions. Both attempted to separate the biological determinism that mapped sex onto gender, and both saw the potential for a new form of gender enactment. The first book, Judith Butler's *Gender Trouble* (1990), introduced the notion of performativity, that process through which gender, no longer understood "as a noun, nor as a set of attributes, but as a 'doing,' a performance that constitutes the identity it purports to be" (Hawkesworth 1997, 663), becomes a continuous negotiation between an individual body and the personal, social, and cultural forces that establish and regulate it. Butler, in denouncing the binary oppositions inherent in the division of the genders into two "natural" categories, embedded the notions of gender and biology within each other, thus freeing them from their binary construct. According to Mary Hawkesworth, this allowed gender to be seen no longer as "an analytic tool used to illuminate a variety of asymmetries in culture but, rather, the process that naturalizes and justifies a particular asymmetry" (ibid., 667).

The second book, *Gender Thinking,* by Stephen Smith, a philosopher of religion also interested in how gender is performed, moved the notion of gender from that of a biologically or culturally determined category to a lifelong negotiated and performed process of gendering. Smith states:

> The more important truth about the genders . . . is that they "express" sex not so much by transcribing sex into character but rather by making representations *about* sex—about the significance of our endowment of sexual difference, about sex-linked regularities in everyday practice, about what constitutes an individual's best use of sexual resources, and about the best adjustment of the sexes to each other and to other important differences. Genders are *theses* on

sex, one could say, and like all theses . . . they speak to their object as an open
question. (1992, 303)

Smith, unlike Butler, still assumes here that genders exist (however defined
culturally) and are used to mark important differences—not only sexual
ones—between humans; like Butler, though, he acknowledges the individual
performative and critical processes of gender construction.

Recent Moments in Feminist Anthropology

The themes of postmodernism had a profound effect on the discipline of
anthropology and, more specifically, on the work of feminist anthropologists.
By 1990 a new anthropology had emerged from the crisis of representation,
a redefining moment that resulted in a critical self-consciousness and self-
reflection of the field during the 1980s. Scholars such as James Clifford and
George Marcus (1986), Clifford Geertz (1988), and others, borrowing and
incorporating the ideas of Derrida, Foucault, and other major postmodern
theorists, came to question their own authority of knowledge.

How could the (usually white, American-trained, male, middle-class)
anthropologist, no matter what his level of knowledge, speak for the other?
What was the truth of other people's lives, and who would best voice this
truth? What were the implications of even writing self-reflexive ethnographies
if postmodernism had declared the death of the author? This questioning led
to some interesting experimentation in ethnographic writing that involved
the use of multiple voices, fictionalized ethnographies, biographies, and other
creative forms of interpretive writing.[6] But more important, ethnographic
writing became an end in itself, a genre of literature, not unlike the novel,
that could lend itself to postmodern literary criticism and deconstruction.

Anthropology in the 1990s also began to take another turn—toward theorizing the global. Thus, for the first time in a generation, basic core values
were questioned. Once defined as a field using a more or less unified theory
of bounded, discrete societies, geographically located, anthropology began to
question *location, field,* and *culture* as defining terms, coming to regard itself
as concerned more or less with a chaos theory of global, constantly shifting,
overlapping, and virtual cultures. Scholars such as Arjun Appadurai (1990),
Bryan Turner (1994), Angela Cheater (1995), and Marilyn Strathern (1995)
point to the profound social, technological, and economic transformations of
the late twentieth century that rendered older, more easily managed concepts
of culture and fieldwork obsolete, for what is the "field" now? As Marilyn
Strathern writes in a critique of older paradigms:

Traditionally, bringing together separate orders of knowledge has been accomplished [in anthropology] through concepts, such as "level" and "context," "structure" and "event," or through the conventions of comparative analysis. Such solutions have in truth rested on the further middle-range constructs of "culture" and "society" which served as reference points for evaluating the significance of diversity and homogeneity. These middle-range constructs no longer seem sufficient in the face of transformations of this kind. (ibid., 3)

Changing concepts of the field have necessarily led to changing methods of data collection and presentation. Henrika Kuklick, in her article "After Ishmael: The Fieldwork Tradition and Its Future," critiques the concerns of the new ethnography as obliterating the "status of the privileged witness" (1997, 60)—the fieldworker—living and interacting on a daily basis with cultural informants in largely unfamiliar cultural contexts. In turning ethnographies into literary works, Kuklick fears that the very essence of anthropology is being subverted: "Though all fieldworkers have been obliged to account for their conclusions in narratives that are strategically phrased to persuade . . . , anthropologists in particular have placed a premium on the literary skill necessary to convey verisimilitude," and she hopes that anthropology can move "even more self-consciously than it has already done toward new modes of representation, without abandoning the interpretive perspective that makes its very essence as a specialized enterprise worthwhile" (ibid., 61, 64).

The irony of the anthropological dance with postmodernism is that, in retheorizing the field, say its feminist critics, it almost completely ignores women and recent feminist and gender-based scholarship (see Moore 1999 and Zalewski 2000). In an article entitled "Why Are There No Great Women Postmodernists?" Geraldine Finn, a Canadian scholar of cultural studies, suggests that the values of postmodernism that rely on texts, technologies, and theories of mass consumption seem to result in the disappearance, or erasure, of actual people from these analyses: "Particular persons, histories and lives are disappeared into texts, screens and machines . . . , into bureaucratic forms and functions and then again into the hermetic patois of abstract universals of those who would make sense of it all" (1993, 140). These conditions, Finn continues, drive an "active process of disappearing people from the collective consciousness, which interprets and shapes our culture and what counts as knowledge of it or even resistance to it. It is a process which disappears not only women, of course. . . . It also disappears Canada" (ibid., 141). Another book with a similar position is Tania Modleski's *Feminism without Women: Culture and Criticism in a "Postfeminist" Age* (1991) that critiques postmodernism as having ultimately fallen into the same pit it had been attempting to destroy: the hegemony of male-dominated theorizing.

Perhaps the most persuasive arguments against postmodern themes have come from those feminist and gender-based anthropologists interested in fieldwork, that quintessential process that critically defines the method of modern anthropology. Fieldwork is not unlike ordinary, everyday life. That is, people sometimes do not show up, cars or cameras break or run out of batteries at the wrong moment, people suddenly stop talking to you, and so on. And unlike library work, where, when the library closes, you are expected to leave, in fieldwork you are always (and sometimes stuck) there. The same person you have been following around and talking to all day may also be responsible for cooking your dinner and providing you with a safe and comfortable place to sleep.[7]

Special problems exist, however, especially for feminist anthropologists doing fieldwork today.[8] By the 1980s, large numbers of women in the field, with an avowedly political agenda, suddenly found themselves face-to-face with other women whose "oppression" seemed strangely familiar. Traditional (mostly male-defined and -theorized) anthropology had historically concerned itself with the other, but, in feminist anthropology, who was the other? Was it even possible, asked Lila Abu-Lughod in 1990, to do a feminist ethnography when political advocacy on behalf of women clearly violated anthropological objectivity?

The irony here is that it was partly in response to the uncoupling of the self-other binary—that hallmark of postmodernism—that feminist anthropology made some of its most significant contributions to postmodernist thought. Yet when theorists such as Geertz, Clifford and Marcus, and Fischer, among others, declared the authority of the ethnographer an illusion and the traditional ethnography dead, they largely ignored the contributions of feminist anthropologists in favor of the theories of European-derived literary criticism and cultural studies, those of multiple perspectives, no fixed truth, and the fragmentation of authority. Women studying women in the field were often all too aware of the truth of specific women's lives (often the truth of their own lives). What caused the disappearing of this knowledge in subsequent ethnographies that turned instead toward globalism and a universalizing of economic and political systems?

According to Diane Bell, "Female anthropologists working with women in societies where the sexual division of labour prescribes separate spaces for women and men in daily and ritual life have been especially clear regarding the relational nature of their enterprise." She suggests a reason feminist ethnographies have been so marginalized in postmodern thought: feminist anthropologists reveal that the "'other' of the feminist—namely the beneficiaries of patriarchy—are the very authors of the 'new ethnography' who, under the guise of democratizing ethnography through plurivocality, avoid scrutiny of their own power" (1993, 8).

The Lineages of Feminist Historical and Ethnomusicology

It should be obvious by now that at least one reason for the relative lack of and acceptance of feminist and gender-based ethnomusicological writing, as compared with that of historical musicology, is related to its postmodern genealogy—its inheritance from a strongly feminist anthropology and from the work of females in the field. In diagram 1 I have attempted to graph this genealogy, as well as that of historical musicology's postmodern inheritance showing the kinds of studies now emerging from both fields.

It is easy to see how ethnomusicology, in inheriting its basic method from anthropology, has had the same difficulties overcoming the problems outlined above in its own musical ethnographies. Many of these are discussed at length in Gregory Barz and Timothy Cooley's *Shadows in the Field* (1997), an examination of special problems inherent in doing fieldwork today within a variety of musical cultures. The only article in this collection dealing explicitly with gender is Carol Babiracki's "What's the Difference? Reflections on Gender and Research in Village India," an article that examines the implications of the fieldworker's gender on the actual experience of fieldwork and the daily interaction with male and female cultural informants it entails.

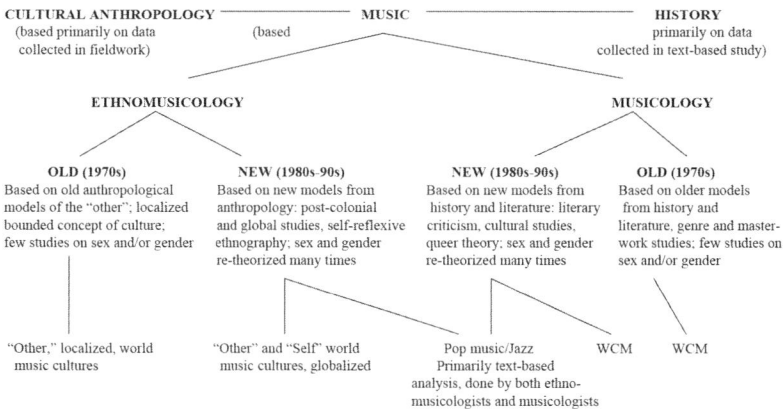

Diagram 1: Postmodern Feminist and Gender Theory, Musicology, and Ethnomusicology, 1970–2004

I suspect, however, there are other reasons that the work of feminist ethnomusicologists has been lessening over the years and that those works that have been written have been largely overlooked or marginalized within the field. First, shifting notions of the field—both the field of ethnomusicology and the field where we collect our data—have resulted in a move toward researching the globalization of musics through commodification; mass media; local, national, and global politics; and quickly changing economic systems that favor Western capitalism. Works such as Veit Erlman's *Music, Modernity, and the Global Imagination* (1999), Mark Slobin's *Subcultural Sounds* (1993), Thomas Turino's *Nationalists, Cosmopolitans, and Popular Music in Zimbabwe* (2000), Timothy Taylor's *Global Pop* (1997), and Lise Waxer's *Situating Salsa* (2002), to name a few recent titles, have examined various non-Western musical cultures (what ethnomusicologists studied in the past), not always using the method of fieldwork (what ethnomusicologists always did in the past), and have begun to theorize their work in terms of cultural studies–derived ideas (what new musicologists do). Rarely is gender considered central to these arguments.

Second, and perhaps more important, in positioning the study of non-Western popular musics in a no-woman's-land between traditional (old) ethnomusicology that relied on fieldwork and a new musicology that relies on analytical models drawn from literary criticism and cultural studies, ethnomusicology has given over part of the "exotic other" to a Western-centric and male-defined theoretical heritage. If we can contextualize all people of the world as now existing in a global economy, manipulated by crass commercial concerns, and caught in tight webs of local and global politics, we do not have to concern ourselves too much with individual people (women or men), especially the regular folks—those not particularly poised to enter the popular music scene or having little access to mass culture.

This is unfortunate because the very lessons learned by feminist anthropologists and ethnomusicologists in the field, those lessons that had to do with everyday, sometimes tedious, sometimes miraculous human interactions, have more to offer than simply their surface messages. They also offer gendered lessons of compassion, respect for the individual, and regard for the process of life that could help us put real people and the truth of their musical lives back into the picture.

In doing this brief survey, I have necessarily simplified the issues and have included only a smattering of the relevant scholarship. Indeed, for every trend in feminist scholarship, a new subfield of theorizing and critiquing has emerged, and I urge readers to search out interesting threads on their own. What appear to be evident in the literature, though, are two interrelated themes, which could be said to characterize the main intellectual tensions of postmodernism. The first theme, reification versus process (stasis versus movement), provides a tension between older-style research paradigms and those of the present and future. Notions of man, woman, gender, sex, and culture as static, bounded categories, existing either alone or in binary constructs, are giving way to process-oriented paradigms favoring movement, negotiation over time, shifting realities, and fluid identities.

The second theme—that of theory versus experience (ideas versus people)—provides, perhaps, a different kind of tension: that between ideas *about* people and the real experiences *of* people and which of these to privilege in our work. Finding a balance between these tensions will, no doubt, be the challenge of our future.

13 Imaginary Conversations

August 1, 2012

I was at a neighborhood meeting recently and was wearing my much-beloved (and now quite old) Feminist Theory and Music II conference T-shirt. As I was leaving the meeting, a young man came up to me and, looking at my T-shirt, asked: "Are you a feminist!?"

"Yes, I am," I answered.

He looked at me with a mixture of wonder and disdain, but curiosity won out: "Did you ever burn your bra?"

"No," I said. "No one did."

*   *   *

Today, when many young people do not know (or care much) about feminism, or see it as some historical relic, it is sometimes difficult to believe that this wonderfully energetic movement still exists. Perhaps it no longer does, at least under the name *feminism*. That word, like *diversity*, and so many others, has picked up its baggage and moved on, no longer signifying its original meaning, now reduced to code. I am not suggesting here that we reclaim it—perhaps its usefulness as a label is over; its usefulness as a political tool for resisting and overthrowing unequal gender relations, however, is not.

I understand the discipline of ethnomusicology to be the study of human music making in all of its social contexts, and, for most of my life, I have used the information-gathering, analytic, and interpretive models of ethnomusicology and anthropology as my scholarly tools. I was initially attracted to ethnomusicology in the 1970s, and have remained so throughout my life, because of its implicit connections to social justice issues and its promotion of tolerance for musical and social difference. Thus, I see ethnomusicology as connected to a wider cultural project, one that celebrates difference, while also remaining aware of the connections of sameness.

Modern feminism emerged from the civil rights movement of the mid–twentieth century as a reaction to social justice issues concerning unequal gender relations and over the decades has reflected this dual focus on sameness and difference. Indeed, sameness and difference have been used explicitly by feminists at times to create new law, to both embrace and resist essentializing and binary-reifying arguments, and, in most recent times, to separate contemporary third-wave feminists from their second-wave parents. From the sameness-difference debates of the 1980s and '90s to the contemporary focus on individual differences between and among women and men of all genders, races, ethnicities, and so on, the issues posed by the interplay between sameness and difference have been a defining feature of both feminism and the work presented here.

In looking back and rethinking the articles in this collection, I have had an unexpected opportunity not only to relive some inspiring, upsetting, and powerfully meaningful moments, but also to rethink my own subject position in relation to my work. What I did not see at the time—and now, in hindsight, virtually pop out of these pages—are underlying assumptions of sameness and difference that I held at various times over the decades and used to structure my work. It is easy, of course, to see this now, in the hindsight provided by this opportunity; my earlier work, like much contemporaneous literature in historical and ethnomusicology, shows the biases of my own culturally inherited and situated subject position, and it is tempting to deconstruct and expose how these biases, largely invisible to me at the time, helped organize and process my fieldwork experiences, interpretations, and analyses.

So, with that in mind, I engage here in three imaginary conversations, the first two between my present-day self and those previous selves who wrote the essays in this collection and the third with those who will read them. I do so not to apologize or to confess personal secrets, but to remain mindful of underlying organizational boundaries and stumbling blocks and to share some of the pitfalls I experienced on my feminist ethnomusicological journey.

The first conversation examines some of my assumptions of difference that seem, in retrospect, to have unconsciously guided the organization of my work with Lubavitchers as well as with that work addressing disciplinary difference. A focus on difference tends to create boundaries and to reify specific differences that are seen in the moment as defining features. The second conversation addresses the assumption of sameness that permeates and structures the cross-cultural work presented here. A focus on sameness tends to erase difference and blur boundaries, connecting larger amounts of data under more general themes. In the third conversation, that with contemporary colleagues and other readers, I propose another way of seeing sameness and difference, using fieldwork as the primary context for grappling with these issues.[1]

A Conversation with My Former Selves, Number 1: Assumptions of Difference

In my dissertation and the work focusing on the Lubavitcher community, I was consciously motivated by many personal and professional goals: to understand my own five-year-old self's strong and immediate attraction to Lubavitcher musical performance; to better understand and speak back to my father and the liberal Jewish American community, whom I felt were burdened by unfortunate stereotypes of Hasidic culture; to accurately document Lubavitcher spiritual and musical lives; and to give a voice to Lubavitcher women, whose musical activities, though different from those of men, were equally meaningful.

In retrospect, I see other, less conscious, assumptions that seemed to privilege difference, allowing a certain amount of exoticism to creep in—perhaps this is a hidden consequence of the assumption of difference. After all, I had chosen the community and field site not only assuming but also wanting difference. I was not like Lubavitchers and did not want to be—at least in the ways I constructed and privileged their differences. My job, as I understood it then, was to document difference, process and organize it, put it into understandable categories, and bring it back to my world in a recognizable form—in short, to reify difference, spin it through current ethnographic theory, and perform it for a (mostly) friendly academic family who also privileged difference. But at the time, I did not see difference itself as a problematic issue.

Much ethnomusicology is, I believe, driven by the desire to uncover, understand, and value difference in the musical cultures with which we engage. But it is sometimes difficult to confront difference. In fact, as you have seen in the articles presented here, my own struggles to deal with social and musical differences did not always go well. I sometimes dismissed what my informants said or argued with them. It has always been easy for me to profess a tolerance for difference, but actually being tolerant, especially when I am strongly connected to an ideology, is far more difficult in the on-the-ground reality of

fieldwork, where one is face-to-face with differences of all kinds. This awareness of difference in the moment of its happening sometimes caused me, I see
in retrospect, to experience uncomfortable feelings, to become destabilized
momentarily, and to retreat into default positions and behaviors. So, if I could
go back to the self first dealing with Lubavitcher research and fieldwork in
the 1970s, I would perhaps caution that Ellen not to go down with the ship
of difference, but to remain more open to sameness. Who knows what would
have resulted if that had been the case at the time?

I have also realized for some time that I have constructed myself as a sort of
ethnomusicology advocate, often using this construction politically to speak
on behalf of disciplinary difference, especially that between ethnomusicology,
my adult (and chosen) academic home, and historical musicology, my early,
culturally inherited home. My resistance to what I saw then as arrogance and
intolerance toward musics and peoples outside the Western art tradition
initially led me away from historical musicology and toward ethnomusicology, which seemed to have a more open evaluative system. This disciplinary
change, though, led me to think more deeply over the years about fundamental underlying differences between these closely related and intertwined
fields that had enabled such different evaluative systems to develop. Some of
that thinking led to the articles you see here, especially chapter 12, "Out in
Left Field/Left Out of the Field."

Much of my early distaste for the values of mid-twentieth-century musicology has faded over the years in light of newer postmodern music research,
especially that focusing on popular and contemporary musics. This literature
has enabled many analytic and interpretive models to be shared between
the disciplines, much to their mutual benefit. However, challenges still exist: ethnomusicology programs have continued to be slow to develop, and
ethnomusicology methods and models have not been fully acknowledged by,
or accepted into, mainstream music research and teaching, Thus, although
I recognize much of the sameness of the two disciplines and value their
collaborative efforts, I still find myself privileging the major difference of
ethnomusicology from historical musicology: fieldwork versus textwork.

A Conversation with My Former Selves, Number 2: Assumptions of Sameness

Here, I turn to the essays dealing with cross-cultural perspectives, seen
through the lenses of feminism and feminist music theory, flipping, for the
moment, to the opposite classificatory pole—sameness. When I first began to
see the potential for a feminist theory applied to social and musical systems

in the early 1980s, I readily accepted the underlying assumption of sameness found in much contemporaneous anthropological feminist literature, that *all women* were, and always had been, the same in one important way: they had all been in the same basic social position vis-à-vis men—secondary, other, on the bottom of unequal power relations, largely invisible in the scholarly literature, especially that of music. Of course, I also recognized at the time that if all women were the same in this way, together they created a bounded set, necessarily implying another, contrasting, set: not women (i.e., men).

I also saw, primarily in the scholarship of feminist theory, the near invisibility of women outside the white American middle class, and, in anthropology, I sensed a certain unease in dealing with music independently as sound and structure. Thus, I was initially motivated to do cross-cultural work in feminist ethnomusicology by the gap created by the lack of research in historical and ethnomusicology on women or gender and music, a general lack of interest in music from anthropology, and almost nothing in feminist theory on non-Western women or music.

I first attempted to fill some of this gap in my introduction to *Women and Music in Cross-Cultural Perspective* (chapter 2 here) by suggesting a nascent model that could help explain this obvious and egregious gap. I continued hoping for a better and better model, adopting different ideas mainly from anthropology, which had had a long-standing engagement with cross-cultural samenesses and differences. Today, I see this activity as overly ambitious and perhaps naive, focusing so exclusively on sameness, but at the time it represented some first attempts to explain, and hopefully correct, what I saw then as a particularly serious situation.

Eventually, though, as we all began rethinking these issues, too much difference seemed to creep in. How could we talk about *all* women and say something useful and nonessentializing? Each musical culture was different in too many ways, and not only were all women supposedly different from all men, but each woman was different from another, and, as we later theorized, each woman was, in fact, her own set of different selves.

A Conversation with My Readers: Sameness and Difference Together

Most of us realize that sameness and difference are not always, if ever, totally opposite categories of classification, but rather are connected and dependent on each other for recognition. They are often experienced as blurred, fuzzy, overlapping, and sometimes inverted, depending on one's level of awareness and mode of discourse. What follows is a discussion of three basic issues that have arisen, for me, over the years concerning problems inherent in exclusively privileging sameness or difference. The issues may seem obvious, but I present them here, nonetheless, again to remind myself of their constant presence as stumbling blocks to a clearer and more openly intersubjective scholarship.

A first issue that I have faced in my research and teaching (as, no doubt, many of you have also) has been finding the right level of sameness or difference in which to present my work. I must construct imaginary readers, providing them with enough specific information at one level of differentiation without becoming too general by blurring distinctions in pursuit of common themes at another level of abstraction. Or in teaching situations, where I might use a certain level of discourse to encourage conversation, one student inevitably responds with a more specific counterexample, thus questioning, perhaps undermining, my assumption of sameness, while another inevitably responds with a "So what?," questioning my assumption of difference.

Thus, certain differences, or samenesses, inevitably become privileged over others; they seem, in the moment, to be more valuable as organizing principles, especially in research and teaching. But it is always easy to jump up or down one or more levels of abstraction or differentiation to make any statement of sameness or difference moot. For me, what leaped out of these chapters was the rigidity with which I held onto difference or sameness, constructing hierarchies based on my own situated position. Is this what scholarship really is? I am not sure what I would have done had I been more aware of this underlying construction when writing these essays, but given an opportunity to go back and to better understand this interplay might have made clear how simply confronting sameness and difference as issues in and of themselves opens up the potential for a more nuanced self and other consciousness.

A second issue for me has been the search for more creative ways to express in writing and speaking—both fairly rigid forms of communication—the sense of sameness<>difference flow as it is experienced in real time.[2] More creative forms of writing have appeared, for example, in some recent scholarship, such as in Deborah Wong's "Moving from Performance to Performative Ethnography and Back Again" (2008), Tomie Hahn's *Sensational Knowledge: Embodying Culture through Japanese Dance* (2007), and Ruth Hellier's "Ixya Herrera: Gracefully Nurturing 'Mexico' with Song in the U.S.A." (2013). These works, and many others, that combine different forms of writing seem to more successfully weave together various perspectives on selves and others and to better express the fluidity of moving from one perspective to another.

The third and perhaps most important issue I have faced has been that of recognizing and uncovering the implicit hierarchy of value inherent in the binary structure of sameness versus difference. There is always the tendency in any binary to privilege one side over the other. Thus, difference and sameness can become valued, *in and of themselves,* as illustrated in the two conversations above. For me, the problem lies not so much in differentiating or merging, per se, but in the value of one *over* the other. One thing that characterizes my earlier work here is that I made a *choice* between sameness and difference, thus privileging one or the other, but missing an opportunity to play with their interconnectedness. As I went along, absorbing some of the new realities of poststructuralist thought, I began to see, as many others did, the potential for embracing both sameness and difference simultaneously and neutrally. Some of the later work presented here reflects this.[3]

So how can we deal more successfully and creatively with sameness and difference? A first step, I believe, is simply becoming aware or conscious of these interconnected classificatory systems in ourselves and how they may underlie and structure human interactions. A second step might be to practice flipping back and forth between the poles, thereby creating a space in between for the performance of intersections between sameness and difference. And a final step, deriving from the second, would be giving up any attachment to either sameness or difference. For me, I think it is probably time to finally, and forever, separate difference and sameness from value, especially when it relates to people and their musics.

The Importance of Fieldwork in Ethnomusicology

As I have asserted throughout this book, for me the fieldwork experience is essential to understanding and more successfully dealing with musical and social sameness and difference and has been the driving methodological practice in all of my work. It is filled with play, allowing me and my field partners to share, reverse, invert, and collapse difference, while at the same time construct new relationships based on sameness. It is difficult to truly objectify a person with whom you have shared a part of your life, with whom you have performed music, or to whom you have told secrets. I privilege fieldwork over other kinds of data gathering because it is, for me, the most direct, immediate, and honest (as well as fun) way to learn about someone else and her or his music. It is not a perfect method, but still more useable than others, and I see it as crucial to a feminist ethnomusicology.

As I have written before, I am grateful to Gregory Barz, Timothy Cooley, and the many authors in their collection *Shadows in the Field: New Perspectives for Fieldwork in Ethnomusicology* (1997) for articulating the importance of ethnographic fieldwork on music, precisely because it creates the potential for intersubjective negotiations between sameness and difference. In their introduction, "Casting Shadows: Fieldwork Is Dead! Long Live Fieldwork!," for example, Barz and Cooley state, "The power of music resides in its liminality, and this is best understood through engaging in the experimental method imperfectly called 'fieldwork,' a process that positions scholars as social actors *within the very cultural phenomena they study.* Ethnographic fieldwork requires meaningful face-to-face interaction with other individuals, and therein lies both the promise and challenge of our endeavors" (2008, 4; emphasis added).

Not specifically focused on feminist or gender issues in music, many of the essays in this collection explore the uses of reflexive and performative ethnography as core ways of knowing music or, as Jeff Titon states, "musical 'being-in-the-world'" (ibid., 31). Two essays stand out for me as being especially helpful: Michelle Kisliuk's "(Un)doing Fieldwork: Sharing Songs, Sharing Lives" and Deborah Wong's "Moving from Performance to Performative Ethnography and Back Again," cited above, each of which was useful to me as I developed my own feminist ethnomusicology.

Describing her work with BaAka performance, Kisliuk writes, "In order to act upon the world we need to continually express our identities; we get to know other people by making *ourselves* known to *them,* and through them to know ourselves again, in a continuous cycle" (2008, 187). Wong, in her beautifully creative and self-reflective essay, describes her relationship to *taiko,* a Japanese drumming tradition now popular in North America. She focuses here, and in her most recent book, *Speak It Louder: Asian Americans Making Music,* on "the play of identification that runs through North American taiko practice: the ways that ideas about race, ethnicity, gender, sexuality, age, and class are discussed, explored, and sometimes hardened in the course of playing these drums" (2004, 77). Moving effortlessly back and forth, through all of the spaces that connect her multiple selves and those of her others, she writes: "As I proceed, I will demonstrate performative ethnography and, simultaneously listen to the issues that it raises. Performativity sets in motion a series of spiraling, discursive responses, and ethnography should, too" (ibid., 79).

The merging and separating of identities suggested by Kisliuk, combined with Wong's flexibility in moving between the experience of flow and the self-consciousness of careful listening, together could become the basis of a new, more creative form of ethnography. I am not suggesting here, like the anthropologists of the 1980s and '90s, that we turn to fiction or question the truths of our ethnographies, but rather that we explore different modes of discourse that can enable more fluid, fuzzier descriptions and also allow for the improvised play between sameness and difference as cognitive models.

A Feminist Ethnomusicology

I am grateful to my 1970s self and to my many colleagues that we were able to imagine a link between social justice, gender inequality, and music. I have learned much from the interplay between these linked knowledges over the decades; each has informed the others in countless scholarly and personal ways, and it would be difficult for me to separate them now. And over the years, I have added other, perhaps even more basic, less visible, knowledges to the mix: my whiteness, my heterosexuality, my economic status, and the access to education that I inherited from my original familial position of privilege. These, too, have contributed to the constellation of knowledges that I have collected and used over a lifetime.

But this was possible for me only because I was lucky enough—also in the early 1970s—to find ethnomusicology, my disciplinary home that has respect for music and cultural difference, yet also acknowledges sameness in the human awareness of music's power and meaning. That I also came to find feminism was serendipitous, but together these disciplinary systems provided an intellectual and emotional safe space for me to work out important issues for myself and, I hope, for my larger communities.

Ethnomusicology is unique within music studies in that it locates its music, its researchers, its researched, and their mutual interactions within a nexus of three interconnected symbolic processes, negotiated simultaneously in real time: making and experiencing music, as in performing and receiving sounds and structures; constructing and performing oneself and one's others, in the sense of performativity; and sharing and merging situating knowledges through intersubjective fieldwork. Each of these processes has a different role to play in understanding human musical interactions: making and experiencing—the *where* of music, not only the physical space, but the symbolic space created together by musical bodies and sounds; constructing—the *how* of performing, not only the music itself, but oneself in the music; and situating—the *what* of performing, not only the specific pieces of music, but also one's position within a set of many intersecting identities.

The triangular model proposed above (in the spirit of Alan Merriam [1964]) is possible because these processes also share other, more general, features that make them compatible partners. First, they share performance, in the sense both of marked performance and of performativity: humans both perform sounds designated as music, as in a performance, and simultaneously create, validate, or protest various aspects of their internalized identities by enacting them outwardly, thereby positioning themselves within their own social webs. Second, they share the feature of embodiment—all are performed through the gendered, racialized, ethnicized, and so forth, body. Third, these processes are all communicative, as all are performed and understood publicly. And, finally, they all share the attribute of improvisation, that seemingly natural process of creating ourselves, our others, our musics, our genders, and our individual and shared realities in real time.[4]

Over the decades, and throughout this collection, my focus has been on feminism as a political stance, enacted and performed through the lens of gendered music and musical activity, as learned through the process of fieldwork. I have concentrated on fieldwork here, as opposed to other scholarly issues, such as analysis, interpretation, or presentation, because it is so basic to the entire ethnographic process. It validates, consciously or unconsciously, one's basic motivations for doing the work; it provides a real-life context for all kinds of performances; and it allows for negotiations of perspective, for self-other overlap, or swapping with real people in real time. For me, a feminist ethnomusicology has been the primary way I have, at different times, discovered, sustained, and shared my self and my core values with others, and fieldwork has been the most direct and honest way I have found to do this. In her book *Feminism Is for Everybody: Passionate Politics,* bell hooks writes, "Imagine living in a world where there is no domination, where females and males are not alike or even always equal, but where a vision of mutuality is the ethos shaping our action. Imagine living in a world where we can all be who we are, a world of peace and possibility. . . . Come closer. See how feminism can touch and change your life and all our lives" (2000, x). Although written more than a decade ago, these words are still powerful to me because they invoke my imagination and fantasy. Imagine such a world! And how can I help to make it happen? The work I have done over the past decades has, I hope, contributed something to this imagining. Throughout these essays, I have sought ways to construct a path that would contribute to this basic personal and professional goal. Together, our understandings of gender and music have grown and become richer and more nuanced, yet I believe there is still work to be done.

Notes

Introduction

1. This term, although in use earlier, was coined in the book *Red Diapers: Growing Up in the Communist Left,* by Judy Kaplan and Linn Shapiro (1998).

2. Hasidim are ultra-Orthodox Jews, who, in addition to following all of the laws and practices of Judaism, also adhere to the teachings of the Ukrainian rabbi Israel ben Eliezer (1698–1760), often called the Ba'al Shem Tov. Lubavitchers are one of many Hasidic groups living today mainly in Israel and the United States. For a full discussion of Lubavitcher Hasidim and their music, see Koskoff 2000.

3. See Morris 1995 and Koskoff 2000 for fuller discussions of Jewish feminism.

4. For an excellent, user-friendly introduction to this history, see Sally J. Scholz's *Feminism: A Beginner's Guide* (2010).

Chapter 1. From Women to Gender

1. These conferences, sponsored by the University of Michigan School of Music, should not be confused with the ongoing Michigan Womyn's Music Festival, held each August since 1976.

2. It is has been suggested that President Kennedy couched his support of this commission within Cold War rhetoric, saying that America needed all of its citizens—men and women—to fight the communist menace.

3. The ERA was actually first introduced in 1904.

4. See Moore 1988; Cole and Phillips 1995; Ortner 1996; and Mascia-Lees and Black 2000. See especially McClaurin 2001 for a good history of black feminist anthropologists.

5. See, for example, early studies by Frazer 1909, 1910; Mead 1928, 1935; and Evans-Pritchard 1951, among many others.

6. See, for example, Reiter 1975; Ardener 1975b; and Moore 1988.

7. See Mascia-Lees and Black 2000 for an excellent summary of different approaches.

8. Some of the more influential writers to address these issues at the time who were most important to me were Rosaldo and Lamphere 1974; Ardener 1975a, 1975b; MacCormack and Strathern 1980; Ortner and Whitehead 1981; and Brown and Jordanova 1981, among many others.

9. See especially Strathern 1980.

10. This last one continues to be unsatisfactorily answered for me, although postcolonialist anthropologist Gayatri Spivak's much-cited (and -critiqued) notion of "strategic essentialism" (1988 [1995]) seems reasonable.

11. For an excellent discussion of Foucault's influence on feminist anthropology, see Armstrong 2005.

12. See especially Carlisle 1973; Kaeppler 1970; Farrer 1975; Wade 1972; Hawes 1974; Coote 1977; Hoch-Smith and Spring 1978; and Cormier 1978, for a good representation in the ethnomusicology of that time.

13. See especially Neuls-Bates 1982; Clément 1988; Bowers and Tick 1986; and Rorich 1989, among others.

14. See Kirkby et al. 2003 for an especially good discussion of this field's interdisciplinarity.

15. Some other articles that were important to me at the time, but are too numerous to discuss here, include Becker 1988; K. Campbell 1985; Avishur 1987; DjeDje 1985; Ellis and Barwick 1990; Keeling 1985; Okafor 1989; Sawa 1987; Schmidt 1989; and Sutton 1984.

Chapter 2. Introduction to Women and Music in Cross-Cultural Perspective

Reprinted with permission from *Women and Music in Cross-Cultural Perspective* (Westport, Conn.: Greenwood Press, 1987).

1. Carolina Robertson was very helpful here, and conversations with her resulted in what some have called the "book ends" of this collection: my introduction and her article "Power and Gender in the Musical Experiences of Women" at the end of the book.

2. See Farrer 1975; Jordan and Kalcik 1985; among others.

3. See especially Ardener 1975a, 1975b; Atkinson 1982; Gornick and Moran 1971; and Schlegel 1972 for general discussions of the impact of feminist anthropology on ethnography.

4. See also Lamphere 1974; Friedl 1967; and Yocom 1985.

5. See especially the citation from a 1970 study by Catherine Ellis in Nettl 1983 that describes her female informants' embarrassment and ensuing strategy to "go away with Ellis," where they could "sing their secret songs without the fear of the men overhearing" (335).

6. See Avery 1977; Burrows 1958; and Wistrand 1969 for some examples. In the hindsight of the past decade of feminist-oriented anthropology, the Wistrand article, especially, highlights missed opportunities in the field (481).

7. Typical of these are studies surrounding such life events as puberty and initiation. See, for example, Blacking's studies among the Venda (1962, 1976); studies of courtship, love, and weddings: Gerson-Kiwi among the Jews of Bokhara (1950) and Wade in North India (1972); women's genres, such as lullabies: Hawes in the United States (1972); laments: Qureshi among Muslims in India (1981), Szirma in Hungary (1967), Caraveli-Chaves in Greece (1980), Hampton among the Ga (1982), and Simon in West Irian (1978); and specific genres associated with healing, shamanistic practices, or spirit possession. See again Blacking among the Venda (1962, 1976); Gourlay in Uganda (1970); Kartomi in central Java (1973); Kealiinohomoku in a comparative study of Hopi and Polynesian dance (1967); Nketia among the Akan, Ashanti, and Ga (1957); Soedarsono in Java (1969); Vander among the Shoshone (1982); and Huhm (1980), Harvey (1980), and Kendall (1985) in Korea.

8. See Martin and Voorhies 1975, 84–108, for an excellent discussion of cross-cultural observations of supernumerary sexes.

9. See Strathern 1980 for a discussion of gender associations that are not dualistic but rather present male and female as symbols of, but not metaphors for, culture and nature (204).

10. See also Cucchiari's (1981) hypothesis that gender hierarchies were first developed when males and females realized the consequences of sexual behavior (i.e., pregnancy and childbirth) and began to construct value systems based on newly developed gender categories; and Patai 1967 for a historical and present-day account of the roles and statuses of women in various world cultures, especially since World War II.

Chapter 3. Both In and Between

Published with permission from *Concilium: International Journal of Theology* (SCM-Canterbury Press) 222 (1990): 97–110.

1. See also Chodorow 1974 for a discussion of the implications of women as primary socializers and Strathern 1972 for a further analysis of the position of women as in between.

2. For a fuller cross-cultural treatment of shamanism, see the classic studies by Eliade 1964 and I. M. Lewis 1971, 1986. See also Rouget 1985 for a discussion of music and trance. For a description of shamanism in Korea, see especially Kendall 1985 and Harvey 1980.

3. Many chosen, professional shamans migrated from North to South Korea during the Korean War (1950–53), and much ritual activity takes place today in and around the Seoul area.

4. Some Western scholars (especially Harvey 1980) have suggested that the extreme sexual repression of Korean women, and their general lack of access to positions of power or authority, can account for the rather high instance of "spirit sickness" and female shamanism in Korea, where, in trance, a *mansin* can act freely in an aggressive or highly sexual manner.

5. See Shimony 1961, 1980; Fenton 1951; and Tooker 1986 for excellent discussions of the Iroquois and their ceremonies.

Chapter 4. Shifting Realities

1. All three of these women were (and continued to be) active at this time in music. Today, Ruth Solie is Sophia Smith Professor Emerita at Smith College; Jane Bowers is professor emerita at the University of Wisconsin, Milwaukee; and Catherine Pickar is currently an adjunct professor in choral studies at George Washington University.

2. The penis was eventually found and rushed to the hospital where it was reattached.

3. Today (2012), women still earn only seventy-eight cents on the dollar that men earn, and although President Obama and the Democratic Party recently tried to pass equal-pay-for-women legislation (June 5, 2012), the Senate successfully blocked this bill.

4. See Pough 2004 and S. Marcus 2010.

5. I am indebted to Beverley Diamond for this insight, as passed on to me by one of her grateful students.

6. Edward Said was also an accomplished pianist and published works discussing Western art music in its social context. See Said and Barenboim 2004.

7. See Collins and Anderson 1992 and Collins's more recent critique of postmodernism from a black feminist perspective (2000).

8. The term *subaltern* is derived from the work of Marxist theorist Antonio Gramsci (1891–1937) and later developed by theorists such as Gayatri Spivak to mean any group disenfranchised on the basis of race, class, gender, and so forth. For excellent discussions of the history and themes of postcolonialism during the 1990s, see Narayan 1997 and Mills 1998.

9. See Gupta and Ferguson 1997 and Strauss 1997 for a fuller discussion.

10. See Manning 1995.

11. See Behar and Gordon 1995 for an excellent discussion and critique.

12. See Whitaker and Downe 2011 for an interesting critique of this moment.

13. See Jones in Pendle 1991; Robertson and Koskoff in Solie 1993; Weiss and Payne in Marshall 1993; Tolbert in Dunn and Jones 1994; and Zheng in Barkin and Hamessley 1999 for some examples.

14. See, for example, among others, McClary 1991; Lewis 1990; Walser 1993; Brett, Wood, and Thomas 1994; Cook and Tsou 1994; Nehring 1997; Whiteley 1997; and Rose 1994.

15. I have edited this list somewhat in the interests of brevity and clarity.

Chapter 5. Gender, Power, and Music

Reprinted with permission from *The Musical Woman: An International Perspective,* vol. 3, *1986–1990,* edited by Judith Laing Zaimont, 769–88 (Westport, Conn.: Greenwood Press, 1990).

1. If we look at the bigger picture, male musicians are also regarded, virtually everywhere, as somewhat out of the mainstream. Many have reputations as bad marriage risks and as sexual aggressors (considered a must in such traditions as rock), and only a few receive real economic independence. It is clear that musicians, as a

separate class, are generally prohibited in most societies from gaining total social and economic acceptance. Female musicians who perform publicly, though, tend to be devalued far more than male musicians and are often thought of in many societies, even today, as similar to prostitutes.

Chapter 6. Miriam Sings Her Song

Reprinted with permission from *Musicology and Difference: Gender and Sexuality in Music Scholarship,* edited by Ruth A. Solie © 1993 by the Regents of the University of California (Berkeley: University of California Press).

1. The masculine plural of *Ba'al Teshuvah* is *Ba'alei Teshuvah,* the feminine singular is *Ba'alat Teshuvah,* and the feminine plural is *Ba'alot Teshuvah.*

2. Orthodox Jews follow all the commandments as set forth in the first five books of the Bible, not only the ten given by God to Moses. There are 365 negative and 248 positive commandments.

3. In Hebrew writings, long vowels are generally omitted, and occasionally definite articles are not given. Thus, the interpretation of texts is often problematic and over the centuries has provided much grist from the scholarly mill.

4. This social and musical hierarchy is presented in a more detailed form in Koskoff 1987b.

5. Indeed, this is the view of many Jewish feminists who have in recent years challenged the historical and legal bases of many of these restrictive laws by becoming rabbis, cantors, and other synagogue and community leaders.

6. See Clifford and Marcus 1986 and Shostak 1981. For a good description and some sample readings in the new ethnography, see Mascia-Lees, Sharpe, and Cohen 1989.

7. However, the very act of having observed and perhaps participated in this scene attests to its implicit value as data.

Chapter 7. The Language of the Heart

Reprinted with permission from *New World Hasidim: Ethnographic Studies of Hasidic Jews in America,* edited by Janet Belcove-Shalin (Albany: State University of New York Press, 1995). All rights reserved.

1. Lubavitchers do not keep accurate statistics on their total population or on the relative size of these two groups. Informally, however, most Lubavitchers agree that with the unprecedented influx of Ba'alei Teshuvah since the late 1960s, this group now outnumbers those who have been Orthodox from birth.

2. For a fuller description of this movement, see Harris 1985 and Steinsaltz 1982.

3. Two recent books present different sides of this controversy: Davidman 1991 and Kaufman 1991.

4. For a fuller explanation of *kol isha* in relation to musical performance, see Cherney 1985 and Koskoff 1976.

5. The word *ervah* in Maimonides's interpretation referred only to a woman of the "forbidden unions," that is, one who was not likely to become a marriage partner, one with whom a man might establish an illicit relationship. Thus, men may listen to their

wives and premenstrual daughters sing. In addition, men may listen to an unmarried woman, with whom a marital relationship could be possible, as well as one's wife while she is a *niddah* (a menstruant)—because sexual intercourse would soon be possible.

6. Mrs. Nadoff resides in Pittsburgh. She has for many years taught in the Lubavitch school there, although she is not herself a Lubavitcher.

Chapter 8. When Women Play

Reprinted with permission from *Canadian University Music Review* 16, no. 1 (1995): 114–27, edited by Regula Berckhart Qureshi.

1. It may seem obvious that male children become men and female children become women, yet examples of the crossing of these two categories exist in the literature. For instance, it is well known that among certain Native American groups, a child of one biological sex is occasionally raised to become the opposite gender so that a young female, socialized to be a man, will take on various masculine behaviors, such as hunting. She may even marry a female, although it is unclear whether such couples engage in homosexual or heterosexual behavior (Allen 1986, 198–200). These so-called midgender roles are common in many societies, and their connection to music awaits further study.

2. See, for example, V. Turner 1969; Basso 1987; and Roseman 1987.

3. See Gourlay 1975; Basso 1987; Murphy and Murphy 1974; and Turnbull 1987.

4. Peggy Reeves Sanday (1981) has characterized merged societies as inner oriented, focusing on the importance of fertility and reproductive powers, while societies at the other end, which she calls outer oriented, are characterized by power, domination, and killing.

5. See Dinnerstein 1976 for an especially cogent examination of this ideology.

6. My female students at Eastman tell me that even today, they will wear heavy shoes at a screened audition, will walk behind the screen with a "male" stride, and will breathe quietly so as not to reveal their gender. Many have told me of the judges' surprise upon finding out they were female when the screen was lifted for the final audition round.

Chapter 9. "Well, That's Why We Won't Take You, Okay?"

1. I am indebted here to the work of sociolinguist Dell Hymes (1974) and others on the ethnography of communication.

2. This scene (but not its analysis) appears in Koskoff 2001.

3. I should point out here that the construction of Miriam I am presenting in this analysis is based on knowledge that I gained about her and about Lubavitcher women generally, not only at the time of the original conversation, but also through many later conversations and through Miriam's own critique of my portrait of her.

Chapter 10. Unresolved Issues

1. See Modleski 1991 for a good discussion of this term.

2. For an excellent and thorough examination of these and other current feminist threads, see "Feminisms at a Millennium" 2000.

3. This article presents a lively discussion of the culture wars in the 1990s.

4. http://science.jrank.org/pages/9469/Gender-Studies-Anthropology-Reping-Ritual-Idea-Performativity.html#ixzz1TgXQwApw.

5. See Kearney 1997 for an especially helpful discussion of the riot-grrrl phenomenon and Keenan 2008 for a lively examination of the intersections of heterosexuality, race, and class in the third wave.

6. See especially Karlyn 2003 and Yamamoto 2000.

7. See also Ramsey 2001 for a parallel discussion within historical musicology.

Chapter 11. The Ins and Outs on In and Out

1. Ba'alei Teshuvah (Masters of Repentance), often referred to (lovingly) by Lubavitchers as BTs, are those who come to Hasidic life as adults.

2. Chana was the first name of the current rebbe's wife.

Chapter 12. Out in Left Field/Left Out of the Field

Reprinted with permission from *Women and Music: A Journal of Gender and Culture* (University of Nebraska Press) 9 (2006).

1. See Bohlman 2009 for an excellent discussion of this topic.

2. See, for example, Crawford 2001, Hamm 1983, and many others on American popular musics.

3. See, for example, Locke 1986, 2011; and Said 1978.

4. Malm 1959 and Hood 1980.

5. See Nettl 1995; Kingsbury 1988; and Sherinian 2000.

6. See Shostak 1981 and Erdrich 1984 for some good examples.

7. To get at the heart and soul of the fieldwork experience, I recommend a wonderful book, *The Wind in a Jar*, by John Farella (1993).

8. See Mascia-Lees, Sharpe, and Cohen 1989; and Mascia-Lees and Black 2000.

Chapter 13. Imaginary Conversations

1. I am indebted to my colleague Jennifer Kyker for this wonderfully evocative word.

2. I am using the print characters <> to show in a more visual way the interactive and overlapping nature of sameness and difference classes.

3. See also my "Afterword" (2013) in Hellier for an example of sameness<>difference flipping.

4. I am thankful to Moisala 1999 for the presentation of five musical ontologies in her article on musical gender, upon which this is partially based.

References

Abbate, Carolyn. 1993. "Opera; or, The Envoicing of Women." In *Musicology and Difference: Gender and Sexuality in Music Scholarship,* edited by Ruth A. Solie, 225–58. Berkeley: University of California Press.

Abu-Lughod, Lila. 1990. "Can There Be a Feminist Ethnography?" *Women and Performance* 5 (1): 7–27.

Adams, Richard N. 1977. "Power in Human Societies: A Synthesis." In *The Anthropology of Power: Ethnographic Studies from Asia, Oceania, and the New World,* edited by Raymond Fogelson and Richard N. Adams, 387–410. New York: Academic Press.

Adler, Guido. 1988. "Umfang, Methode und Ziel der Musikwissenschaft." In *Music in European Thought, 1851–1912,* edited by Bojan Bujic, 348–55. Cambridge Readings in the Literature of Music. Cambridge: Cambridge University Press.

Alcoff, Linda Martín. 2000. "Philosophy Matters: A Review of Recent Work in Feminist Philosophy." *Signs* 25 (3): 841–82.

———. 2006. *Visible Identities: Race, Gender, and the Self.* Oxford: Oxford University Press.

Allen, Paula Gunn. 1986. *The Sacred Hoop: Recovering the Feminine in American Indian Traditions.* Boston: Beacon.

Ames, David W. 1973. "Igbo and Hausa Musicians: A Comparative Examination." *Ethnomusicology* 17 (2): 250–78.

Ammer, Christine. 1980. *Unsung: A History of Women in American Music.* Contributions in Women's Studies 14. Westport, Conn.: Greenwood Press.

Anderson, Elizabeth. 2011. "Feminist Social Epistemology." In *Stanford Encyclopedia of Philosophy.* http://plato.stanford.edu/archives/win2003/entries/davidson/.

Antelis, M. 1990. *Radical Rappin' Rebbes.* Mantelis Records Studio, R3 Productions, 3242.

Aparicio, Frances R. 2002. "Toward a Feminist Genealogy of Salsa Music." In *Situating Salsa: Global Markets and Local Meaning in Latin Pop Music,* edited by Lise Waxer. New York: Routledge.

Appadurai, Arjun. 1990. "Disjuncture and Difference in the Global Cultural Economy." *Public Culture* 2 (2): 1–24.

Ardener, Edwin. 1975a. "Belief and the Problem of Women." In *Perceiving Women,* edited by Shirley Ardener, 1–18. London: Malaby.

———. 1975b. "The 'Problem' Revisited." In *Perceiving Women,* edited by Shirley Ardener, 19–28. London: Malaby.

Armstrong, Aurelia. 2005. "Foucault and Feminism." In *Internet Encyclopedia of Philosophy.* Article last modified July 8. http://www.iep.utm.edu.

Asad, Talal, ed. 1973. *Anthropology and the Colonial Encounter.* Atlantic Highlands, N.J.: Humanities Press.

Atkinson, Jane Monnig. 1982. "Anthropology." *Signs: Journal of Women in Culture and Society* 8 (2): 236–58.

Auerbach, Susan. 1987. "From Singing to Lamenting: Women's Musical Role in a Greek Village." In *Women and Music in Cross-Cultural Perspective,* edited by Ellen Koskoff, 25–43. Westport, Conn.: Greenwood Press.

Austin, J. L. 1975. *How to Do Things with Words.* 2nd ed. Oxford: Oxford University Press.

Avery, Thomas L. 1977. "Mamaindé Vocal Music." *Ethnomusicology* 21 (3): 359–77.

Avishur, Yitzhak, ed. and trans. 1987. *Women's Folk Songs in Judeo-Arabic from Jews in Iraq.* Or Yehuda, Israel: Iraqi Jews Traditional Culture Center.

Babiracki, Carol. 1997. "What's the Difference? Reflections on Gender and Research in Village India." In *Shadows in the Field: New Perspectives for Fieldwork in Ethnomusicology,* edited by Gregory F. Barz and Timothy J. Cooley, 121–38. 2nd ed. New York: Oxford University Press.

Barkin, Elaine, and Lydia Hamessley, eds. 1999. *Audible Traces: Gender, Identity, and Music.* Zurich: Carciofoli Verlagshaus.

Bartók, Béla, and Albert Lord. 1951. *Serbo-Croatian Folk Songs.* New York: Columbia University Press.

Barwick, Linda. 1990. "Central Australian Women's Ritual Music: Knowing through Analysis versus Knowing through Performance." *Yearbook for Traditional Music* 22: 60–79.

Barz, Gregory F., and Timothy J. Cooley. 2008. "Casting Shadows: Fieldwork Is Dead! Long Live Fieldwork!" Introduction to *Shadows in the Field: New Perspectives for Fieldwork in Ethnomusicology,* edited by Gregory F. Barz and Timothy J. Cooley, 3–24. 2nd ed. New York: Oxford University Press.

Basso, Ellen B. 1987. "Musical Expression and Gender Identity in the Myth and Ritual of the Kalapalo of Central Brazil." In *Women and Music in Cross-Cultural Perspective,* edited by Ellen Koskoff, 163–76. Westport, Conn.: Greenwood Press.

Bauman, Richard, and Charles L. Briggs. 1990. "Poetics and Performance as Critical Perspectives on Language and Social Life." *Annual Review of Anthropology* 19: 59–88.

Baumgardner, Jennifer, and Amy Richards. 2000. *Manifesta: Young Women, Feminism, and the Future.* New York: Farrar, Straus, and Giroux.

Beauvoir, Simone de. 1953. *The Second Sex.* Translated and edited by H. M. Parshley. Reprint, New York: Vintage Books, 1989.

Becker, Judith. 1988. "Earth, Fire, *Sakti,* and the Javanese Gamelan." *Ethnomusicology* 32 (3): 385–91.

———. 2004. *Deep Listeners: Music, Emotion, and Trancing.* Bloomington: Indiana University Press.

Behar, Ruth, and Deborah A. Gordon. 1995. *Women Writing Culture.* Berkeley: University of California Press.

Bell, Diane. 1981. "Women's Business Is Hard Work." *Signs* 7: 314–37.

———. 1993. "Introduction 1: The Context." In *Gendered Fields: Women, Men, and Ethnography,* edited by Diane Bell, Patricia Caplan, and Wazir Jahan Karim, 1–18. London: Routledge.

Bender, Wolfgang. 1991. "Great Female Singers: Mali." In *Sweet Mother: Modern African Music.* Translated by Wolfgang Freis. Chicago Studies in Ethnomusicology. Chicago: University of Chicago Press.

Berger, Harris M. 2008. "Phenomenology and the Ethnography of Popular Music: Ethnomusicology at the Juncture of Cultural Studies and Folklore." In *Shadows in the Field: New Perspectives for Fieldwork in Ethnomusicology,* edited by Gregory Barz and Timothy J. Cooley. 2nd ed. Oxford: Oxford University Press.

Bergeron, Katherine, and Philip V. Bohlman, eds. 1992. *Disciplining Music: Musicology and Its Canons.* Chicago: University of Chicago Press.

Bernstein, Jane A., ed. 2004. *Women's Voices across Musical Worlds.* Boston: Northeastern University Press.

Berry, Venise. 1994. "Feminine or Masculine: The Conflicting Nature of Female Images in Rap Music." In *Cecilia Reclaimed: Feminist Perspectives on Gender and Music,* edited by Susan C. Cook and Judy S. Tsou. Urbana: University of Illinois Press.

Blacking, John. 1962. "Musical Expeditions of the Venda." *African Music: Journal of the African Music Society* 3 (1): 54–72.

———. 1976. "The Value of Musical Experience in Venda Society." *World of Music* 18 (2): 23–28.

———, ed. 1977. *The Anthropology of the Body.* Association of Social Anthropologists of the Commonwealth. London: Academic Press.

Bloch, Adrienne, and Carol Neuls-Bates. 1979. *Women in American Music: A Bibliography of Music and Literature.* Westport, Conn.: Greenwood Press.

Blumer, Herbert. 1969. *Symbolic Interaction: Perspective and Method.* Englewood Cliffs, N.J.: Prentice Hall.

Bohlman, Philip V. 2009. *The Music of European Nationalism: Cultural Identity and Modern History.* 2nd ed. New York: Routledge.

Borroff, Edith. 1982. "A Conference on Women in Music: A Progress Report." *College Music Symposium* (College Music Society) 22 (2): 161–65.

Bourdieu, Pierre. 1977. *Outline of a Theory of Practice.* Translated by Richard Nice. Cambridge: Cambridge University Press.

Bowers, Jane, and Judith Tick, eds. 1986. *Women Making Music: The Western Art Tradition, 1150–1950.* 2nd ed. Urbana: University of Illinois Press.

Brett, Philip, Elizabeth Wood, and Gary C. Thomas, eds. 1994. *Queering the Pitch: The New Gay and Lesbian Musicology.* New York: Routledge.

Briggs, Charles L. 1993. "Personal Sentiments and Polyphonic Voices in Warao Women's Ritual Wailing: Music and Poetics in a Critical and Collective Discourse." *American Anthropologist* 95: 929–57.

Brown, Penelope, and L. J. Jordanova. 1981. "Oppressive Dichotomies: The Nature/Culture Debate." In *Women in Society: Interdisciplinary Essays,* edited by the Cambridge Women's Studies Group, 224–41. London: Virago.

Brownmiller, Susan. 1975. *Against Our Will: Men, Women, and Rape.* New York: Simon and Schuster.

———. 1984. *Femininity.* New York: Simon and Schuster.

Bufwack, Mary A., and Robert K. Oermann. 1993. *Finding Her Voice: The Saga of Women in Country Music.* New York: Crown.

Burns, Lori, and Mélisse Lafrance. 2001. *Disruptive Divas: Feminism, Identity, and Popular Music.* New York: Routledge.

Burrows, Edwin Grant. 1958. "Music on Ifaluk Atoll in the Caroline Islands." *Ethnomusicology* 2 (1): 9–22.

Butler, Judith P. 1990. *Gender Trouble: Feminism and the Subversion of Identity.* New York: Routledge.

———. 1993. *Bodies That Matter: On the Discursive Limits of "Sex."* New York: Routledge.

———. 1996. "Gender as Performance." In *A Critical Sense: Interviews with Intellectuals,* edited by Peter Osborne. New York: Routledge.

Cadar, Usopay H. 1973. "The Role of Kulintang Music in Maranao Society." *Ethnomusicology* 17 (2): 234–50.

Campbell, Carol A., and Carol M. Eastman. 1984. "Ngoma: Swahili Adult Song Performance in Context." *Ethnomusicology* 28 (3): 467–93.

Campbell, K. H. 1985. "Saudi Arabian Women's Music." *Habibi* 9: 33–59.

Caraveli-Chaves, Anna. 1980. "Bridge between Worlds: The Greek Women's Lament as Communicative Event." *Journal of American Folklore* 93 (368): 129–57.

Carby, Hazel V. 1991. "In Body and Spirit: Representing Black Women Musicians." *Black Music Research Journal* 11 (2): 177–92.

Carlisle, Roxane Connick. 1973. "Women Singers in Darfur, Sudan Republic." *Anthropos* 68, facs. 516: 785–814. Reprinted in *The Garland Library of Readings in Ethnomusicology.* Vol. 7, *A Century of Ethnomusicological Thought,* edited by Kay Kaufman Shelemay. New York: Garland, 1990.

Cavanagh, Beverley. 1989. "Music and Gender in the Sub-Arctic Algonkian Area." In *Women in North American Indian Music,* edited by Richard Keeling, 55–67. Special Series 6. Bloomington, Ind.: Society for Ethnomusicology.

Cheater, Angela P. 1995. "Globalization and the New Technologies of Knowing: Anthropological Calculus or Chaos?" In *Shifting Contexts: Transformations in Anthropological Knowledge,* edited by Marilyn Strathern, 117–27. London: Routledge.

Cherney, Ben. 1985. "Kol Isha." *Journal of Halacha and Contemporary Society* 10: 57–75.

Chesler, Phyllis. 1972. *Women and Madness.* New York: Doubleday.

Chodorow, Nancy. 1971. "Being and Doing: A Cross-Cultural Examination of the Socialization of Males and Females." In *Woman in Sexist Society: Studies in Power and Powerlessness,* edited by Vivian Gornick and Barbara K. Moran, 173–97. New York: Basic Books.

———. 1974. "Family Structure and Feminine Personality." In *Women, Culture, and Society,* edited by Michelle Zimbalist Rosaldo and Louise Lamphere, 43–66. Stanford, Calif.: Stanford University Press.

Chuse, Loren. 2003. *The Cantaoras: Music, Gender, and Identity in Flamenco Song.* New York: Routledge.

Citron, Marcia J. 1993. *Gender and the Musical Canon.* Cambridge: Cambridge University Press.

Clément, Catherine. 1988. *Opera; or, The Undoing of Women.* Translated by Betsy Wing. Minneapolis: University of Minneapolis Press.

Clifford, James. 1986. "Introduction: Partial Truths." In *Writing Culture: The Poetics and Politics of Ethnography,* edited by James Clifford and George E. Marcus. Berkeley: University of California Press.

———. 1988. *The Predicament of Culture: Twentieth-Century Ethnography, Literature, and Art.* Cambridge, Mass.: Harvard University Press.

Clifford, James, and George E. Marcus, eds. 1986. *Writing Culture: The Poetics and Politics of Ethnography.* Berkeley: University of California Press.

Coaldrake, A. Kimi. 1996. *Women's Gidayu and the Japanese Theatre Tradition.* New York: Routledge.

Code, Lorraine, ed. 2000. *Encyclopedia of Feminist Theories.* New York: Routledge.

Cole, Sally, and Lynne Phillips. 1995. *Ethnographic Feminisms: Essays in Anthropology.* Women's Experience Series. Montreal: McGill-Queen's University Press.

Collins, Patricia Hill. 2000. "What's Going On? Black Feminist Thought and the Politics of Postmodernism." In *Working the Ruins: Feminist Poststructural Theory and Methods in Education,* edited by Elizabeth St. Pierre and Wanda S. Pillow, 41–74. New York: Routledge.

Collins, Patricia Hill, and Margaret Anderson. 1992. *Creating Race, Class, and Gender: An Anthology.* New York: Wadsworth.

Conboy, Katie, et al. 1997. *Writing on the Body: Female Embodiment and Feminist Theory.* Cambridge: Cambridge University Press.

Cook, Susan C., and Judy S. Tsou, eds. 1994. *Cecilia Reclaimed: Feminist Perspectives on Gender and Music.* Urbana: University of Illinois Press.

Coote, Mary P. 1977. "Women's Songs in Serbo-Croatian." *Journal of American Folklore* 90: 331–38.

Cormier, Holly, comp. 1978. *Women and Folk Music: A Select Bibliography.* Washington, D.C.: Smithsonian Institution Press.

Covell, Alan. 1986. *Folk Art and Magic: Shamanism in Korea.* Seoul: Hollym.

Crawford, Richard. 2001. *America's Musical Life: A History.* New York: W. W. Norton.

Cucchiari, Salvatore. 1981. "The Gender Revolution and the Transition from Bisexual Horde to Patrilocal Band: The Origins of Gender Hierarchy." In *Sexual Meanings: The Cultural Construction of Gender and Sexuality,* edited by Sherry B. Ortner and Harriet Whitehead, 31–79. Cambridge: Cambridge University Press.

Cusick, Suzanne. 1994. "On a Lesbian Relationship with Music: A Serious Effort Not to Think Straight." In *Queering the Pitch: The New Gay and Lesbian Musicology*, edited by Philip Brett, Elizabeth Wood, and Gary C. Thomas, 67–83. New York: Routledge.

———. 1995. Personal communication. September.

———. 1999. "On Musical Performance of Gender and Sex." In *Audible Traces: Gender, Identity, and Music*, edited by Elaine Barkin and Lydia Hamessley. Zurich: Carciofoli Verlagshaus.

Danielson, Virginia. 1997. *The Voice of Egypt: Umm Kulthum, Arabic Song, and Egyptian Society in the Twentieth Century*. Chicago Studies in Ethnomusicology. Chicago: University of Chicago Press.

———. 1999. "Moving toward Public Space: Women and Musical Performance in Twentieth-Century Egypt." In *Hermeneutics and Honor: Negotiating Female "Public" Space in Islamic/ate Societies*, edited by Asma Afsaruddin, 116–39. Cambridge, Mass.: Harvard University Press.

Davidman, Lynn. 1991. *Tradition in a Rootless World: Women Turn to Orthodox Judaism*. Chicago: University of Chicago Press.

Davis, Angela Y. 1981. *Women, Race, and Class*. New York: Random House.

Densmore, Frances. 1910–13. *Chippewa Music*. 2 vols. Smithsonian Institution Bureau of American Ethnology Bulletin 45 and 53. Washington, D.C.: Government Printing Office.

Derrida, Jacques. 1976. *Of Grammatology*. 1st American ed. Baltimore: Johns Hopkins University Press.

Dinnerstein, Dorothy. 1976. *The Mermaid and the Minotaur: Sexual Arrangements and Human Malaise*. New York: HarperCollins.

DjeDje, Jacqueline Codgell. 1985. "Women and Music in Sudanic Africa." In *More than Drumming: Essays on African and Afro-Latin American Music and Musicians*, edited by Irene Jackson, 67–89. Westport, Conn.: Greenwood Press.

Doubleday, Veronica. 1990. *Three Women of Herat*. Austin: University of Texas Press.

———. 1999. "The Frame Drum in the Middle East: Women, Musical Instruments, and Power." *Ethnomusicology* 43 (1): 101–34.

———. 2008. "Sounds of Power: An Overview of Musical Instruments and Gender." Special issue, *Ethnomusicology Forum: Journal of the British Forum for Ethnomusicology* 17 (1): 3–39.

Drinker, Sophie. 1948. *Music and Women: The Story of Women in Their Relation to Music*. New York: Coward-McCann.

Driscoll, Margarette. 2008. "The Day Feminist Icon Alice Walker Resigned as My Mother." *New York Times*, Sunday ed., May 4.

Dunn, Leslie C., and Nancy A. Jones, eds. 1994. *Embodied Voices: Representing Female Vocality in Western Culture*. Cambridge: Cambridge University Press.

Dworkin, Andrea. 1981. *Pornography: Men Possessing Women*. London: Women's Press.

Dworkin, Andrea, and Catharine A. MacKinnon. 1988. *Pornography and Civil Rights: A New Day for Women's Equality*. Minneapolis: Organizing against Pornography.

Eliade, Mircea. 1964. *Shamanism: Archaic Techniques of Ecstasy.* Princeton, N.J.: Princeton University Press.

Ellis, C. J., and L. Barwick. 1990. "Antikirinja Women's Song Knowledge, 1963–1972: Its Significance in Antikirinja Culture." In *Women, Rites, and Sites: Aboriginal Women's Cultural Knowledge,* edited by Peggy Brock, 21–40. Sydney: Allen & Unwin.

El-Mallah, Issam. 1997. *The Role of Women in Omani Musical Life.* Tutzing, Germany: Hans Schneider Verlag.

Elson, Arthur, and Everett E. Truette. 1903. *Woman's Work in Music: Being an Account of Her Influence on the Art, in Ancient as Well as Modern Times.* Boston: L. C. Page.

Engels, Friedrich. 1942. *The Origin of the Family, Private Property, and the State.* Translated by Alec West. Edited by Eleanor Burke Leacock. New York: International Publishers, 1972.

Enslin, Elizabeth. 1994. "Beyond Writing: Feminist Practice and the Limitations of Ethnography." *Cultural Anthropology* 9 (4): 537–68.

Erdrich, Louise. 1984. *Love Medicine.* New York: Bantam Books.

Ericson, Margaret D. 1996. *Women and Music: A Selective Annotated Bibliography on Women and Gender Issues in Music, 1987–1992.* New York: G. K. Hall.

Erlmann, Veit. 1999. *Music, Modernity, and the Global Imagination: South Africa and the West.* New York: Oxford University Press.

Evans-Pritchard, E. E. 1951. *Social Anthropology.* London: Cohen and West.

Falk, Nancy A., and Rita M. Gross, eds. 1980. *Unspoken Worlds: Women's Religious Lives in Non-Western Cultures.* New York: Harper and Row.

Farella, John R. 1993. *The Wind in a Jar.* Albuquerque: University of New Mexico Press.

Farrer, Claire R. 1975. Introduction to *Women and Folklore,* edited by Claire R. Farrer, vii–xvii. American Folklore Society Series 28. Austin: University of Texas Press.

Feld, Steven. 1982. *Sound and Sentiment: Birds, Weeping, Poetics, and Song in Kaluli Expression.* Philadelphia: University of Pennsylvania Press.

"Feminisms at a Millennium." 2000. Special issue, *Signs* 25 (4).

Fenton, William N., ed. 1951. *Symposium on Local Diversity in Iroquois Culture.* Bureau of American Ethnology Bulletin 149. Washington, D.C.: Government Printing Office, Smithsonian Institution Press.

Finn, Geraldine. 1993. "Why Are There No Great Women Postmodernists?" In *Relocating Cultural Studies: Developments in Theory and Research,* edited by Valda Blundell, John Shepherd, and Ian Taylor, 123–54. London: Routledge.

Fletcher, Alice C., and Francis La Flesche. 1911. *The Omaha Tribe.* Smithsonian Institution Bureau of American Ethnology Annual Report 27. Washington, D.C.: Smithsonian Institution Press.

Fogelson, Raymond, and Richard N. Adams, eds. 1977. *The Anthropology of Power: Ethnographic Studies from Asia, Oceania, and the New World.* New York: Academic Press.

Foucault, Michel. 1972. *The Archaeology of Knowledge and the Discourse of Language.* Translated by A. M. Sheridan Smith. New York: Pantheon Books.

———. 1977. *Power and Knowledge: Selected Interviews and Other Writings, 1972–1977.* Edited by Colin Gordon. New York: Pantheon Books.

———. 1978. *History of Sexuality.* Vol. 1, *An Introduction.* Translated by Robert Hurley. New York: Random House.

———. 1995. *Discipline and Punish.* 2nd ed. New York: Vintage.

Fraser, Jane. 1984. *Women Composers: A Discography.* Detroit: Information Coordinators.

Fraser, Nancy. 1989. *Unruly Practices: Power, Discourse, and Gender in Contemporary Social Theory.* Minneapolis: University of Minnesota Press.

Frazer, James George. 1909. *Psyche's Task: A Discourse Concerning the Influence of Superstition on the Growth of Institutions.* London: Macmillan.

———. 1910. *Totemism and Exogamy: A Treatise on Certain Early Forms of Superstition and Society.* London: Macmillan.

Friedan, Betty. 1963. *The Feminine Mystique.* New York: W. W. Norton.

Friedl, Ernestine. 1967. "The Position of Women: Appearance and Reality." *Anthropological Quarterly* 40 (3): 97–108.

———. 1975. *Women and Men: An Anthropologist's View.* New York: Holt, Rinehart, and Winston.

Friedson, Steven M. 1996. *Dancing Prophets: Musical Experience in Tumbuka Healing.* Chicago: University of Chicago Press.

Frisbie, Charlotte J. 1967. *Kinaalda: A Study of the Navajo Girl's Puberty Ceremony.* Middletown, Conn.: Wesleyan University Press.

———. 1980. "Vocables in Navajo Ceremonial Music." *Ethnomusicology* 24 (3): 347–92.

———. 1989. "Gender and Navajo Music: Unanswered Questions." In *Women in North American Indian Music: Six Essays,* edited by Richard Keeling, 22–38. Special Series 6. Bloomington, Ind.: Society for Ethnomusicology.

———. 1991. "Women and the Society for Ethnomusicology: Roles and Contributions from Formation through Incorporation (1952/53–1961)." In *Comparative Musicology and Anthropology of Music: Essays on the History of Ethnomusicology,* edited by Bruno Nettl and Philip V. Bohlman, 244–65. Chicago: University of Chicago Press.

Frith, Simon, and Angela McRobbie. 1978. "Rock and Sexuality." *Screen Education* 29: 3–19.

Fritsch, Ingrid. 1992. "Blind Female Musicians on the Road: The Social Organization of 'Goze' in Japan." *CHIME: European Foundation for Chinese Music Research* 5 (March): 58–64.

Fuller, S. Margaret. 1845. *Woman in the Nineteenth Century.* New York: Greeley & McElrath.

Fuller, Sophie, and Lloyd Whitesell, eds. 2002. *Queer Episodes in Music and Modern Identity.* Urbana: University of Illinois Press.

Ganzfried, Solomon. 1963. *Code of Jewish Law* [Kitzur Shulhan Arukh]: *A Compilation of Jewish Laws and Customs.* Translated by Hyman E. Goldin. Rockaway Beach, N.Y.: Hebrew Publishing.

Geertz, Clifford. 1967. *Interaction Ritual: Essays on Face-to-Face Behavior.* New York: Anchor Books.

———. 1988. *Works and Lives: The Anthropologist as Author.* Stanford, Calif.: Stanford University Press.

Gergis, Sonia. 1993. "The Power of Women Musicians in the Ancient and Near East: The Roots of Prejudice." *British Journal of Music Education* 10 (3): 189–96.

Gerson-Kiwi, Edith. 1950. "Wedding Dances and Songs of the Jews of Bokhara." *Journal of the International Folk Music Council* 2: 17–18.

Giglio, Virginia. 1994. *Southern Cheyenne Women's Songs.* Norman: University of Oklahoma Press.

Gilkes, Cheryl Townsend. 1985. "'Together and in Harness': Women's Traditions in the Sanctified Church." *Signs* 10 (4): 678–99. Reprinted in *Black Women in America: Social Science Perspectives,* edited by Micheline R. Malson, Elisabeth Mudimbe-Boyi, Jean F. O'Barr, and Mary Wyer, 223–44. Chicago: University of Chicago Press, 1990.

Gilligan, Carol. 1982. *In a Different Voice: Psychological Theory and Women's Development.* Cambridge, Mass.: Harvard University Press.

Gillis, Stacy, et al. 2007. Introduction to *Third Wave Feminism: A Critical Exploration,* edited by Stacy Gillis et al., xxi–xxxiv. 2nd ed. New York: Palgrave Macmillan.

Goffman, Erving. 1959. *The Presentation of Self in Everyday Life.* New York: Doubleday, Anchor Books.

Goodale, Jane C. 1971. *Tiwi Wives: A Study of the Women of Melville Island, North Australia.* Seattle: University of Washington Press.

Goode, Gloria Davis. 1990. "Preachers of the Word and Singers of the Gospel: The Ministry of Women among Nineteenth Century African-Americans." Ph.D. diss., University of Pennsylvania.

Gornick, Vivian, and Barbara K. Moran. 1971. Introduction to *Woman in Sexist Society: Studies in Power and Powerlessness,* edited by Vivian Gornick and Barbara K. Moran. New York: Basic Books.

Gourlay, Ken A. 1970. "Trees and Anthills: Songs of Karimojong Women's Groups." *African Music* 4 (4): 114–21.

———. 1975. *Sound-Producing Instruments in Traditional Society: A Study of Esoteric Instruments and Their Role in Male-Female Relations.* Port Moresby: New Guinea Research Unit, Australian National University.

Grame, Theodore C. 1962. "Bamboo and Music: A New Approach to Organology." *Ethnomusicology* 6 (1): 8–14.

Greer, Germaine. 1970. *The Female Eunuch.* New York: Farrar, Straus, and Giroux.

Grosz, Elizabeth. 1994. *Volatile Bodies: Toward a Corporeal Feminism.* Bloomington: Indiana University Press.

Gupta, Akhil, and James Ferguson. 1997. "Discipline and Practice: 'The Field' as Site, Method, and Location in Anthropology." In *Anthropological Locations: Boundaries and Grounds of a Field Science,* edited by Akhil Gupta and James Ferguson, 1–46. Berkeley: University of California Press.

Hahn, Tomie. 2007. *Sensational Knowledge: Embodying Culture through Japanese Dance.* Middletown, Conn.: Wesleyan University Press.

Halperin, David. 2005. "The Normalizing of Queer Theory." *Journal of Homosexuality* 45: 343.

Hamm, Charles. 1983. *Music in the New World.* New York: W. W. Norton.

Hampton, Barbara. 1982. "Music and Ritual Symbolism in the Ga Funeral." *Yearbook for Traditional Music* 14: 75–105.

Handelman, S. S. 1981. "On Being Single and Jewish." In *The Modern Jewish Woman.* Brooklyn: Lubavitch Educational Foundation for Jewish Marriage Enrichment.

Handler, Richard. 1998. "Raymond Williams, George Stocking, and Fin-de-Siecle U.S. Anthropology." *Cultural Anthropology* 13 (4): 447–63.

Haraway, Donna. 1988. "Situated Knowledges: The Science Question in Feminism and the Privilege of Partial Perspective." *Feminist Studies* 14 (3): 575–99.

Harding, Sandra. 1986. *The Science Question in Feminism.* Ithaca, N.Y.: Cornell University Press.

Harris, Lis. 1985. *Holy Days: The World of the Hasidic Family.* New York: Touchstone.

Harris, Marvin. 1964. *The Nature of Cultural Things.* New York: Random House.

Harvey, Youngsook Kim. 1980. "Possession Sickness and Women Shamans in Korea." In *Unspoken Worlds: Women's Religious Lives in Non-Western Cultures,* edited by Nancy A. Falk and Rita M. Gross, 41–52. San Francisco: Harper and Row.

Hatton, Orin T. 1986. "In the Tradition: Grass Dance Musical Style and Female Pow-Wow Singers." *Ethnomusicology* 30 (2): 197–222.

Hawes, Bess Lomax. 1974. "Folksongs and Function: Some Thoughts on the American Lullaby." *Journal of American Folklore* 87 (344): 140–48.

Hawkesworth, Mary. 1997. "Confounding Gender." *Signs* 22 (3): 649–85.

Hayes, Eileen M. 2006. "Theorizing Gender, Culture, and Music." *Women and Music: A Journal of Gender and Culture* 10: 71–79.

———. 2010. *Songs in Black and Lavender: Race, Sexual Politics, and Women's Music.* Urbana: University of Illinois Press.

Hayes, Eileen M., and Linda Williams, eds. 2007. *Black Women and Music: More than Just the Blues.* Urbana: University of Illinois Press.

Headland, Thomas N., Kenneth L. Pike, and Marvin Harris, eds. 1990. *Frontiers of Anthropology.* Vol. 7. Newbury Park, Calif.: Sage.

Hellier, Ruth. 2013. "Ixya Herrera: Gracefully Nurturing 'Mexico' with Song in the U.S.A." In *Female Singers in Contemporary Global Contexts,* edited by Ruth Hellier. Urbana: University of Illinois Press.

Hernandez, Deborah P. 1990. "Cantando la Cama Vacia: Love, Sexuality, and Gender Relationships in Dominican Bachata." *Popular Music* 9 (3): 351–67.

Herndon, Marcia. 1990. "Biology and Culture: Music, Gender, Power, and Ambiguity." In *Music, Gender, and Culture,* edited by Marcia Herndon and Susanne Ziegler, 11–26. Wilhelmshaven, Germany: Florian Noetzel Verlag.

———. 1993. "Insiders, Outsiders: Knowing Our Limits, Limiting Our Knowledge." *World of Music* 35 (1): 63–80.

———. 2000. "Epilogue: The Place of Gender within Complex, Dynamic Musical Systems." In *Music and Gender,* edited by Pirkko Moisala and Beverley Diamond, 347–60. Urbana: University of Illinois Press.

Herndon, Marcia, and Susanne Ziegler, eds. 1990. *Music, Gender, and Culture.* International Council for Traditional Music Study Group on Music and Gender. Wilhelmshaven, Germany: Florian Noetzel Verlag.

———. 1991. "Women in Music and Music Research." Special issue, *World of Music* 33 (2).

Heskes, Irene. 1992. "Miriam's Sisters: Jewish Women and Liturgical Music." *Notes* 48 (4): 1193–1202.

Heywood, Leslie, and Jennifer Drake. 2007. "'It's All about the Benjamins': Economic Determinants of Third Wave Feminism in the United States." In *Third Wave Feminism: A Critical Exploration,* edited by Stacy Gillis et al., 114–24. London: Palgrave Macmillan.

Hill, Jonathan. 1979. "Kamayura Flute Music: A Study of Music as Meta-Communication." *Ethnomusicology* 23 (3): 417–32.

Hoch-Smith, Judith, and Anita Spring. 1978. Introduction to *Women in Ritual and Symbolic Roles,* edited by Judith Hoch-Smith and Anita Spring, 1–23. New York: Plenum Press.

Hood, Mantle. 1980. Foreword to *Musics of Many Cultures: An Introduction,* edited by Elizabeth May. Berkeley: University of California Press.

hooks, bell. 1981. *Ain't I a Woman? Black Women and Feminism.* Cambridge, Mass.: South End Press.

———. 1984. *Feminist Theory: From Margin to Center.* Cambridge, Mass.: South End Press.

———. 1989. *Talking Back: Thinking Feminist, Thinking Black.* Toronto: Between the Lines Press.

———. 2000. *Feminism Is for Everybody: Passionate Politics.* Cambridge, Mass.: South End Press.

Howard, Judith A., and Carolyn Allen. 2000. "Feminisms at a Millennium." *Signs* 25 (4): xiii–xxx.

Huhm, Halla Pai. 1980. *Kut: Korean Shamanist Rituals.* Elizabeth, N.J.: Hollym International.

Hull, Gloria, Patricia Bell Scott, and Barbara Smith, eds. 1982. *All the Women Are White, All the Blacks Are Men, but Some of Us Are Brave.* Old Westbury, N.Y.: Feminist Press.

Hymes, Dell. 1974. *Foundations of Sociolinguistics: An Ethnographic Approach.* Philadelphia: University of Pennsylvania Press.

Jankovic, Danica S., and Ljubica S. Jankovic. 1962. "Serbian Folk Dance Tradition in Prizren." *Ethnomusicology* 6 (2): 115–25.

Jardine, Alice, and Paul Smith, eds. 1987. *Men in Feminism.* New York: Routledge.

Johnson, Anna. 1990. "The Sprite in the Water and the Siren of the Woods: On Swedish Folk Music and Gender." In *Music, Gender, and Culture,* edited by Marcia Herndon and Susanne Ziegler, 27–40. Wilhelmshaven, Germany: Florian Noetzel Verlag.

Jones, Alexander, ed. 1966. *The Jerusalem Bible*. Garden City, N.Y.: Doubleday.

Jones, Claire. 2008. "Shona Women Mbira Players: Gender, Tradition, and Nation in Zimbabwe." Special issue, "'Sounds of Power': Musical Instruments and Gender." *Ethnomusicology Forum* 17 (1): 125–39.

Jones, Judy. 1995. "Nez Perce Women, Music, and Cultural Change." *Women of Note Quarterly* 3 (3): 6–19.

Jones, L. JaFran. 1991. "Women in Non-Western Music." In *Women and Music: A History,* edited by Karin Pendle, 314–30. Bloomington: Indiana University Press.

Jordan, Rosan A., and Susan J. Kalçik, eds. 1985. *Women's Folklore, Women's Culture.* Philadelphia: University of Pennsylvania Press.

Joseph, Rosemary M. F. 1987. "Zulu Women's Bow Songs: Ruminations on Love." *Bulletin of the School of Oriental and African Studies* 50 (1): 90–119.

Joseph, Terri Brint. 1980. "Poetry as a Strategy of Power: The Case of Riffian Berber Women." *Signs* 5 (3): 418–34.

Junghare, Indira. 1983. "Songs of the Mahars: An Untouchable Caste of the Maharashtra, India." *Ethnomusicology* 27 (2): 271–95.

Kaeppler, Adrienne L. 1970. "Tongan Dance: A Study in Cultural Change." *Ethnomusicology* 14 (2): 266–77.

Kaeppler, Adrienne L., Linda Barwick, Helen Payne, Nancy C. Lutkehaus, James F. Weiner, and Judith Macdonald. 1998. "Music and Gender." In *The Garland Encyclopedia of World Music.* Vol. 9, *Australia and the Pacific,* edited by J. W. Love and Adrienne L. Kaeppler, 241–50. New York: Garland.

Kaplan, Judy, and Linn Shapiro. 1998. *Red Diapers: Growing Up in the Communist Left.* Urbana: University of Illinois Press.

Karlyn, Kathleen Rowe. 2003. "Scream, Popular Culture, and Feminism's Third Wave: 'I'm Not My Mother.'" *Genders* 38. http://www.genders.org/g38/g38_rowe_karlyn .html.

Kartomi, Margaret J. 1973. "Music and Trance in Central Java." *Ethnomusicology* 17 (2): 163–208.

Kaufman, Debra. 1991. *Rachel's Daughters.* New Brunswick, N.J.: Rutgers University Press.

———. 1995. "Engendering Orthodoxy: Newly Orthodox Women and Hasidism." In *New World Hasidim: Ethnographic Studies of Hasidic Jews in America,* edited by Janet S. Belcove-Shalin, 135–60. Albany: State University of New York Press.

Kealiinohomoku, Joann W. 1967. "Hopi and Polynesian Dance: A Study in Cross-Cultural Comparison." *Ethnomusicology* 11 (3): 343–68.

Kearney, Celeste. 1997. "The Missing Links: Riot Grrrl–Feminism-Lesbian Culture." In *Sexing the Groove: Popular Music and Gender,* edited by Sheila Whitely, 207–29. London: Routledge.

Keeling, Richard. 1985. "Contrast of Song Performance Style as a Function of Sex Role Polarity in the Hupa Brush Dance." *Ethnomusicology* 29 (2): 185–212.

———, ed. 1989. *Women in North American Indian Music: Six Essays.* Special Series 6. Bloomington, Ind.: Society for Ethnomusicology.

Keenan, Elizabeth K. 2008. "If Liz Phair's 'Exile in Guyville' Made You a Feminist, What Kind of Feminist Are You? Heterosexuality, Race, and Class in the Third Wave." *Women and Music: A Journal of Gender and Culture* 14: 45–71.

Keesing, Roger M. 1981. *Cultural Anthropology: A Contemporary Perspective.* New York: Harcourt.

Keightley, Keir. 1996. "'Turn It Down!' She Shrieked: Gender, Domestic Space, and High Fidelity, 1948–59." *Popular Music* 15 (2): 149–77.

KellyGadol, Joan. 1976. "The Social Relation of the Sexes: Methodological Implications of Women's History." *Signs* 1 (4): 809–23.

Kendall, Laurel. 1985. *Shamans, Housewives, and Other Restless Spirits: Women in Korean Shamanism.* Studies of the East Asian Institute. Honolulu: University of Hawaii Press.

Kendall, Laurel, and Mark Peterson. 1983. "Traditional Korean Women: A Reconsideration." In *Korean Women: View from the Inner Room,* edited by Laurel Kendall and Mark Peterson, 5–21. Cushing, Maine: East Rock.

Kiefer, Thomas M. 1968. "A Note on Cross-Sex Identification among Musicians." *Ethnomusicology* 12 (1): 107–9.

Kingsbury, Henry. 1988. *Music, Talent, and Performance: A Conservatory Cultural System.* Philadelphia: Temple University Press.

Kingsolver, Ann E. 2010. "Foucault and Power." In *Encyclopedia of Social and Cultural Anthropology,* edited by Alan Barnard and Jonathan Spencer. New York: Routledge.

Kingsolver, Barbara. 2000. *Small Wonder: Essays.* New York: HarperCollins.

Kirkby, Joan, et al., eds. 2003. *Gender Studies: Terms and Debates.* New York: Palgrave Macmillan.

Kisliuk, Michelle. 2000. "Performance and Modernity among BaAka Pygmies: A Closer Look at the Mystique of Egalitarian Forgers in the Rainforest." In *Music and Gender,* edited by Pirkko Moisala and Beverley Diamond, 25–50. Urbana: University of Illinois Press.

———. 2008. "(Un)doing Fieldwork: Sharing Songs, Sharing Lives." In *Shadows in the Field: New Perspectives for Fieldwork in Ethnomusicology,* edited by Gregory F. Barz and Timothy J. Cooley, 183–206. 2nd ed. New York: Oxford University Press.

Kondo, Dorinne. 1990. *Crafting Selves: Power, Gender, and Discourses of Identity in a Japanese Workplace.* Chicago: University of Chicago Press.

Koskoff, Ellen. 1976. "The Concept of Nigun among Lubavitcher Hasidism in the United States." Ph.D. diss., University of Pittsburgh.

———. 1987a. "An Introduction to Women, Music, and Culture." In *Women and Music in Cross-Cultural Perspective,* edited by Ellen Koskoff. Westport, Conn.: Greenwood Press.

———. 1987b. "The Sound of a Woman's Voice: Gender and Music in a New York Hasidic Community." In *Women and Music in Cross-Cultural Perspective,* edited by Ellen Koskoff, 213–23. Westport, Conn.: Greenwood Press.

———. 1989a. "Both In and Between: Women's Musical Roles in Ritual Life." *Concilium: International Journal for Theology.* Vol. 2, *Music and the Experience of God* (202): 82–93.

———, ed. 1989b. *Women and Music in Cross-Cultural Perspective.* 2nd ed. Urbana: University of Illinois Press.

———. 1991. "Gender, Power, and Music." In *The Musical Woman, an International Perspective.* Vol. 3, *1986–1990*, edited by Judith Laing Zaimont, 769–88. Westport, Conn.: Greenwood Press.

———. 1993. "Miriam Sings Her Song: The Self and the Other in Anthropological Discourse." In *Musicology and Difference: Gender and Sexuality in Music Scholarship*, edited by Ruth A. Solie, 149–63. Berkeley: University of California Press.

———. 1995. "The Language of the Heart: Music in Lubavitcher Life." In *New World Hasidism: Ethnographic Studies of Hasidic Jews in America*, edited by Janet S. Belcove-Shalin, 87–106. Albany: State University of New York Press.

———. 1996. "When Women Play: Musical Instruments and Gender Ideology." In *Voices of Women: Essays in Honour of Violet Archer*, edited by Brenda Dalen, Regula Qureshi, and A. La France, 34–49. Edmonton: University of Alberta Press.

———. 2000. "Gender and Music." In *The Garland Encyclopedia of World Music.* Vol. 8, *Europe*, edited by Timothy Rice, James Porter, and Chris Goertzen, 191–204. New York: Garland.

———. 2001. *Music in Lubavitcher Life.* Music in American Life. Urbana: University of Illinois Press.

———. 2002. "Is Female to Male as Postmodern Is to Modern? Implications for a New Ethnomusicology." In *Encomium Musicae: A Festschrift in Honor of Robert J. Snow*, edited by Robert J. Snow, David Crawford, and George Grayson Wagstaff. Festschrift Series. Hillsdale, N.Y.: Pendragon Press.

———. 2006. "(Left Out in) Left (the Field): The Effects of Post-postmodern Scholarship on Feminist and Gender Studies in Musicology and Ethnomusicology, 1990–2000." *Women and Music: A Journal of Gender and Culture* 9: 90–98.

———. 2013. Afterword to *Female Singers in Contemporary Global Contexts*, edited by Ruth Hellier. Urbana: University of Illinois Press.

Kristeva, Julia. 1979. "Women's Time." Translated by Alice Jardine and Harry Blake. In *The Kristeva Reader*, edited by Yoril Moi, 187–213. Oxford: Basil Blackwell.

Kuklick, Henrika. 1997. "After Ishmael: The Fieldwork Tradition and Its Future." In *Anthropological Locations: Boundaries and Grounds of a Field Science*, edited by Akhil Gupta and James Ferguson, 47–65. Berkeley: University of California Press.

Kurath, Gertrude P. 1960. "Dance, Music, and the Daily Bread." *Ethnomusicology* 4 (1): 1–9.

Lamm, Y. 1988. *Yisroel Lamm and the Philharmonic Experience.* Jerusalem: Holyland Records and Tapes.

Lamphere, Louise. 1974. "Strategies, Cooperation, and Conflict among Women in Domestic Groups." In *Woman, Culture, and Society*, edited by Michelle Zimbalist Rosaldo and Louise Lamphere, 97–112. Stanford, Calif.: Stanford University Press.

Lange, Barbara Rose. 1996. "Gender Politics and Musical Performers in the Isten Gyulekezet: A Fieldwork Account." *Journal of American Folklore* 109 (Winter): 60–76.

Leacock, Eleanor Burke. 1981. *Myths of Male Dominance: Collected Articles on Women Cross-Culturally*. New York: Monthly Review Press.

Lee, Byong Won. 1979. "Evolution of the Role and Status of Korean Professional Female Entertainers (Kisaeng)." *World of Music* 21 (2): 75–81.

Leonardo, Micaela di, ed. 1991. *Gender at the Crossroads of Knowledge: Feminist Anthropology in the Postmodern Era*. Berkeley: University of California Press.

Lerner, Gerda. 1986. *The Creation of Patriarchy*. New York: Oxford University Press.

Lewis, I. M. 1971. *Ecstatic Religion: A Study of Shamanism and Spirit Possession*. New York: Penguin Books.

———. 1986. *Religion in Context: Cults and Charisma*. Cambridge: Cambridge University Press.

Lewis, Lisa. 1990. *Gender Politics and MTV: Voicing the Difference*. Philadelphia: Temple University Press.

Lincoln, Bruce. 1991. *Emerging from the Chrysalis: Rituals of Women's Initiation*. New York: Oxford University Press.

Lipsker, Eli. 1990. Interview. April 22.

Lock, Margaret. 1993. "Cultivating the Body: Anthropology and Epistemologies of Bodily Practice and Knowledge." *Annual Review of Anthropology* 22: 133–55.

Locke, Ralph. P. 1986. *Music, Musicians, and the Saint Simonians*. Chicago: University of Chicago Press.

———. 2011. *Musical Exoticism: Images and Reflections*. Cambridge: Cambridge University Press.

Lomax, Alan. 1968. *Folksong Style and Culture*. Washington, D.C.: American Association for the Advancement of Science.

Lubavitch Foundation of Great Britain. 1970. *Challenge: An Encounter with Lubavitch Chabad in Israel*. London: Lubavitch Foundation of Great Britain.

MacArthur, Sally. 2002. *Feminist Aesthetics in Music*. Westport, Conn.: Greenwood Press.

MacCormack, Carol P. 1980. "Nature, Culture, and Gender: A Critique." In *Nature, Culture, and Gender,* edited by Carol P. MacCormack and Marilyn Strathern, 1–24. Cambridge: Cambridge University Press.

MacCormack, Carol P., and Marilyn Strathern, eds. 1980. *Nature, Culture, and Gender*. Cambridge: Cambridge University Press.

Mackay, Mercedes. 1955. "The Shantu Music of the Harims of Nigeria." *African Music* 1 (2): 56–57.

MacKinnon, Catharine A. 1982. "Feminism, Marxism, Method, and the State: An Agenda for Theory." *Signs* 7 (3): 515–44.

———. 1987. *Feminism Unmodified: Discourses on Life and Law*. Cambridge, Mass.: Harvard University Press.

———. 1989. *Toward a Feminist Theory of the State*. Cambridge, Mass.: Harvard University Press.

Magrini, Tullia. 2003. *Music and Gender: Perspectives from the Mediterranean*. Chicago: University of Chicago Press.

Maimonides [Maimon, Moses ben]. 1965. *The Code of Maimonides (Mishneh Torah)*. Bk. 5, *The Book of Holiness*. Edited by Leon Nemoy. Translated by Louis I. Rabinowitz and Philip Grossman. Yale Judaica Series. New Haven, Conn.: Yale University Press.

Malm, William P. 1959. *Japanese Music and Musical Instruments*. Rutland, Vt.: C. E. Tuttle.

Manning, Peter K. 1995. "The Challenges of Postmodernism." In *Representation in Ethnography*, edited by J. Van Maanen, 245–72. London: Sage.

Marcus, George E., and Dick Cushman. 1982. "Ethnographies as Texts." *Annual Review of Anthropology* 11: 25–69.

Marcus, George E., and Michael M. J. Fischer. 1986. *Anthropology as Cultural Critique: An Experimental Moment in the Human Sciences*. Chicago: University of Chicago Press.

Marcus, Sara. 2010. *Girls to the Front: The True Story of the Riot Grrrl Revolution*. New York: Harper Perennial.

Markoff, Irene. 1975. "Two-Part Singing from the Razlog District of Southwestern Bulgaria." *Yearbook of the International Folk Music Council* 7: 134–44.

Marshall, Kimberly, ed. 1993. *Rediscovering the Muses: Women's Musical Traditions*. Boston: Northeastern University Press.

Martin, M. Kay, and Barbara Voorhies. 1975. *Female of the Species*. New York: Columbia University Press.

Marx, Karl. 1967. *Capital: A Critique of Political Economy*. Vol. 1, *The Production Process of Capital*. New York: International Publishers.

Mascia-Lees, Frances E., and Nancy Johnson Black. 2000. *Gender and Anthropology*. Prospect Heights, Ill.: Waveland Press.

Mascia-Lees, Frances E., Patricia Sharpe, and Colleen Ballerino Cohen. 1989. "The Postmodern Turn in Anthropology: Cautions from a Feminist Perspective." *Signs* 15 (1): 7–33.

May, Elizabeth, and Stephen Wild. 1967. "Aboriginal Music on the Laverton Reservation, Western Australia." *Ethnomusicology* 11 (2): 207–17.

McClary, Susan. 1991. *Feminine Endings: Music, Gender, and Sexuality*. Minneapolis: University of Minnesota Press.

McClaurin, Irma. 2001. *Black Feminist Anthropology: Theory, Politics, Praxis, and Poetry*. New Brunswick, N.J.: Rutgers University Press.

McLeod, Norma, and Marcia Herndon. 1975. "The Bormliza: Maltese Folksong Style and Women." In *Women and Folklore*, edited by Claire R. Farrer, 81–100. Austin: University of Texas Press for the American Folklore Society.

Mead, Margaret. 1928. *Coming of Age in Samoa: A Psychological Study of Primitive Youth for Western Civilization*. New York: W. Morrow.

———. 1935. *Sex and Temperament in Three Primitive Societies*. New York: W. Morrow.

———. 1963. *Sex and Temperament in Three Primitive Societies*. New York: Morrow Quill Paperbacks.

Merriam, Alan P. 1964. *The Anthropology of Music*. Evanston, Ill.: Northwestern University Press.

Merrill-Mirsky, Carol. 1984. "Judeo-Spanish Song from the Island of Rhodes: A Musical Tradition in Los Angeles." Master's thesis, University of California, Los Angeles.

Millett, Kate. 1970. *Sexual Politics.* Urbana: University of Illinois Press.

Mills, Sara. 1998. "Postcolonial Feminist Theory." In *Contemporary Feminist Theories,* edited by S. Jackson and J. Jones, 98–112. Edinburgh: Edinburgh University Press.

Mindel, Nissan. 1969. *Rabbi Schneur Zalman.* Vols. 1–3. New York: Kehot.

Mintz, Jerome R. 1968. *Legends of the Hasidim: An Introduction to Hasidic Culture and Oral Tradition.* Chicago: University of Chicago Press.

Modleski, Tania. 1991. *Feminism without Women: Culture and Criticism in a "Post-feminist" Age.* New York: Routledge.

Mohammed, Patricia. 1991. "Reflections on the Women's Movement in Trinidad: Calypsos, Changes, and Sexual Violence." *Feminist Review* 38 (Summer): 33–47.

Mohanty, Chandra. 1991. "Under Western Eyes: Feminist Scholarship and Colonial Discourse." In *Third World Women and Feminism,* edited by Chandra Mohanty, Ann Russo, and Lourdes Torres, 51–80. Bloomington: Indiana University Press.

Moisala, Pirkko. 1999. "Musical Gender in Performance." *Women and Music: A Journal of Gender and Culture* 3: 1–16.

Moisala, Pirkko, and Beverley Diamond, eds. 2000. *Music and Gender.* Urbana: University of Illinois Press.

Monts, Lester P. 1989. "Vai Women's Roles in Music, Masking, and Ritual Performance." In *African Musicology: Current Trends, a Festschrift Presented to J. H. Kwabena Nketia,* edited by Jacqueline C. DjeDje and William G. Carter, 1:219–35. Berkeley: University of California.

Moore, Henrietta L. 1988. *Feminism and Anthropology.* Minneapolis: University of Minnesota Press.

———. 1993. "The Differences Within and the Differences Between." In *Gendered Anthropology,* edited by Teresa del Valle, 193–204. London: Routledge.

———. 1999. "Whatever Happened to Women and Men? Gender and Other Crises in Anthropology." In *Anthropological Theory Today,* edited by Henrietta L. Moore, 151–71. Oxford: Polity Press.

———. 2006. "The Future of Gender or the End of a Brilliant Career?" In *Feminist Anthropology: Past, Present, and Future,* edited by Pamela L. Geller and Miranda K. Stockket, 23–42. Philadelphia: University of Pennsylvania Press.

Morgan, Robin. 1970. *Sisterhood Is Powerful: An Anthology of Writings from the Women's Liberation Movement.* New York: Random House.

Morris, Bonnie. 1995. "Agents or Victims of Religious Ideology: Approaches to Locating Hasidic Women in Feminist Studies." In *New World Hasidim: Ethnographic Studies of Hasidic Jews in America,* edited by Janet S. Belcove-Shalin, 161–80. Albany: State University of New York Press.

Morton, David. 1976. *The Traditional Music of Thailand.* Berkeley: University of California Press.

Murphy, Yolanda, and Robert F. Murphy. 1974. *Women of the Forest.* New York: Columbia University Press.

Narayan, Uma. 1997. *Dislocating Cultures: Identities, Traditions, and Third-World Feminism*. New York: Routledge.

Nash, Dennison. 1961. "The Role of the Composer (Part 1)." *Ethnomusicology* 5 (2): 81–94.

Nehring, Neil. 1997. *Popular Music, Gender, and Postmodernism: Anger Is an Energy*. Thousand Oaks, Calif.: Sage.

Nettl, Bruno. 1983. *The Study of Ethnomusicology: Twenty-Nine Issues and Concepts*. Urbana: University of Illinois Press.

———. 1995. *Heartland Excursions: Ethnomusicological Reflections on Schools of Music*. Urbana: University of Illinois Press.

Neuls-Bates, Carol, ed. 1982. *Women in Music: An Anthology of Source Readings from the Middle Ages to the Present*. New York: Harper and Row.

Newcomb, Anthony. 1986. "Courtesans, Muses, or Musicians? Professional Women Musicians in Sixteenth-Century Italy." In *Women Making Music: The Western Art Tradition, 1150–1950*, edited by Jane Bowers and Judith Tick, 90–115. Urbana: University of Illinois Press.

Newman, L. I. 1944. *The Hasidic Anthology: Tales and Teachings of the Hasidim*. New York: Block.

Nketia, J. H. Kwabena. 1957. "Possession Dances in African Societies." *Journal of the International Folk Music Council* 9: 4–9.

Nochlin, Linda. 1971. "Why Have There Been No Great Women Artists?" *ARTnews* 69 (January): 22–39.

Ntarangwi, Mwenda. 2003. *Gender, Performance, and Identity: Understanding Swahili Cultural Realities through Songs*. Trenton, N.J.: Africa World Press.

Okafor, Richard C. 1989. "Women in Igbo Musical Culture." *Nigerian Field* 54 (3–4): 133–40.

O'Kelly, Charlotte G., and Larry S. Carney. 1986. *Women and Men in Society: Cross-cultural Perspectives on Gender Stratification*. 2nd ed. Belmont, Calif.: Wadsworth.

Olsen, Dale A. 1980. "Japanese Music in Peru." *Asian Music* 11 (2): 41–51.

Olsen, Hope A. 2001. "Sameness and Difference: A Cultural Foundation of Classification." *Library Resources and Technical Services* 45 (3).

Olsen, Miriam Rovsing. 2002. "Contemporary Issues of Gender and Music." In *The Garland Encyclopedia of World Music*. Vol. 6, *The Middle East*, edited by Virginia Danielson, Scott Marcus, and Dwight Reynolds, 299–307. New York: Routledge.

Orbell, Margaret. 1990. "'My Summit Where I Sit': Form and Content in Maori Women's Love Songs." *Oral Tradition* 5 (2–3): 185–204.

Ortner, Sherry B. 1974. "Is Female to Male as Nature Is to Culture?" In *Woman, Culture, and Society*, edited by Michelle Zimbalist Rosaldo and Louise Lamphere, 67–87. Stanford, Calif.: Stanford University Press.

———. 1996. *Making Gender: The Politics and Erotics of Culture*. Boston: Beacon Press.

Ortner, Sherry B., and Harriet Whitehead. 1981. "Introduction: Accounting for Sexual Meanings." In *Sexual Meanings: The Cultural Construction of Gender and Sexuality*, edited by Sherry B. Ortner and Harriet Whitehead, 1–28. Cambridge: Cambridge University Press.

Parker, Arthur C. 2008. *The Code of Handsome Lake, the Seneca Prophet.* 1913. Reprint, Charleston, S.C.: Bibliobazaar.

Pasternak, Velvel, ed. 1960. *Songs of the Chassidim.* New York: Bloch.

Patai, Raphael, ed. 1967. *Women in the Modern World.* New York: Free Press.

Payne, Helen. 1993. "The Presence of the Possessed: A Parameter in the Performance Practice of the Music of Australian Aboriginal Women." In *Rediscovering the Muses: Women's Musical Traditions,* edited by Kimberly Marshall, 1–20. Boston: Northeastern University Press.

Pendle, Karen, ed. 1991. *Women and Music: A History.* Bloomington: Indiana University Press.

Pike, Kenneth L. 1947. *Phonemics: A Technique for Reducing Languages to Writing.* Ann Arbor: University of Michigan Press.

———. 1967. *Language in Relation to a Unified Theory of the Structure of Human Behavior.* The Hague: Mouton.

———. 1982. *Linguistic Concepts: An Introduction to Tagmemics.* Lincoln: University of Nebraska Press.

———. 1990. "On the Etics and Emics of Pike and Harris." In *Emics and Etics: The Insider/Outsider Debate,* edited by Thomas Headland, Kenneth Pike, and Marvin Harris, 28–47. Newbury Park, Calif.: Sage.

Post, Jennifer C. 1987. "Professional Women in Indian Music: The Death of the Courtesan Tradition." In *Women and Music in Cross-Cultural Perspective,* edited by Ellen Koskoff, 97–110. Westport, Conn.: Greenwood Press.

———. 1994. "Erasing the Boundaries between Public and Private in Women's Performance Traditions." In *Cecilia Reclaimed: Feminist Perspectives on Gender and Music,* edited by Susan C. Cook and Judy S. Tsou, 35–51. Urbana: University of Illinois Press.

———. 2000. "Women and Music." In *The Garland Encyclopedia of World Music.* Vol. 5, *South Asia: The Indian Subcontinent,* edited by Alison Arnold, 407–17. New York: Garland.

Pough, Gwendolyn D. 2004. *Check It while I Wreck It: Black Womanhood, Hip-Hop Culture, and the Public Sphere.* Boston: Northeastern University Press.

Price, Janet, and Margrit Shildrick. 1999. *Feminist Theory and the Body: A Reader.* New York: Routledge.

Price, Sally. 1983. "Sexism and the Construction of Reality: An Afro-American Example." *American Ethnologist* 10 (3): 460–76.

Qureshi, Regula. 1981. "Islamic Music in an Indian Environment: The Shi'a Majlis." *Ethnomusicology* 25 (1): 41–71.

———. 2000. "How Does Music Mean? Embodied Memories and the Politics of Affect in the Indian *Sarangi.*" *American Ethnologist* 27 (4): 805–38.

Qureshi, Regula, et al., eds. 1995. "Voices of Women: Essays in Honor of Violet Archer." Special issue, *Canadian University Music Review* 16 (1).

Rabinowicz, H. 1970. *The World of Hasidism.* Hartford, Conn.: Hartford House.

Racy, Ali Jihad. "Funeral Songs of the Druzes of Lebanon." Master's thesis, University of Illinois.

Ramsey, Guthrie P., Jr. 2001. "Who Hears Here? Black Music, Critical Bias, and the Musicological Skin Trade." *Musical Quarterly* 85 (1): 1–52.

———. 2003. *Race Music: Black Cultures from Bebop to Hip-Hop.* Berkeley: University of California Press.

Rashomon. 1950. Directed by Akira Kurasawa. Tokyo.

Rasmussen, Anne K. 2010. *Women, the Recited Qur'an, and Islamic Music in Indonesia.* Berkeley: University of California Press.

Reiter, Rayna R, ed. 1975. *Toward an Anthropology of Women.* New York: Monthly Review Press.

———. 1979. "Review Essay: Anthropology." *Signs* 4 (3): 497–513.

Rice, Timothy. 1980. "A Macedonian Sobor: Anatomy of a Celebration." *Journal of American Folklore* 93 (368): 113–28.

Rich, Adrienne. 1980. "Compulsory Heterosexuality and Lesbian Existence." *Signs* 5: 631–60.

Riley, Joanne. 1980. "Women in World Music: Straining Our Ears to the Silence." Special issue, "Women and Music." *Heresies: A Feminist Publication on Art and Politics* (Heresies Collective) 10 (2): 30–35.

Roark-Calnek, Sue. 1977. "Indian Way in Oklahoma: Transaction in Honoring and Legitimacy." Ph.D. diss., Bryn Mawr College.

Roberts, Helen H., and Morris Swadesh. 1955. *Songs of the Nootka Indians of Western Vancouver Island.* Vol. 45, pt. 3 of *Transactions of the American Philosophical Society, New Series.* Philadelphia: American Philosophical Society.

Robertson, Carol E. 1984. "Response to Feld and Roseman." *Ethnomusicology* 28 (3): 449–52.

———. 1987. "Power and Gender in the Musical Experiences of Women." In *Women and Music in Cross-Cultural Perspective,* edited by Ellen Koskoff, 225–44. Westport, Conn.: Greenwood Press.

———. 1989. "Singing Social Boundaries into Place: The Dynamics of Gender and Performance in Two Cultures, Part I." *Sonus* 10 (1): 59–71.

———. 1990. "Singing Social Boundaries into Place: The Dynamics of Gender and Performance in Two Cultures, Part II." *Sonus* 10 (2): 1–13.

———. 1993. "The Ethnomusicologist as Midwife." In *Musicology and Difference: Gender and Sexuality in Music Scholarship,* edited by Ruth Solie, 107–24. Berkeley: University of California Press.

Rorich, Mary. 1989. "Shebeens, Slumyards, and Sophiatown: Black Women, Music, and Cultural Change in Urban South Africa, c. 1920–1960." *World of Music* 31 (1): 78–104.

Rosaldo, Michelle Zimbalist. 1980. "The Use and Abuse of Anthropology: Reflections on Feminism and Cross-Cultural Understanding." *Signs* 5 (3): 389–418.

Rosaldo, Michelle Zimbalist, and Louise Lamphere, eds. 1974. *Woman, Culture, and Society.* Stanford, Calif.: Stanford University Press.

Rose, Tricia. 1994. *Black Noise: Rap Music and Black Culture in Contemporary America.* Middletown, Conn.: Wesleyan University Press.

Roseman, Marina. 1987. "Inversion and Conjuncture: Male and Female Performance among the Temiar of Peninsular Malaysia." In *Women and Music in Cross-Cultural Perspective,* edited by Ellen Koskoff, 13150. Westport, Conn.: Greenwood Press.

Rosenblum, Miriam. 1975. Interview. November 16.

Rosenblum, R. Ephraim. 1975. Interview. September 13.

Rossen, Jane Mink. 1990. "Politics and Songs: A Study in Gender on Mungiki." In *Music, Gender, and Culture,* edited by Marcia Herndon and Susanne Ziegler, 173–90. Wilhelmshaven, Germany: Florian Noetzel Verlag.

Rouget, Gilbert. 1985. *Music and Trance: A Theory of the Relations between Music and Possession.* Translated by Brunhilde Biebuyck. Chicago: University of Chicago Press.

Rubin, Gayle S. 1975. "The Traffic in Women: Notes on the 'Political Economy' of Sex." In *Toward an Anthropology of Women,* edited by Rayna R. Reiter, 157–210. New York: Monthly Review Press.

———. 1993. "Misguided, Dangerous, and Wrong: An Analysis of Anti-pornography Politics." In *Bad Girls and Dirty Pictures: The Challenge to Reclaim Feminism,* edited by Alison Assiter and Avedon Carol, 18–40. Boulder, Colo.: Pluto Press.

Sachs, Curt. 1940. *The History of Musical Instruments.* New York: W. W. Norton.

Said, Edward W. 1978. *Orientalism.* New York: Vintage Books.

Said, Edward W., and Daniel Barenboim. 2004. *Parallels and Paradoxes: Explorations in Music and Society.* New York: Vintage.

Sakata, Hiromi Lorraine. 1976. "The Concept of Musician in Three Persian-Speaking Areas of Afghanistan." *Asian Music* 8 (1): 1–28.

———. 1989. "Hazara Women in Afghanistan: Innovators and Preservers." In *Women and Music in Cross-cultural Perspective,* edited by Ellen Koskoff, 85–96. 2nd ed. Urbana: University of Illinois Press.

Saldaña, Nancy H. 1966. "La Malinche: Her Representation in Dances of Mexico and the United States." *Ethnomusicology* 10 (3): 298–309.

Sanday, Peggy Reeves. 1974. "Female Status in the Public Domain." In *Women, Culture, and Society,* edited by Michelle Zimbalist Rosaldo and Louise Lamphere, 189–206. Stanford, Calif.: Stanford University Press.

———. 1981. *Female Power and Male Dominance: On the Origins of Sexual Inequality.* Cambridge: Cambridge University Press.

Sarkissian, Margaret. 1992. "Gender and Music." In *Ethnomusicology: An Introduction,* edited by Helen Myers, 337–48. London: Macmillan.

———. 1999. "Thoughts on the Study of Gender in Ethnomusicology: A Pedagogical Perspective." *Women and Music: A Journal of Gender and Culture* 3: 17–27.

Sawa, Suzanne Meyers. 1987. "The Role of Women in Musical Life: The Medieval Arabo-Islamic Courts." *Canadian Women's Studies* 8 (1): 23–35.

Schieffelin, Edward L. 1985. "Performance and the Cultural Construction of Reality." *American Ethnologist* 12 (4): 707–24.

———. 1998. "Problematising Performance." In *Ritual, Performance, Media,* edited by Felicia Hughes-Freeland, 194–207. London: Routledge.

Schippers, Mimi. 2002. *Rockin' Out of the Box: Gender Maneuvering in Alternative Hard Rock*. New Brunswick, N.J.: Rutgers University Press.

Schlegel, Alice. 1972. *Male Dominance and Female Autonomy: Domestic Authority in Matrilineal Societies*. New Haven, Conn.: Human Relations Area File.

Schmidt, Cynthia E. 1989. "Womanhood, Work, and Song among the Kpelle of Liberia." In *African Musicology: Current Trends, a Festschrift Presented to J. H. Kwabena Nketia*, edited by Jacqueline C. DjeDje and William G. Carter, 1:237–63. Berkeley: University of California Press.

Scholz, Sally J. 2010. *Feminism: A Beginner's Guide*. Oxford: One World Publications.

Schworer-Kohl, Gretel. 1990. "Considering Gender Balance in Religion and Ritual Music among the Hmong and Lahu in Northern Thailand." In *Music, Gender, and Culture*, edited by Marcia Herndon and Susanne Ziegler, 143–56. Wilhelmshaven, Germany: Florian Noetzel Verlag.

Sedgwick, Eve K. 1990. *Epistemology of the Closet*. Berkeley: University of California Press.

Seeger, Anthony. 1980. "Sing for Your Sister: The Structure and Performance of Suya Akia." In *The Ethnography of Musical Performance*, edited by Norma McLeod and Marcia Herndon, 7–43. Norwood, Pa.: Norwood.

Seeger, Charles. 1977. "The Musicological Juncture: Music as Value." In *Studies in Musicology, 1935–1975*, edited by Charles Seeger, 51–63. Berkeley: University of California Press.

Seigel, Richard, Michael Strassfeld, and Sharon Strassfeld, eds. 1973. *The First Jewish Catalog: A Do-It-Yourself Kit*. Philadelphia: Jewish Publication Society of America.

Seitz, Barbara. 1991. "Songs, Identity, and Women's Liberation in Nicaragua." *Latin American Music Review* 12 (1): 21–41.

Shapiro, Anne Dhu. 1991. "A Critique of Current Research on Music and Gender." *Worlds of Music*: 3–15.

Shapiro, Anne Dhu, and Inés Talamantez. 1986. "The Mescalero Apache Girls' Puberty Ceremony: The Role of Music in Structuring Ritual Time." *Yearbook for Traditional Music* 18: 17–90.

Shelemay, Kay Kaufman. 2007. "The Power of Silent Voices: Women in the Syrian Jewish Musical Tradition." In *Music and the Play of Power in the Middle East, North Africa, and Central Asia*, edited by Laudan Nooshin, 269–88. Surrey, United Kingdom: Ashgate.

Shepherd, John. 1977. *Whose Music? A Sociology of Musical Languages*. Rutgers, N.J.: Transaction.

———. 1987. "Music and Male Hegemony." In *Music and Society: The Politics of Composition, Performance, and Reception*, edited by Richard Leppert and Susan McClary, 151–72. Cambridge: Cambridge University Press.

Sherinian, Zoe C. 2000. "k. d. lang and Gender Performance." In *The Garland Encyclopedia of World Music*. Vol. 3, *The United States and Canada*, edited by Ellen Koskoff, 107–10. New York: Routledge.

———. 2005. "Re-presenting Dalit Feminist Politics through Dialogical Musical Ethnography." *Women and Music: A Journal of Gender and Culture* 9: 1–12.

Shimony, Annemarie Anrod. 1961. *Conservatism among the Iroquois at the Six Nations Reserve.* Yale University Publications in Anthropology 65. New Haven, Conn.: Yale University Department of Anthropology.

———. 1980. "Women of Influence and Prestige among the Native American Iroquois." In *Unspoken Worlds: Women's Religious Lives in Non-Western Cultures,* edited by Nancy A. Falk and Rita M. Gross, 243–59. San Francisco: Harper and Row.

Shostak, Marjorie. 1981. *Nisa: The Life and Words of a !Kung Woman.* Cambridge, Mass.: Harvard University Press.

Silberbauer, George. 1982. "Political Process in G/Wi Bands." In *Politics and History in Band Societies,* edited by Eleanor Leacock and Richard Lee, 23–35. Cambridge: Cambridge University Press.

Simon, Artur. 1978. "Types and Functions of Music in the Eastern Highlands of West Irian." *Ethnomusicology* 22 (3): 441–55.

Slobin, Mark. 1984. "Europe/Peasant Music-Cultures of Eastern Europe." In *Worlds of Music: An Introduction to the Music of the World's Peoples,* edited by Jeff Todd Titon, 167–207. New York: Schirmer Books.

———. 1993. *Subcultural Sounds: Micromusics of the West.* Hanover, N.H.: Wesleyan University Press.

Slocum, Sally. 1975. "Woman the Gatherer: Male Bias in Anthropology." In *Toward an Anthropology of Women,* edited by Rayna R. Reiter, 36–50. New York: Monthly Review Press.

Small, Christopher. 1998. *Musicking: The Meanings of Performing and Listening.* Middletown, Conn.: Wesleyan University Press.

Smith, Gordon E., and Robin Elliott. 2010. *Music Traditions, Cultures, and Contexts.* Waterloo, Ontario: Wilfrid Laurier University Press.

Smith, Stephen G. 1992. *Gender Thinking.* Philadelphia: Temple University Press.

Soedarsono. 1969. "Classical Javanese Dance: History and Characterization." *Ethnomusicology* 13 (3): 498–506.

Solie, Ruth A., ed. 1993. *Musicology and Difference: Gender and Sexuality in Music Scholarship.* Berkeley: University of California Press.

Spivak, Gayatri Chakravorty. 1995. "Can the Subaltern Speak?" In *The Postcolonial Studies Reader,* edited by Bill Ashcroft et al. London: Routledge. First published in *Marxism and the Interpretation of Culture,* edited by Cary Nelson and Lawrence Grossberg. London: Macmillan, 1988.

Srivastava, I. 1991. "Woman as Portrayed in Women's Folk Songs of North India." *Asian Folklore Studies* 50 (2): 269–310.

Stack, Carol B., et al. 1975. "Anthropology." *Signs* 1 (1): 147–59.

Steinsaltz, Adin. 1982. *Teshuvah: A Guide for the Newly Observant Jew.* New York: Free Press.

Stobart, Henry. 2006. "Devils, Daydreams, and Desire: Siren Traditions and Musical Creation in the Central-Southern Andes." In *Music of the Sirens,* edited by Linda

Phyllis Austern and Inna Naroditskaya, 105–39. Bloomington: Indiana University Press.

Stone, Ruth M. 2008. *Theory for Ethnomusicology.* Upper Saddle River, N.J.: Pearson Prentice Hall.

Strathern, Marilyn. 1972. *Women in Between: Female Roles in a Male World—Mount Haven, New Guinea.* Napier, New Zealand: Seminar Press.

———. 1980. "No Nature, No Culture: The Hagen Case." In *Nature, Culture, and Gender,* edited by Carol P. MacCormack and Marilyn Strathern, 174–222. Cambridge: Cambridge University Press.

———. 1987. "An Awkward Relationship: The Case of Feminism and Anthropology." *Signs: Journal of Women in Culture and Society* 12 (2): 276–92.

———. 1995. *Shifting Contexts: Transformations in Anthropological Knowledge.* London: Routledge.

Strauss, Claudia. 1997. "Partly Fragmented, Partly Integrated: An Anthropological Examination of 'Postmodern Fragmented Subjects.'" *Cultural Anthropology* 12 (3): 362–404.

Strossen, Nadine. 1994. *Defending Pornography: Free Speech, Sex, and the Fight for Women's Rights.* New York: Simon and Schuster.

Sugarman, Jane. 1989. "The Nightingale and the Partridge: Singing and Gender among Prespa Albanians." *Ethnomusicology* 33 (2): 191–215.

———. 1997. *Engendering Song: Singing and Subjectivity at Prespa Albanian Weddings.* Chicago: University of Chicago Press.

Sutton, R. Anderson. 1984. "Who Is the Pesindhèn? Notes on the Female Singing Tradition in Java." *Indonesia* 37: 119–33.

Szirma, Palma. 1967. "A Csango-Hungarian Lament." *Ethnomusicology* 11 (3): 310–25.

Taylor, Timothy D. 1997. *Global Pop: World Music, World Markets.* New York: Routledge.

Tewari, Laxmi G. 1988. "'Sohar': Childbirth Songs of Joy." *Asian Folklore Studies* 47 (2): 257–76.

Tick, Judith. 1986. "Passed Away Is the Piano Girl: Changes in American Musical Life, 1870–1900." In *Women Making Music: The Western Art Tradition, 1150–1950,* edited by Jane Bowers and Judith Tick, 325–48. Urbana: University of Illinois Press.

Tick, Judith, Margaret Ericson, and Ellen Koskoff. 2001. "Women in Music." In *The New Grove Dictionary of Music and Musicians,* edited by Stanley Sadie. 2nd ed. London: Macmillan.

Tilly, Margaret. 1947. "The Psychoanalytical Approach to the Masculine and Feminine Principles in Music." *American Journal of Psychiatry* 103: 477–83.

Titon, Jeff Todd. 2008. "Knowing Fieldwork." In *Shadows in the Field: New Perspectives for Fieldwork in Ethnomusicology,* edited by Gregory F. Barz and Timothy J. Cooley, 25–42. 2nd ed. New York: Oxford University Press.

Tolbert, Elizabeth. 1990a. "Magico-religious Power and Gender in the Karelian Lament." In *Music, Gender, and Culture,* edited by Marcia Herndon and Susanne Ziegler, 41–56. Wilhelmshaven, Germany: Florian Noetzel Verlag.

———. 1990b. "Women Cry with Words: Symbolization of Affect in the Karelian Laments." *Yearbook for Traditional Music* 22: 80–105.

———. 1997. "Negotiating the Fault Lines: Ethnomusicology, Feminist Theory, and Cultural Difference." Paper presented at the Third Conference on Feminist Theory and Music, Riverside, Calif.

Tooker, Elisabeth, ed. 1986. *Native North American Spirituality of the Eastern Woodlands: Sacred Myths, Dreams, Visions, Speeches, Healing Formulas, Rituals, and Ceremonies.* Mahwah, N.J.: Paulist Press.

Topp Fargion, Janet. 1993. "The Role of Women in *Taarab* in Zanzibar: An Historical Examination of a Process of 'Africanization.'" *World of Music* 35 (2): 109–25.

Turino, Thomas. 2000. *Nationalists, Cosmopolitans, and Popular Music in Zimbabwe.* Chicago: University of Chicago Press.

———. 2008. *Music as Social Life: The Politics of Participation.* Chicago: University of Chicago Press.

Turnbull, Colin. 1987. *The Forest People.* New York: Touchstone.

Turner, Bryan S. 1994. *Orientalism, Postmodernism, and Globalism.* New York: Routledge.

Turner, Victor W. 1969. *The Ritual Process: Structure and Anti-Structure.* Chicago: Aldine Press.

Tylor, E. B. 1871. *Primitive Culture: Researches into the Development of Mythology, Philosophy, Religion, Art, and Custom.* 2 vols. 1871. Reprint, Cambridge: Cambridge University Press, 2010.

Valdez, Avelardo. 1996. "Gender in the Culture of Mexican American Conjunto Music." *Gender and Society* 10 (2): 148–67.

Vander, Judith. 1982. "The Song Repertoire of Four Shoshone Women: A Reflection of Cultural Movements and Sex Roles." *Ethnomusicology* 26 (1): 73–83.

———. 1988. *Songprints: The Musical Experience of Five Shoshone Women.* Urbana: University of Illinois Press.

Van Nieuwkerk, Karin. 1995. *A Trade Like Any Other: Female Singers and Dancers in Egypt.* Austin: University of Texas Press.

Wade, Bonnie C. 1972. "Songs of Traditional Wedding Ceremonies in North India." *Yearbook of the International Folk Music Council* 4: 57–65.

Walker, Alice. 1983. *In Search of Our Mothers' Gardens: Womanist Prose.* New York: Harcourt.

Walker, Rebecca. 1992. "Becoming the Third Wave." *Ms.,* January–February.

———, ed. 1995. *To Be Real: Telling the Truth and Changing the Face of Feminism.* New York: Anchor Books.

Walley, Christine J. 1997. "Searching for 'Voices': Feminism, Anthropology, and the Global Debate over Female Genital Operations." *Cultural Anthropology* 12 (3): 405–38.

Walser, Robert. 1993. *Running with the Devil: Power, Gender, and Madness in Heavy Metal Music.* Hanover, N.H.: Wesleyan/University Press of New England.

Washabaugh, William, ed. 1998. *The Passion of Music and Dance: Body, Gender, and Sexuality.* Oxford: Berg.

Waxer, Lise. 2002. *Situating Salsa: Global Markets and Local Meanings in Latin Popular Music*. New York: Routledge.

Weathers, Mary Ann. 1969. "An Argument for Black Women's Liberation as a Revolutionary Force." *No More Fun and Games: A Journal of Female Liberation* 1 (2).

Weidman, Amanda. 2003. "Gender and the Politics of Voice: Colonial Modernity and Classical Music in South India." *Cultural Anthropology* 18 (2): 194–232.

Weiss, Sarah. 1993. "Gender and *Gender:* Gender Ideology and the Female *Gender* Player in Central Java." In *Rediscovering the Muses: Women's Musical Traditions,* edited by Kimberly Marshall, 21–48. Boston: Northeastern University Press.

———. 2006. *Listening to an Earlier Java: Aesthetics, Gender, and the Music of Wayang in Central Java*. Leiden: KITLV Press.

West, Candace, and Don H. Zimmerman. 1987. "Doing Gender." *Gender and Society* 1 (2): 125–51.

Whitaker, Robin, and Pamela J. Downe. 2011. "Introduction: Feminist Anthropology Confronts Disengagement." *Anthropology in Action* 18 (1): 2–4.

Whiteley, Shrila, ed. 1997. *Sexing the Groove: Popular Music and Gender*. New York: Routledge.

Wikipedia. n.d.a. "Black Feminism." http://en.wikipedia.org/w/index.php?title=Black_feminism&oldid=431287872.

———. n.d.b. "Presidential Commission on the Status of Women." http://en.wikipedia.org/wiki/Presidential_Commission_on_the_Status_of_Women.

———. n.d.c. "Queer Theory." http://en.wikipedia.org/wiki/Queer_theory.

Wistrand, Lila M. 1969. "Music and Song Texts of Amazonian Indians." *Ethnomusicology* 13 (3): 469–88.

Wolf, Margery. 1992. *A Thrice-Told Tale: Feminism, Postmodernism, and Ethnographic Responsibility*. Stanford, Calif.: Stanford University Press.

Wollstonecraft, Mary. 1792. *A Vindication of the Rights of Women: With Strictures on Political and Moral Subjects*. Boston: Thomas and Andrews, 1792.

"Women in Music." 1980. Special issue, *Heresies: A Feminist Publication on Art and Politics* (Heresies Collective) 10 (2).

Wong, Cynthia P. 2002. "Women and Music I." In *The Garland Encyclopedia of World Music*. Vol. 7, *East Asia: China, Japan, and Korea,* edited by Robert C. Provine, Yosihiku Tokumaru, and J. Lawrence Witzleben, 401–4. New York: Routledge.

Wong, Deborah. 2001. *Sounding the Center: History and Aesthetics in Thai Buddhist Performance*. Chicago: University of Chicago Press.

———. 2004. *Speak It Louder: Asian Americans Making Music*. New York: Routledge.

———. 2006. "Ethnomusicology and Difference." *Ethnomusicology* 50 (2): 259–79.

———. 2008. "Moving: From Performance to Performative Ethnography." In *Shadows in the Field: New Perspectives for Fieldwork in Ethnomusicology,* edited by Gregory F. Barz and Timothy J. Cooley, 76–90. 2nd ed. New York: Oxford University Press.

Wood, Elizabeth. 1980. "Review Essay: Women in Music." *Signs* 6: 283–97.

Wrazen, Louise. 1983. "The Folk Music of the Polish Highlanders in Canada." *Canadian Folk Music Journal* 11: 18–28.

Yamamoto, Traise. 2000. "Millennial Bodies." Special issue, "Feminisms at a Millennium." *Signs* 25 (4): 1243–46.

Yocom, Margaret R. 1985. "Woman to Woman: Fieldwork and the Private Sphere." In *Women's Folklore, Women's Culture,* edited by Rosan A. Jordan and Susan J. Kalçik, 45–53. Publications of the American Folklore Society New Series 8. Philadelphia: University of Pennsylvania Press.

Zaimont, Judith Laing, ed. 1984. *The Musical Woman: An International Perspective.* Vol. 1, *1983.* Westport, Conn.: Greenwood Press.

Zalewski, Marysia. 2000. *Feminism after Postmodernism: Theorising through Practice.* London: Routledge.

Zalman, Rabbi Shneur. 1969. *Likutei Amarim (Tanya).* Translated by Nissan Mindel. New York: n.p.

Zalmanoff, R. S., ed. 1948. *Sefer ha-nigunim.* Vol. 1. New York: Nichoach.

Zborowski, Mark, and Elizabeth Herzog. 1952. *Life Is with People: The Culture of the Shtetl.* New York: International Universities Press.

Zheng, Su. 2002. "Women and Music II." In *The Garland Encyclopedia of World Music.* Vol. 7, *East Asia: China, Japan, and Korea,* edited by Robert C. Provine, Yosihiku Tokumaru, and J. Lawrence Witzleben, 405–10. New York: Routledge.

Index

ELLEN KOSKOFF is a professor of ethnomusicology at the University of Rochester's Eastman School of Music, director of ethnomusicology programs, and general editor of the Eastman/Rochester Studies in Ethnomusicology series. She is the editor of *Music Cultures in the United States* and author of *Music in Lubavitcher Life.*

New Perspectives on Gender in Music

The University of Illinois Press
is a founding member of the
Association of American University Presses.

Composed in 10.5/13 Adobe Minion Pro
at the University of Illinois Press
Manufactured by Sheridan Books, Inc.

University of Illinois Press
1325 South Oak Street
Champaign, IL 61820-6903
www.press.uillinois.edu